D1610529

C014997329

FRONT COVER

A detail from a coloured map of Woodmancott area showing Augustus Kinchin's house – in the centre marked by a 'A'.

(*By kind permission of the Warden and Scholars of Winchester College*)

REAR COVER AND SPINE

The parchment-over-boards binding of Mary Bacon's ledger.

(*Hampshire Record Office* 28M82/F1)

MARY BACON'S WORLD

RUTH FACER

Mary Bacon's World

A farmer's wife in eighteenth-century Hampshire

THRESHOLD PRESS

First published 2010 by
Threshold Press Ltd
Norfolk House, 75 Bartholomew Street
Newbury Berks RG14 5DU
Phone 01635-230272 and fax 01635-44804
email: publish@threshold-press.co.uk
www.threshold-press.co.uk

British Library Cataloguing in Publication Data
A catalogue record for this book is available from the British Library
ISBN 978–1–903152–28–7

Printed in England by
MPG Biddles Ltd, Kings Lynn

Contents

List of illustrations

For Roger, with love

Acknowledgements

IN THE WRITING of this book, I have been particularly indebted to the staff of the Hampshire Record Office, the British Library, Museum of English Rural Life, Reading, and Suzanne Foster, Archivist and the Warden and Scholars of Winchester College. I would like to thank staff at Chawton House Library, especially Helen Scott the previous librarian and Jacqui Grainger, the present one.

I am grateful to Chawton House Library, for the image of a page from *Primitive physick: or, an easy and natural method of curing most diseases* by John Wesley, taken by their photographer, Steve Shrimpton. I am also grateful to the Trustees of Carisbrooke Castle Museum for the image of 'J. N. 1788 (John Nixon) J. N. and Richard N pulling off their boots through the banisters in their room at Shanklin, Isle of Wight'. I am very grateful to Tim and Gill Bannerman for the image of Aylesfield Farm'. I would like to thank Janice Hadlow for advising me on the epistle sent by Queen Charlotte to the King of Prussia, and Brian Southam for an interesting exchange on a charm to cure the ague.

Every effort has been made to trace the copyright holders and we apologise in advance for any unintentional omissions. The author and the publishers would be pleased to insert the appropriate acknowledgement in any subsequent edition.

My deepest thanks are due to Margaret and John Winckler for their support and encouragement throughout this project and for their very helpful work as editors of this book. I would like to add special thanks to my two grandsons, Jamie Hamill and Lochlann Facer-Floate for their ongoing interest. Above all, my very grateful thanks to my husband, Roger Facer for all the love and support he has given me throughout my research and writing about Mary Bacon.

Maps

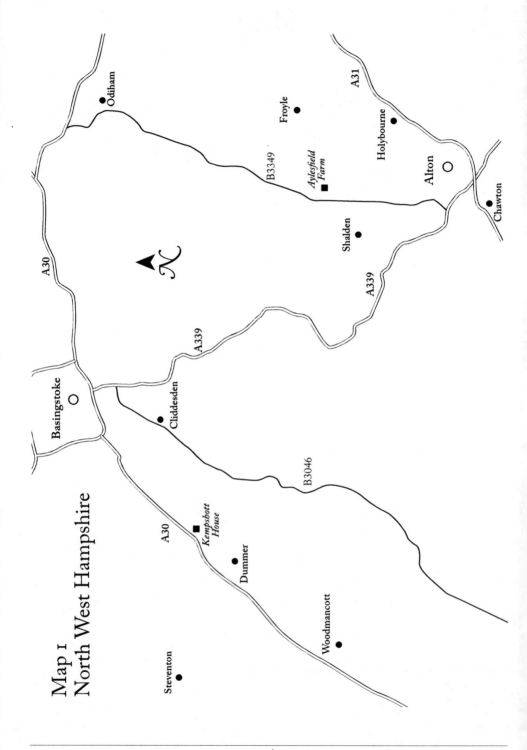

Map 1
North West Hampshire

Map 2 from Thomas Milne's map, 1791

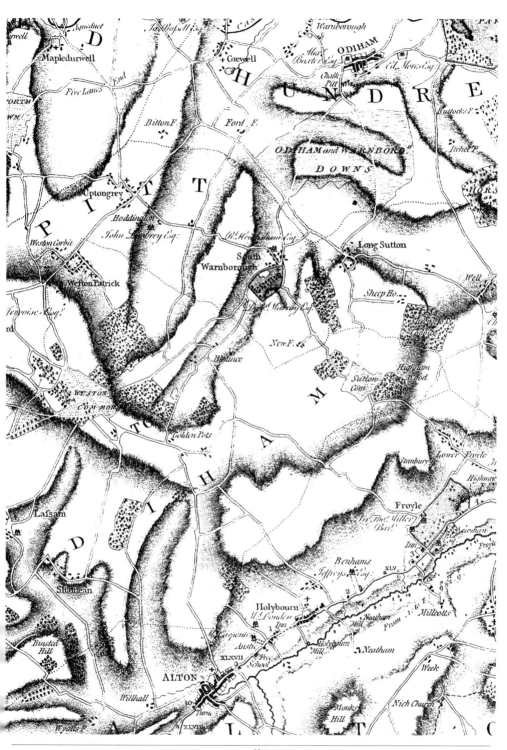

Introduction

W E LIVE IN an age of curiosity about other people. Politicians' love lives are splashed across the pages of the newspapers, reports of scandals have become part of our daily conversation, but we also peruse the actions of others with serious intent – to inform, to debate and to learn. We do not confine ourselves to the present age but show an avid interest in people of the past, reading biographies, watching history programmes and costume dramas on television, visiting stately homes inhabited by aristocrats of the period, and generally wondering about those long dead. The eighteenth century, an age of contradictions, of growing prosperity, of fashion and frivolity, of new ideas and enduring literature, underlain by dirt, personal ruin and poverty, with an all-pervading threat of war with both France and America, constantly compels its students to find out more. The secret love lives and inner thoughts of duchesses, queens and courtesans are speculated upon, and serious studies of the wisdom, or stupidity, are made of kings, statesmen, explorers, and generals.

But what of those who are not remembered, many of whom are not even recorded in the burial grounds of their churches? Our attitudes to those whose fame does not live after them is beginning to change. Until recently an important social group had been seriously ignored and it is only in the last ten to fifteen years that historians researching into aspects of the eighteenth century have shown a growing interest in the lives of middle-class women, the 'middling sort'. A number of books have been written on their daily lives, education, occupations, religious views, reading habits, and attitudes to love and marriage. Historians now realise that a significant contribution to the growth of industry in the eighteenth century was made by women. But despite this interest, one important group of women has continued to be largely ignored. Farmers' wives have remained relatively unknown in their rural retreats, and their archives, such as they are, prove difficult to retrieve. Nicola Verdon, one of the few historians who has written about these women, expresses this view:

> The farmer's wife remains one of the most elusive figures in agrarian history. Her labour on the farm (and in the farmhouse) was largely unpaid, and therefore unrecorded. Historians have acknowledged the contribution made by farmers' wives, but no attempt has yet been made to examine in detail the whole range of tasks usually

undertaken by them and the value attached to that work.[1]

Although Verdon has gone a long way to remedy this omission, it is still easier to find books or articles on the work of a woman farm labourer than it is to discover the role of her employer's wife. In exploring attitudes towards this little known group of women within the patriarchal society of the eighteenth century, and by discussing any contemporary expectations of their role as assistants in the production of the farm and in their local community, this book discusses their importance to both the rural economy and middle-class intellectual life. Do we really know so little about eighteenth-century farmers' wives and the work they did? How were they viewed by their contemporaries and what records did they leave behind? Were they appreciated as contributors to the economy? It must be said that those most guilty of ignoring their work, on paper at least, were their own husbands. There are many farmers' notebooks, memorandum books, and account books extant, but little reference is made to the work of the farmer's wife; payments went unrecorded, for none were made. Farmers habitually, though sometimes haphazardly, jotted down details of agricultural work in their notebooks, recording the number of working horses used each day and on which part of the farm, and the sale and purchase of livestock, grains, and other produce. An unnamed farmer's diary from the Liverpool area is a typical example.[2] Each man was named in relation to his work for the day while the women's tasks were only enumerated – there were seven women gathering stones, nine women hoeing potatoes, nine women making hay and hoeing cabbages. Women also cut straw, spread manure, planted potatoes, pulled docks and thistles, and cleaned turnips. There is no mention of a wife, sister, daughter, nor any indication of who was in charge of the dairy and poultry, although there is an entry, 'Betty Hankinson took charge of Milk House.'

George Brigham of Lindy Hill Farm, Cleveland, Yorkshire kept a very detailed diary from 1799 to 1810 in which he recorded the work to be done for each month of the year.[3] He listed tasks traditionally undertaken by the farmer's wife, noting that it was 'extracted from Moore's Almanac'.

January: kill and cure bacon, hanging beef and hams. Feed your bees if weak. Feed pigeons.

February: Feed your bees, brew best beer.

March: kill no bacon pigs after this nor hang beef nor hams towards the end of this month if the weather be good.

1   N. Verdon, 'Subject deserving of highest praise: farmers' wives and the farm economy in England, *c.* 1700–1850', *Agricultural History Review* Vol. 51, Part 1 (2003) 23.
2   Museum of English Rural Life (MERL) LAN 1.1.
3   MERL YOR 13.1.

May: look after bees they now begin to swarm.

September: take care of your bees, straighten the entrance into their hives, destroy wasps and drones. Put up hogs for pork and bacon.

It is possible that he had no wife or female family member to help with the work; in any event, no reference was made to the fact that these tasks were usually done by women.

Patriarchal attitudes were also to be found in many of the books on farming and in agricultural journals. There are very few references to women in the *Farmers' Magazine* between 1800 and 1803, apart from occasional mention of dairymaids. Again, wives and their traditional responsibilities on the farm were ignored, although there was room for criticism. A letter from a 'Young Farmer' to his father is quite scathing about women in farming:

> Not many led-farms, as they are called, are therefore managed judiciously ... the same remark applies to farms possessed by widows, especially if they interfere in the executive department. Unless a very steady and clear-headed overseer is procured, it would, in nine cases out of ten, be more for the interest of those concerned, even for the landlord, that such farms were instantly sublet than to remain under the feeble management and imperfect husbandry generally exercised.[4]

The eighteenth century was an age of instruction books: there were conduct books for young ladies, volumes of advice on household management, new cookery books for middle-class women, and a range of farming manuals from general advice to specialised books on farriery. Whereas some of these acknowledged the role of the farmer's wife, others did not. Although it had long been recognised that wives were traditionally in charge of the dairy, they did not always get the credit for it. *Rural Recreations or Modern Farmer's Calendar and Monthly Instructor,* by A Farmer, acknowledged the asset of a dairy.[5] 'The profits arising to the farmer from a well-regulated Dairy, are usually admitted to be greater than what can be obtained by any other mode of husbandry,' but those profits are attributable to the 'farmer or dairyman', not the wife. And of poultry, traditionally in the wife's domain: 'we contend that Poultry if judiciously managed, may prove a source of great profit to the farmer.' John Billingsby was critical in his Somerset report to the Board of Agriculture:

> I think dairies should be encouraged; for the arduous domestic labor and incessant employment which they bring in the female part of a farmer's family, will always prevent undue increase thereof, unless their profits on a comparison are

---

4 *Farmer's Magazine* (1807) 470.
5 A Farmer, *Rural Recreations or Modern Farmer's Calendar and Monthly Instructor* (1802) 65.

very great indeed. But whilst I recommend encouragement to the pail, I must do it with this proviso, that a different mode of management be adopted from that now practised.[6]

In many books two of the main areas of work for the farmer's wife are omitted. Poultry is ignored altogether, as if it had no impact on the profitability of the farm, and, although cattle are frequently mentioned, their produce of milk, butter and cheese is barely referred to. That it is the farmer who dominates the scene is aptly illustrated in a description of the ideal position of the farmhouse in *Rural Recreations*. It must be 40–50 yards distant from the offices, because of fire risk, and living near the cattle and dung-heap. The farmer must hold sway: the house must not be, 'in such a situation as to preclude the eye of the master from commanding a distinct view of all the operations that are going forward in his home-stead.'[7] Was there any positive recognition of the expected tasks of these shadowy women voiced in the masculine world of farming literature? Was it shown that they *were* expected to contribute to the economic production of goods from the farm and was their task made clear? *The Farmer's Kalendar* by Arthur Young, does acknowledge the work of the wife.

> Now begins the hurry of the dairyman's business: this is one of the most ticklish parts of the Farmer's business. Unless he has a very diligent and industrious wife, who sees minutely to her dairy…he will assuredly lose money by his dairy: trusted to common servants. [8]

In some of these manuals the responsibilities of the farmer's wife are clearly outlined. *The Farmer's Wife or Complete Country Housewife* emphases its purpose on the title page:

> Instructions full and plain we give
> To teach the Farmer's Wife
> With satisfaction how to live,
> The happy Country life.[9]

The manual contains detailed instructions for the care of poultry, beekeeping, making beer, country wines and cooking recipes. A farmer named William Ellis was a popular mid eighteenth-century writer giving both agricultural and horticultural advice. In *The Country Housewife's Family Companion* he instructs the farmer's wife that

The keeping of Salves and other Remedies in the House, so as to have them always

6   J. Billingsley, *A General View of the Agriculture in the County of Somerset* (1794) 112.

7   A Farmer, *Rural Recreations* (1802) 2.

8   A. Young, *The Farmers' Kalendar* (1771) May.

9   Anon, *The Farmer's Wife, or Complete Country Housewife* (1780).

Figure 1   A farmer's wife in her yard with the chickens.

From René Antoine Ferchault de Reamur *The art of hatching and bringing up domestic fowls.* (1750)

(Museum of English Rural Life)

in Readiness, is of such Importance in Gentlemen's, Yeomen's and Farmers' Families, that none should be without them, by reason of the many Accidents that a Country Family is more liable to than most others …'[10]

A wife also needed a wide range of culinary expertise, especially useful at harvest time; she was expected to make brawn, pickle pork, skim milk from her dairy and grains from her brewings, and preserve vegetables and fruit. Ellis also told her how to make butter and wean the calves. His book is an excellent example of a manual for farmers' wives, acknowledging their role, and making sure they know how to carry it out. The care of poultry being the wife's province, she would have done well to take the advice of Edward Lisle from Crux Easton in Hampshire who published *Observations in Husbandry* in 1757. 'Ducks I am informed, generally lay in the night, wherefore a careful dame drives them then into a lower coop … she can then keep on feeding them and those which have not laid can be kept in and she will not lose their eggs.'[11] It is difficult to assess the work of these women in relation to their expected roles as outlined in the manuals. Some evidence that they undertook some of their tasks is to be found scattered among diaries, notebooks and other documents. Material which illustrates fully the range of their daily lives as cooks, brewers, apothecaries and veterinarians, with responsibility for servants, poultry and dairy produce, is scarce. The diary of a female member of the Sutton

10 William Ellis, *The Country Housewife's Family Companion* (1750) viii.

11 Edward Lisle, *Observations in Husbandry* (1757) 346.

family[12] from near Tavistock, contains an inventory of 'my things', a few recipes for curing people, bullocks and horses, some farming accounts, and an arrangement that Edward Muchmore, a servant, would have his woollen clothes made and mended in the house. Mary Hardy, the daughter of a prominent Norfolk yeoman farmer, kept a diary from 1773 to 1809. She made some weather records, kept an account of servants, and in October 1774 wrote: 'hired W. Crane for a year at £2. 10 exclusive of hiring money, as he is a good boy'. She was also involved with the killing of pigs and the keeping of poultry.[13]

In order to understand the lives of these forgotten wives of the 'middling sort' their own writings are important. But this is not enough to put them in context and set them against the background of their time. Some insight into their inner worlds, as in literary taste, or religious thinking, is needed. Documents containing both practical and literary insight into the life of a working farmer's wife are extremely scarce; even the large collection in the Museum of English Rural Life library has proved unproductive. There is, however one such document in the Hampshire Record Office which offers insight into the inner world of a farmer's wife of the 'middling sort', as well as illustrating all her practical responsibilities in the day-to-day running of the farm. Because of the scarcity of material in this field of research, it is a very valuable contribution to the limited knowledge we have of this group of women. This book examines this evidence and sets it against the background of the time.

The author was Mary Bacon (1743–1818), a farmer's wife who lived approximately seven miles north of Alton in Hampshire. This, her legacy to future historians, is a very unusual, if not unique, document in the form of a ledger in which she made entries from 1789 to 1807.[14] The book illustrates her work on the farm and adds a further dimension by giving an insight into her literary taste and religious meditations, showing, through her own reading list and copied written material, a background of both education and rusticity. She used an old account book belonging to her uncle Augustin Kinchin, a yeoman farmer, in which to make her entries. At first glance the book appears to be a ledger but only about half has been used for this purpose. As a result the document gives a remarkable insight into the work and mind of a farmer's wife and contributes to what is known of both eighteenth-century reading and agriculture.

The ledger illustrates the role of a farmer's wife in her everyday life and as an

---

12 MERL DEV 3/8/1.
13 *Mary Hardy's Diary*, ed. B. Cozens Hardy, Norfolk Record Society (1968). First written 1773 to 1809. 19 September, 1774.
14 Hampshire Record Office (HRO) 28M82/F1.

assistant on the farm. It includes accounts which were usually kept by men, but in this ledger it was the wife who entered sales of wheat, oats and barley, butter, wool and honey, her records ranging from the cows and horses her husband purchased, to household items such as the exact number of nails needed to repair the house. It is not surprising that she mentioned the weather in her ledger as diaries, newspapers, and letters written in the eighteenth century habitually contained such news. It was a subject as popular then as it is today. She also recorded farming reports, dates of fairs, and some indications of sale of stock. Her very full inventory, which includes all the brewing equipment she used, yields a colourful, detailed and very useful description of the entire contents of a late eighteenth-century farmhouse. A large section, 'My Book of Receipts', contains her favourite recipes together with cures to give family and friends for their sick animals and their own illnesses. 'Twelve True Old Golden Rules' is a conduct book in miniature, instructing a middle-class woman, who is doing much of her own housekeeping, how to look after her house economically.

Second, and of equal importance, is the light the ledger sheds on reading by middle-class eighteenth-century rural women. The document illustrates a wide range of taste in reading, both through a list of 59 books and the material which Mary Bacon copied into it. This includes long narrative renderings in prose and poetry of well loved Bible stories, a popular, amusing and moral tale of a soldier and a pack of cards, together with religious musings and hymns. Religion was important to Mary and she owned weighty tomes of sermons and meditations, prayer books and bibles. Although the ledger is not a diary, it includes the kind of almanac material frequently found at the beginning and end of diaries of the period, such as information about the West Indies, and the moon and planets, both popular subjects at the time. In a lighter vein, a disaster story, a trial, and a voyage, are included in her book list, and she also copied out a letter purported to be from Queen Charlotte to the King of Prussia complaining about his treatment of her native state of Mecklenburg, an unusual document which was in circulation at the time.

The ledger was started on 31 October 1748 by Mary Bacon's uncle, Augustin Kinchin, a yeoman farmer who lived at Woodcote Farm (Woodcut, or Woodcott) in Woodmancott, a small village in north-west Hampshire. He continued making entries up to 11 October 1765, by which time his writing had become shaky and he may have been unwell. His records are concerned with both farming and personal accounts and give brief, sometimes tantalising, glimpses into rural life in the mid-eighteenth century. His farming accounts itemise the crops he sold, the number of sheep and pigs he kept, the servants he employed, and what their exact functions were. Notes of loans, signed by both parties, were recorded, some concerning sums lent to servants. His personal accounts include problems he was having with his wife's patrimony, the amounts he paid for wine, newspapers, different kinds of footwear and clothing, horses, mortgages and the repair of his wife's stays. At some point in the late 1780s his niece took over the book.

When Mary Bacon started making her entries, she and her husband William were farming in Cliddesden, a village immediately south of Basingstoke; they cover a further fourteen years after the family moved to Aylesfield farm, which is situated approximately three miles north of Alton. A ledger with entries by two separate people can be confusing. When turning the pages, such is the mixture that one is never sure what to expect next. Part of the accounts written by Augustin Kinchin from 1748 to 1775, in his elaborate, almost indecipherable, curling hand, may occupy a third of a page, while accounts in Mary's neat sloping writing fill the rest. Another page turned at random contains some Kinchin accounts and a couple of loan notes, followed by the date of the Bacons' daughter's wedding. Yet more accounts are suddenly interrupted by Mary's 'My Book of Receipts', at the end of which she turned the whole ledger upside down and started again from the back.

Because entries in the ledger are often jumbled and haphazard, the material has been rearranged by subject matter for the purposes of this book. Augustin Kinchin, his ancestors, land and farming practices, provided Mary Bacon with a centuries-old background of rural life which had changed little. Inclusion of his accounts is important as they offer small insights into the daily life of a mid eighteenth-century yeoman farmer from the south of England. This background, symbolised in the keeping of her Woodmancott Prayer Book throughout her life, was obviously important to Mary, contributed to her early formative years, and is the subject of Chapter One. Chapter Two covers her married life, her children, and house, Aylesfield farm, with all its contents. I am guilty of speculation as to her fears and pleasures, but certain events are discussed which may have been experienced, if not by her, then by those around her. There were periods of rejoicing, most of them concerned with national celebrations well recorded in newspapers, farming events, and local betting on the hop returns for the country. The continual cloud of war hung over the 1790s, resulting in bread shortages, escaped prisoners in the neighbourhood, and the pressure on farmers due to the increasing recruitment of men into the services, bleeding the land of much needed labour. The first part of Chapter Three considers the farming accounts, alongside material from reports to the Board of Agriculture. The second part of the chapter discusses the weather, a vital subject for farmers. Mary's own reports are interspersed with records from contemporary diarists, graphically illustrating the biting cold of an eighteenth-century winter. Chapters Four, Five, and Six

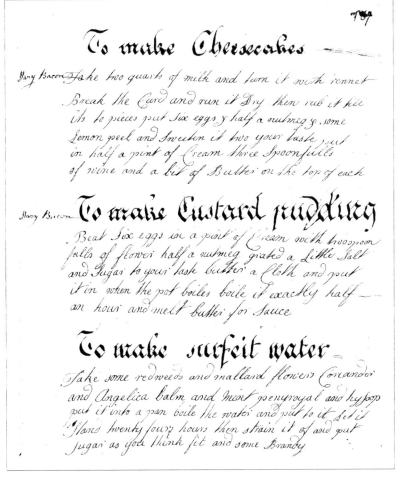

Figure 2   A page from Mary Bacon's 'My Book of Receipts'

(HRO 28M82/F1)

are concerned with 'My Book of Receipts' which contains a long list of food recipes, and cures for animals and humans. Interspersed is information from contemporary documents which sets the 'receipts' in context, relates them to other similar writers and gives some idea as to how they were made. In Chapter Seven Mary Bacon's list of books is examined and her own writing and copying of miscellaneous material discussed. Chapter Eight is concerned with religion and includes both writings in the ledger and an analysis of the books on Mary's list which come under this heading. One section relates to an Oedipal version of the story of Judas Iscariot, which she copied out and which has been traced to a tract in the British Library and before that to a medieval source. The chapter concludes with some speculation as to the end of her life, and her musings on the soul. A series of appendices includes a family tree, a table of measures, the full list of books owned by Mary Bacon with bibliographical notes, and an annotated list of the plants most commonly used in her recipes. The original spelling and grammar has been kept in all quotations from the ledger.

When put together, the document offers a remarkable insight into the mental world of a middle-class farmer's wife together with glimpses of her everyday life. Although this book is about a Hampshire woman, it is not confined to that county but is generally relevant to rural southern England. It contributes to the study of literacy in the eighteenth-century, giving some indication of the kind of reading material of interest to a busy farmer's wife. It is about those women who were gradually gaining the freedom to read, middle-class women who were expanding their horizons and learning about their world on a much wider level than before. It is a history which many people leave, small facts about themselves, important dates in their lives, their likes and dislikes, and what they are paid, or spend their money on. This is only a small part of the story of Mary Bacon, a relatively unknown farmer's wife, but these little histories add to our knowledge of the past. History is what we make it. We can never get back into the past, but we can get a little nearer in an effort to understand it. No written work can stand alone; it is part of its time and must be considered in relation to the people and events of the period. Fascinating and useful though this ledger is (and no doubt an edition of it might have found some limited interest), its value is far greater when set against a contemporary background. In trying to bridge the gap in time, I have used the work of many contemporary writers, some printed and some in manuscript. They include newspaper editors, diarists, agriculturalists, and writers about a diversity of subjects, who were much closer to the age of Mary Bacon than we are today.

Chapter One

Mary Kinchin

I N T H E H A M L E T of Woodmancott,[1] in north Hampshire, stands a little Victorian chapel. Next to it is a modern farmhouse complete with shiny grain hoppers where once house, barns, wagon sheds, and stables for the draught and riding horses belonging to the Kinchin family were situated. Although Woodmancott is a small village, the parish consisting of approximately 1,404 acres, it is not as isolated as it appears. It is near the county town of Winchester and within easy reach of Basingstoke, described by Celia Fiennes as 'a large town for to entertaine travellers and commodious.'[2]

Little remains in Woodmancott from the eighteenth-century. The Kinchins' original house has been pulled down; only the front flint and brick boundary wall remains. The property is shown in outline on an eighteenth-century map preserved in the archives of Winchester College, depicting a large, double-gabled building, an appropriate dwelling for a yeoman whose father was a 'gentleman'.[3] The house, with about 650 acres, including copses and downland for sheep, had been in the family since 1649. It is possible that there was a short gap in tenure as a house, almost certainly the same property, was advertised to let through a detailed description in *Henry's Winchester Journal* on 9 March 1747.

To be LETT

And Enter'd upon at Michaelmas next

A Farm at Woodmancott in Hampshire, within nine Miles of Winchester, seven of Basingstoke, and five of Aylesford, three Market Towns. The Farm consists of near 610 Acres of arable Land in exceeding good Condition; 35 Acres of Pasture and Meadow, and about 53 Acres of Wood; all inclosed (except 30 Acres in the Common Fields of Woodmancott aforesaid) with Right of Common on a Down

---

1   Sometimes referred to as Woodcut, or Woodcott.
2   C. Fiennes, *The Journeys of Celia Fiennes*, ed. C. Morris (1949) 28. First published on or before 1696.
3   Winchester College Archives 21448 (1761).

called Beckhurst Down adjoining to the said arable land for 400 Sheep, and Underwood sufficient for fuel and other Uses for the Tennant. The Mansion-house, Barns and all Out-houses in very good Repair – For further Particulars enquire of the Town Clerk of Winchester; Mr. Noyes of Andover; Mr. Beale of Newbury, or a Mr. Kinchin of Woodmancott aforesaid. N.B . All manner of Utensils in Husbandry likewise to be disposed of.

This land had been in the Kinchin family for several generations. It was very appropriate that in marrying William Bacon Mary was to become a farmer's wife herself.

There is nothing left of the medieval church of St James, in which Mary Bacon's ancestors, the Kinchins, worshipped, married and were sometimes buried; it was burnt in a fire on Easter Day 1854. Until 1838 the church was a chapelry dependent upon the nearby parish of Brown Candover, where Mary Kinchin's baptism was registered on 15 December 1743. Now the only part of the original site that remains is the churchyard where very few tombstones are left with which to remember those long dead.

Farming was very heavy work and life was hard in the eighteenth-century, yet people found time and energy to enjoy celebrations, which often took place on a national scale; the Kinchins' centre for these jollifications was Winchester. Perhaps Augustin Kinchin took his family to watch the festivities there in October 1746? Did his niece then only three years old, go too? *Henry's Winchester Journal* reported that,

> Thursday last being the Day appointed for a general thanksgiving, the same was observed here with great solemnity by People of all Ranks. In the morning a most excellent Sermon suitable to the occasion, was preached at the Cathedral by the Rev. Dr. Sykes. In the Evening there were the Grandest Illuminations accompanied with Bonfires, and various kinds of Fireworks, that had been known for many years. And, in short, nothing was Wanting to express the sincerity of our Day.[4]

Relationships are part of a family background and Mary Bacon had many relatives. She came from a large family of Kinchins, most of whom lived in towns and villages situated in north Hampshire. Her paternal grandfather, Mr Augustine Kinchin, is referred to as 'Gent' in all the documents concerning him, whereas her uncle, Augustin Kinchin, from whom she inherited the ledger, was a 'yeoman'. Her paternal grandmother was a Terry (Thierry) and came from a gentry family said to date back to the time of William the Conqueror. The Terrys were well known in the neighbourhood and were acquaintances of Jane Austen's family. The birth of James, Augustin Kinchin's younger brother and Mary Kinchin's father, is entered in the family page of the Woodmancott parish register thus: 'ye son of Mr Augustine Kinchin & Anne his wife was born ye 2d June about 8 at night, & was baptised ye 8th day of ye same month 1713.' James became a grocer in Dummer, possibly with the help of the Terry family who lived there, although at the time of his marriage in Winchester Cathedral to Sarah Wake on 22 February 1742 he was described as a yeoman of Woodmancott.[5] There were two children of the marriage, Ann and Mary. James died at the age of 33, and his widow married Joseph Husbands, the Dummer Parish Clerk who was to become the young Mary's stepfather.

It is difficult to know how well Mary Kinchin knew individual members of her extended family, but she certainly had strong connections with Augustin Kinchin and Woodmancott, including in the list of books which she owned, 'Woodmancut Common Prayer book'. Although still very young when she moved to Dummer with her parents, it is likely that contact with her uncle would have continued. Kinchin was principally an arable, sheep and pig farmer and made careful records of his stock. In 1751 he noted in his ledger, 'an account of my Hogs and Pigs' and listed '9 great shoots 3 sows 22 pigs and 3 great shoots out of old Knight's sow 1 dead pig since 4 more pigs since.'[6] The price of a pig averaged 12s. 6d. per animal. Black pigs were said to taste better and Kinchin sold 'a pigg of the black sort' for £1. There is no description of his ordinary pigs; they were probably 'the native hog of this county… a coarse, raw boned, flat-sided animal,' as described by Charles Vancouver. [7] It was not until the 1770s when the Chinese pig was introduced that commercial breeds began to change from their close resemblance to wild boar. Kinchin also farmed sheep, listing a total of 682 animals in November 1755. There are very few entries of the sale of sheep, but he did record that in 1748 he sold 40 lambs at 3s. 6d. each. Wool and sheepskins were the main products from sheep and in July 1755 Kinchin recorded 'sold sheep and lamb wool.' There is no record of any particular breed, but W. and A. Driver in their *General View of the Agriculture of the County of Hants*, gave some indication of what kind of sheep might have been grazing in the vicinity of Woodmancott. 'The original Hampshire sheep is horned, and for the most part with a white face, though some few have speckled faces; they were formerly long-legged and narrow…'.[8] Horse skins were also sold – did Mary Kinchin know Jolly and Diamond whose hides were sold for 10s. in 1756? Money was also earned by

5 As a 'grocer' James Kinchin probably sold a variety of goods, an eighteenth-century version of a supermarket, rather than a village shop.
6 A 'shoot' was a pig of ¾ years and was considered to be the best for pork while those of 1–1½ years were used for bacon.
7 C. Vancouver, *General View of the Agriculture of Hampshire including the Isle of Wight*, Board of Agriculture (1813) 350.
8 Abraham and William Driver, *General View of the Agriculture of the county of Hants* (1794) 23.

wintering other people's cattle: 'John Martin's cow came to wintring at 6*d*. a week', a farming practice followed by Mary and William Bacon when they had their own farm.

Much of the land was used to grow grain; Kinchin recorded various crops, noting the amount of barley and wheat sent to the mill, but also that some of it was kept 'for my own winnowing.' He grew peas, but beans are not recorded, and also made money from selling wood for fuel, either as faggots, long faggots, or bavins.[9] The grounds around Woodmancott Farm are spacious and it appears from the Winchester map that in Kinchin's time there was a garden. He bought 200 plants for 8*d*. and paid a gardener. He also purchased 400 cabbage plants for the same amount and at a later date 'colly flower plants'. Most eighteenth-century farms, however small, would have had some apple trees, and so it is surprising that a Mrs. Chamberlain was paid 8*s*. for a sack of apples in 1751. The only other food item recorded was cheese bought at Winchester Fair. Although mainly for the sale of sheep, cattle (including oxen) and horses, the fair was particularly well known for the sale of cheeses.

There were household expenses too. Circulating libraries, where newspapers were commonly read, were only just beginning to open in 1748; Kinchin had his newspaper delivered. This is confirmed by a record included in the list of disbursements for 1748, which noted that he paid the newsman 21*s*. although he does not give the period this covered. The entry for 10 January 1752 was more specific: 'pd Mr Collins the newsman in full to St Thomas Day last past for newspapers and Ink 0 9 0.'[10] Candles were needed to read the newspaper and on 10 January 1752 Kinchin paid 3*s*. 2*d*. for three iron candlesticks. There were more personal purchases including articles of clothing; in 1751 Kinchin paid 3*s*. 7*d*. for gloves and breeches and 17*s*. 6*d*. for a Great Coat. Two further entries show that a variety of footwear was bought. In the same year, 'Jany 6th pd Freeborn for my cork shoes 0 6 0' and in 1753 'bought a pair of pattens'.[11] There is one enigmatic entry on 12 May 1748: 'pd Mrs. Wheeler for redeeming the wifes stays'. Kinchin paid to be shaved, although there is only one entry for this recorded in 1767, when he was quite an elderly man. Beds had to be renovated and in 1751 £1 5*s*. 8*d*. was spent on 11 yards of bed ticking. Other purchases included a chopping block and a trivet in 1767, but the prices are not given. Both cinnamon water, and white wine at 1*s*. 6*d*. a bottle, were favourites of the Kinchins as they appear several times in the accounts. In January 1752 Augustin Kinchin

9 Bavin: bunch of untrimmed brushwood tied with two withies. Faggots: tied with one withy.
10 St. Thomas's Day was the 21st December. Payment was therefore for three weeks; unfortunately it
    is impossible to calculate the price of Kinchin's newspapers as a purchase of ink was included.
11 Shoes which had a wooden sole mounted on an iron ring, raising the foot off the ground. They
    were secured with a leather strap, which passed over the instep.

may have depleted his cellars over Christmas as his wine purchasing increased. He bought 16 bottles of wine on 10 January, 16 on 28 January and another 16 on 10 February, this time at a guinea a time. It is interesting that the accounts actually specify white wine, as wine in the eighteenth century frequently meant port or Madeira. Mary Bacon may have learnt to brew beer from visits to her uncle as he recorded purchases of malt and hops.

Money was also spent travelling and there is an entry in a very neat hand, possibly that of Mrs. Kinchin:

1757	16 febry by porter turnpike & expenses	0	6	6
	23 by porter turnpike & expenses		4	6
	27 by porter turnpike &		5	0

The cost of the turnpike itself was not very great in comparison with the total amount spent on travelling on each of these days. Although at a later date, and therefore possibly reflecting an increase in price, figures recorded in the *Hampshire Chronicle* on 11 March 1793 give some indication as to cost. Had Mrs Kinchin had her own transport, her payment would have come under the category of 'every coach, berlin, landau, chariot, chaise, calash, chair, caravan, or hearse, drawn by six horses, mares, geldings, or mules'; for which the turnpike toll was one shilling. However, she travelled 'by porter' and the turnpike cost could have been as little as 3*d*.

Riding horses were very high on Augustin Kinchin's list of priorities. He spent large sums on them, and in October 1751 travelled the long distance to Rugby fair where he bought three horses, which he carefully described and entered into his ledger. There was 'a Bald Sorrel Gelding 2 years old at £8 10*s*', a 'Little black mare 3 white leggs 1 yr old' at £6 4*s*. and most expensive of all, a 'Bay Nagg 4 years old' at £14 1*s*. By 1700 £8 was considered a fairly high figure to pay for a mare[12] and therefore it may be assumed that Kinchin's new horses were for riding. His taste had become more expensive as in 1748 he had only paid £6 for a mare and gelding. Thomas Turner, a village grocer at East Hoathly, Sussex, received only £2 10*s*. in 1756 for his riding horse, which he sold after it threw him.[13] Buying a horse was an important piece of business and Augustin Kinchin would have been well advised to treat the matter with great care and attention. Listed among Mary Bacon's books is *The English Horseman and Complete Farrier*, a title which I have been unable to trace. She was not always accurate in copying and it is possible that she in fact possessed the *Compleat Horseman or Perfect Farrier*, a manual which may have belonged to her uncle. It is to be hoped that if so, he read the chapter 'After what manner a Man should mount and try a Horse he intends to buy', before setting off to Rugby. He

12 J. Thirsk, *The Rural Economy of England* (1984) 397.
13 Thomas Turner, *The Diary of Thomas Turner 1754–1765* ed. D. Vaisey (1994) 41.

would have been advised to,

> Take the Horse as he comes out of the Stable, and if possible before he hath been
> rid that day, and without animaling, or in the least frightening him with your Legs
> or Rod, slack your bridle-hand about four Finger's breadth, more than is necessary
> to feel him on the Hand, letting him go at a Step according to his own Fancy and
> Humour, with his head lolling if he will, and you no ways troubling him: Now if you
> can have but Patience to let him walk thus for a quarter of an Hour, if he incline to
> stumble, he will trip more than once, and perhaps salute the Ground with his Nose,
> if he be very subject to it. If he be heavy on the Hand, he will rest wholly upon the
> Bit, and be a burden to the Bridle-hand. If he be dull and lazy, he will diminish
> insensibly the train of his Walk, and will at last stand still. [14]

A final, wise piece of advice is given, of which all purchasers of horses should take
heed, 'Lastly, when you are buying a Horse, take care not to fall in love with him, for
when this Passion hath once seized you, you are no longer in a Condition to judge
of his Imperfections.' Equine accessories were included in the accounts: Robert
Ricketts was paid 8*s.* 6*d.* for 'Bridle whip & Comb'.

Mary was thus the child of a large north Hampshire family; she had a strong
farming background and church connections. Her father died when she was very
young and, although her mother remarried, links were undoubtedly kept up with
the Woodmancott branch of the family. It is possible that she and her sister Anne
spent some time on the farm there with their aunt and uncle during their childhood. After all, it was Mary who took over her uncle's ledger for her own use, and
the tie with him may have been a close one. She was ideally suited to become a
farmer's wife.

Mary Bacon's life almost certainly began at Woodmancott; her baptism appears
in the Brown Candover register on the family page with all her aunts and uncles:
'Mary daughter of James and Mary Kinchin[15] was baptised Dec 15 1743.' At some
point the family moved to Dummer, home of the Terry family, where James Kinchin
became a grocer. It was a parish known to have connections with royalty. In about
1788 the Prince of Wales rented the nearby Kempshott House as a hunting lodge to
which he took Mrs. Fitzherbert and is said to have furnished it to her taste. 'Seraglio'
apparently existed and certainly the Prince's conduct scandalised the village and
the neighbourhood.[16] There is no evidence of Mary Kinchin's education although
she must have gone to school. Her writing is neat and clear, but her grammar and

---

14 Sieur de Sollysell, *Compleat Horseman: or Perfect Farrier*, trans. Sir William Hope, 4th edition
  (1729) 60–61, 69.

15 James Kinchin's wife was named Sarah, not Mary and it is likely that this was an error of the clerk
  who made the entry in the register.

16 *Hampshire Treasures*, Hampshire County Council (1979).

spelling are often inaccurate; her accounting usually adds up, but it was irregularly maintained.

James Kinchin did not live to a great age and the evidence of his will is that he had little money to leave. In the eighteenth-century wills were rarely made until death was imminent and survival unlikely; James was only 33 when he signed the document in which he bequeathed his daughter Mary his tea kettle. Unfortunately, it does not appear in her extremely detailed inventory and it is not known what happened to it.

Will of James Kinchin May 8th, 1746

Dummer in the county of Southampton, grocer

I will that my debts and funeral charges be paid and discharged and that my household goods be sold to pay it except the Tea kettle which I give to my Daughter Mary, my wife having the use of it during her widowhood ... I give to my loving wife Sarah Kinchin all my linen and two silver teaspoons mark'd with D.K. and as for my woollen clothes I give it to my two children Mary & Ann, if it be not sold to pay debts. I give to my Brother Stephen my Gun I desire my Brother Stephen and my Brother-in-law Thomas Wolveridge of lower Froyle to be Trustees to my children but not to take them from their mother without her consent and in case one of my children should die the other shall inherit her share. I nominate and appoint my brother Stephen and my Brother Woolveridge Joint Executors of this will witness my hand and seal this eighth day of May 1746.[17]

James's widow Sarah married Joseph Husbands, Parish Clerk, in Dummer on 27 July 1747.

Although not everyone went to church in the eighteenth-century, Mary Kinchin was undoubtedly brought up as a good Christian within the Established church, as is well endorsed by the number of religious books she owned. Such books often contained detailed advice on how children should be brought up to fear the Lord. It is not possible to speculate as to what kind of a child Mary Kinchin was, but there is evidence from the number of religious books she owned, which included her mother's Bible, and the religious writings she copied into her ledger, to suggest she was brought up in this faith. Mary probably met her future husband through friends and relatives. At some time before her marriage, she went to stay in Cliddesden, a small village with scattered farms south of Basingstoke, where William Bacon and his family lived and farmed. In February 1765, four months before her own wedding, she was witness to another marriage there, presumably that of a friend. She also had relatives in Cliddesden and may have attended a Kinchin marriage recorded

17 HRO Wills Index: 1748B/063.

in the parish register in 8 June 1765. And so Mary Kinchin started her life as Mrs. Bacon in a place she knew, where she had friends, and where she was to live as a farmer's wife, a way of living with which she was thoroughly conversant.

Chapter Two

Mrs. Bacon

MARY AND WILLIAM Bacon were married at Cliddesden, a small farming village two miles south of Basingstoke, dominated by Hackwood House, the seat of the Duke of Bolton. The marriage, conducted by Christopher Fox the curate, took place on 25 June 1765 and was by licence, indicating that Mary was not a long-term resident of the parish. How she met William Bacon, and where, remains unknown. As there was a Kinchin living in Cliddesden, the introduction probably took place through relatives. William and Mary Bacon had six children and farmed tenanted land in Cliddesden for the next 26 years. The Bishop's visitation of 1788 recorded a population of 310 in the parish of Cliddesden which contained 3,000 acres.[1] It is difficult to assess the size or exact situation of the Bacons' farm, but it was certainly productive, as the sale of grains totalled approximately £578 from September 1790 to June 1791. Apple and pear grafting seemed to have been of some importance to the residents and a document in the parish records some of their names.[2] Broad Nose Pippin, Honey Comb, Strawberry, Lemon Pippin, Margill, Pelly Con, and French Bennec were all apples grafted in 1786. Green Catherine and Autumn Bergamot were the only pears recorded.

Many of the farms in the area belonged to the Earl of Portsmouth and his leases serve as a good example of the arrangements made between landlord and tenant in the eighteenth century and the kind of farming practised.[3] Although not William Bacon's actual lease, his would have been very similar. The document describes the land 'Buildings Barns Stables Outhouses Orchards Gardens feedings Sheeplights ways paths passages water ponds profits privileges advantages and appurtenances whatsoever to the said demised premises.' The landlord had the right to trees and saplings, to cut, pollard and take away. The leaseholder, had to keep in good repair 'the said Messuage Barns Stables Buildings Walls Gates Posts Pales Rails Stiles

1   Visitation return. HRO 21M65B4/3/35.
2   Cliddesden Parish records. HRO 44M69M/2/6/1.
3   Lease of Swallick farm to Charles Hoare for 14 years. HRO 15M84/3/1/39.

Hedges Ditches Mounds Bounds and fences of and belonging to the said demised premises.' Straw and fodder had to be consumed on the premises; manuring was an important part of eighteenth-century husbandry and instructions for this were carefully spelt out in the lease. 'And the Dung Soil and Compost from then aris-ing as made shall and will spread lay and bestow thereon in a proper husbandlike manner'. Instructions were also given in relation to the sheep. 'And shall and will during the said term pen and fold on the said premises his or their whole flock of sheep which he or they shall keep and depasture thereon in the usual manner.' and in the last year of the term 'will pen and fold thereon one hundred and twenty sheep at the least and from and after the twelfth day of May in such last year will fold the same on such parts of the said premises …'. The arable lands were subjected to a 'proper and regular course of Husbandry and not more than three parts in five thereof in any one year. And in the last year of the said term will leave one fifth part of the said arable lands of one years lay and one other fifth part thereof of two years lay.' Finally, the landlord was to be permitted to sow grass seeds with the summer and Lenten grain. Nothing is stated in this lease about land tax but some landlords either paid all taxes or those levied by Parliament. The tenant might then pay those levied by the parish, or sometimes the cost was split between landlord and tenant. There is nothing in the Bacon accounts to give any indication of arrangements made regarding the payment of these taxes.

William, John, Mary, James, Sarah and another James, who died when he was only a few months old, were all born in Cliddesden. There is little in the ledger that gives any information as to their upbringing but it may be assumed that they attended the village school, which was endowed with £10 a year by the Earl of Portsmouth. As a farmer's children, they would have been expected to work on the farm as well as attending school. Their strong Christian upbringing is indicated by the inclusion of religious works for young people in the booklist which Mary wrote out in her ledger. (see Appendix Two)

The production of books written specifically for children was increasing rapidly during the eighteenth century and Mary had a little book, *Divine Songs, in easy language for the use of children*, in her collection which was one of the most popu-lar of these publications.[4] The songs cover the usual range of moral teaching and include such subjects as lying, quarrelling, fighting, scoffing and calling each other names. Children are exhorted not to swear, curse or take God's name in vain and they are not to keep evil company. There are dark and awful warnings of what will happen to naughty children in the after life. If they are holy, they will go to heaven when they die, but sinners are condemned to a dreadful hell 'and everlasting pains',

4 Isaac Watts, *Divine Songs: attempted in easy language for the use of children* (1715).

dwelling with devils, darkness, and chains, and burning in brimstone and fire. The wrath of God, if a child is hardened in sin, will bring 'one stroke of his almighty rod' which will 'send young sinners quickly to hell.' That, with the idea that there was no repentance after death, must have been a terrifying prospect for young minds. Some of these *Divine Songs* lasted well into the twentieth century and as a child in the 1940s, I remember my father reciting three of them. 'Let dogs delight to bark and bite' and 'Birds in their little nests agree' are phrases that remain with me still. A song for very young children included in the book, is gentler and encourages the little singers to be busy and virtuous. Although there is mention of Satan, it does not contain the frightening threats of eternal damnation made to older children.

> How doth the little busy bee
> Improve the shining hour,
> And gather honey all the day,
> From every opening flower.
>
> How skilfully she builds her Cell,
> How neat she spreads her wax
> And labours hard to store it well
> With the sweet food she makes.
>
> In works of labour or of skill,
> I would be easy too;
> For Satan finds some mischief still,
> For idle hands to do.
>
> In books, or works, or healthful play,
> Let my first years be past,
> That I may give for every day
> Some good account at last.

It is to be hoped that the Bacon children were also given lighter material to read, or to have read to them, although none was included in the list. There were many cheap tracts and chapbooks in circulation during their childhood, which included fables, fairy tales and romanticised history among other subjects. *The History of Jack and the Giants*[5] was one of the most popular and described 'Jack's Birth and Parentage, his Dispute with a Country Vicar etc. How he slew a Monstrous Giant on the Mount of Cornwall, by which Achievement he obtained the name of Jack the Giant-killer. How King Arthur's Son met Jack, and the wonderful things they performed in their travels...' and so on. Also published in tracts or chapbooks, *The Sleeping Beauty in*

---

5   There are a number of versions of this tract appearing in the late eighteenth and early nineteenth centuries, printed in different parts of the country.

the Wood, and *The History of the two Children in the Wood*, were popular stories for children in circulation at the time.

In 1791 the family moved to Aylesfield farm, renting arable, hop growing and sheep farming land of approximately 165 acres in the north of the parish of Alton. Mary recorded in her ledger: '1791 June 22 we came to Ailesfield farm to Live we took it for fourteen years & the time will be expired in the year 1805'. Leases were commonly made for seven years or a multiple of seven. The land was described by Driver and Driver as 'high and chalky with a thin staple'.[6] At the end of the eighteenth century the farming land in the parish consisted of 3,556 acres of arable, 132 acres devoted to hops, and 87 acres of meadow, a surprisingly small amount, and finally, 201 acres of woodland. The parish was mainly divided into small farms, the average value being approximately 14s. an acre.

Aylesfield farm is strikingly situated on the ridge of the Downs in front of a panoramic view over north Hampshire. It is not possible to tell the size of the original house from the map, but the total area of buildings was quite extensive. The house dates back to the seventeenth century and is of two stories with a half-hipped clay tile roof and a central chimney; nothing of the old farmyard remains.[7] The owner of a property was expected to ensure that at the change of a lease everything was handed over in good order, but when William and Mary Bacon moved in they found that there was work to do. Mary recorded that 'When we come to Ailesfield farm' they spent £43 15s. She then went on to list items needed for repairs and included the amount paid to the workman.

1791 June Edwards Bill		
27	4 holdfast 7d & brush 6d	0 = 1 = 1
	/2 a pint of Linseed oil	0 = 0 = 3/2
28	6 holdfast at 1 /2	0 = 0 = 9
	2 Do at 2	0 = 0 = 4
	1 staple 2 & /4 dore nayls 2d /2	0 = 0 = 4
29	100 = 8 nails & file 2 /2	0 = 0 = 10 /2
July 2	4 hundred nails	0 = 0 = 2
	3 staples at 2d and 1 Do 3d	0 = 0 = 9
		0 = 4 = 7
Andrews Bill		1 = 17 = 8
Do - - - -		0 = 5 = 6

Hurdles were also needed and 8 dozen were purchased in October at £2. Added to this a further £3 12s. 6d. was spent on chips, '5 cord of Grub wood', and another cord

6 Abraham and William Driver, *General View of the Agriculture of the county of Hants* (1794) 285–6.
7 *Hampshire Treasures* (1982) 297.

FRONTISPIECE.
Engraved for Henderson's Housekeepers Instructor

THE
·HOUSEKEEPER's INSTRUCTOR;
OR,
UNIVERSAL FAMILY COOK.
BEING AN AMPLE AND CLEAR DISPLAY OF THE
ART OF COOKERY
IN ALL ITS VARIOUS BRANCHES.
CONTAINING
Proper Directions for Dressing all Kinds of
BUTCHER's MEAT, POULTRY, GAME, FISH, &c.
ALSO, THE METHOD OF PREPARING
SOUPS, HASHES, AND MADE DISHES;
WITH THE WHOLE ART OF
CONFECTIONARY, PRESERVING, PICKLING, &c.
Likewise, The Making and Keeping in Perfection
BRITISH WINES;
AND CERTAIN
RULES FOR BREWING MALT LIQUOR,
As well for Family Consumption as the Regale of private Visitants;
TO WHICH IS ADDED,
The Complete Art of Carving,
ILLUSTRATED WITH ENGRAVINGS,
Explaining, by proper References, the Manner in which the Young Practitioner may acquit himself at Table with Elegance and Ease.
ALSO,
BILLS OF FARE FOR EVERY MONTH IN THE YEAR;
WITH *COPPER PLATES,* DISPLAYING THE BEST
MANNER OF DECORATING A TABLE;
Whereby every Person will be enabled to add to the Art of Cookery the proper Disposition of each Article in its respective Season.
TOGETHER WITH
DIRECTIONS FOR MARKETING,
AND THE
·. MANAGEMENT OF THE KITCHEN AND FRUIT-GARDEN.
The Whole formed on so NEW a PLAN, that the Inexperienced will be instructed, and the professed Cook receive that Information which has never been made known by any preceding Publication.

THE TENTH EDITION.

By WILLIAM AUGUSTUS HENDERSON,
Who has made the CULINARY *Art his Study for upwards of Forty Years.*

LONDON: PRINTED AND SOLD BY J. STRATFORD,
No. 112, HOLBORN-HILL.

Figure 3 *'The Housekeeper's Instruction or universal family cook.' W. A. Henderson (London c.1800 J. Stratford)*(Museum of English Rural Life)

of wood, presumably for heating.[8]

Furnishing the house was, of course, the Bacons' responsibility and it must have required several cartloads to move their furniture from Cliddesden to Aylesfield judging from the very full inventory which Mary included in her ledger. They may have sold some of their possessions prior to the move, a common custom in the eighteenth century. Her inventory gives a picture of a prosperous couple, owning good quality furniture and other artefacts, which indicate a good standard of living. Much of the furniture was made of mahogany, an expensive wood at the time which was fashionable among the middle classes. It was also the wood favoured by Parson Woodforde, the Norfolk diarist, who recorded some prices. In 1789 he paid 12s. 6d. for two large second-hand mahogany dressing tables with drawers, 2 guineas for a new mahogany washstand and 10s. 6d. for another mahogany washstand, all of

8 Cord: measure of cut wood, usually 128 cubic feet. Grub was roots or branches lying on the ground.

which he thought was very cheap.[9]

There is no plan of Aylesfield farm as it was in the eighteenth-century. The building has been greatly altered since the Bacon's time, but from the amount of bedroom furniture it probably had three bedrooms, together with a kitchen and a parlour or sitting room. There may have been attic rooms and extensions to the kitchen in the form of a dairy and some combination of brewery, washhouse and bake house. The upstairs rooms contained 'three feather Beds and three bolsters', one bed having red and white check coverings, and another patchwork. Bed hangings in check were fashionable at the time and were usually made of Madras cotton, reflecting the increasing trade with India. A drawing in Carisbrooke Castle museum shows the check on bed furnishings as quite large. A third bed, belonging to Mary's sister-in-law, who appears to have lived with the family, had a brown quilt underneath it. One warming pan, which seems hardly enough to heat so many beds when eighteenth-century winters were so cold, was included. There were enough mirrors for several bedrooms, which were listed as 'a Larg looking Glass in a brown frame', 'a looking Glass with two drawers in a mahogony frame', two small looking glasses and a dressing glass. Mary clearly had a love of pillows as she had seven in her room, in which there was also a large chest, a travelling trunk and a small chest with one drawer. 'two Long hair brushes' and a nest of drawers were also listed with the bedroom furniture together with a clock and a weather glass (a long, thin barometer). Not all the inventory is in order, and these last two items were probably to be found downstairs.

It is difficult to know how the furniture listed fitted into the space downstairs and it is only possible to guess in which room individual items were placed. The furnishings of the parlour or sitting room indicate that the Bacons did their share of entertaining, certainly in respect of tea drinking, and that Mary had some time for leisure. China, probably blue and white, as this was the ware she gave to her daughter, would have been displayed on the 'beaufet' (buffet).[10] A Japan tea board (a lacquered tray), two waiters (more salvers or trays), a mahogany tea board, and two tea tables, one of which was made of mahogany, are listed and would have been used for guests, as would the tea chest, or tea caddy. Sadly, the tea kettle, which Mary's father had left her in his will, is missing from the inventory. The Bacons also drank coffee and owned two coffee pots, one of copper and one of tin, as well as a coffee mill to grind the beans. Made of wood, this would have been cube-shaped with a

9 Woodforde, James, *The Diary of a Country Parson: the Reverend James Woodforde, 1758–1802*, ed. J. Beresford (1924–31) 363.

10 Buffet: 'a side board or side-table often ornamental, for the disposition of china, plate etc.' *Oxford English Dictionary*.

metal mechanism inside. 'A Dozen of knives & forks in a box' were almost certainly those used for entertaining. Not surprisingly, for someone who clearly enjoyed literary pursuits, Mary had a 'beaurow' (bureau, or small lady's writing desk), which together with her bookstand would have made it easy for her to copy material into her ledger. There is no indication as to where she kept her 59 books, but there were shelves on either side of the parlour fireplace. As many of the books were quite small, several of them being thin tracts, they might have fitted into that space. A number of chairs are listed in the inventory, several of which were used with the square dining table. They varied in both shape and quality. Some were made of ash, two had reeded seats, and others, 'two arm chairs' and 'a old low chair', were more obviously for relaxing in. Children, or by this time, grandchildren, were not forgotten and there was also a 'Childs Chair'. Candlesticks were part of every household and two pairs of brass and two of iron, together with a pair of snuffers, are listed. Even the furnishings of the fireplace are recorded; they consisted of a fire pan, a pair of tongs with a brass head, a poker, and a bellows. If William Bacon smoked a pipe, he could use the pair of steel tobacco tongs to pick up an ember from the hearth with which to light it. Snuff was commonly taken in the eighteenth century and, as Mary included a 'Japan Snuff tray' in her inventory, perhaps she, her husband, or both indulged in this habit. Finally, at the side of the hearth was a pair of 'angers', local dialect for anjur-dogs or andirons, on which the logs were supported.[11] The contents of the kitchen are also fully listed and are described in Chapter Five.

Not all the items in the inventory were brought from Cliddesden and having got the building repairs done to the outside of the house in July, the Bacons added a few more possessions to the inside on 3 August 1791. Some may have been bought at Alton market, which was held every Saturday. Mary recorded in her ledger that she 'bought a pair of Princes metle Candlesticks 7s. snuffers & boat 8s., a table 18s. a tea tray 12s.' In November, there was another shopping expedition when she bought more things for the house. A dressing box and glass cost her 13s.; she also added another table, a chaffing dish, a brass kettle, a brass skillet and a quart skillet. On 20 December she purchased a Weather Glass (16s.), a huckmuck (1s. 7d.), and a tun bowl (4s.). She appears to have completed her household purchases in July 1793 with a dripping pan (4s.), and a cullender (3s. 6d.) Nothing further is recorded in the way of new purchases for the house.[12] It is impossible to know Mary's thoughts

---

11 W. H. Long, *A Dictionary of the Isle of Wight Dialect* (1886).

12 An advertisement in the *Hampshire Chronicle* (9 January 1801) confirms some of the contents of a house in the period and adds to some of the details. 'The Household Furniture comprises Four-post and other Bedsteads, with Flowered Cotton, Moreen, and Check Furnitures; Goose and other Feather Beds, Mattresses, Blankets, Quilts, and Counterpanes; Draw-up Window Curtains; Mahogany Dining, Card, Claw, and side-board Tables; Mahogany and other Chairs; Pier and

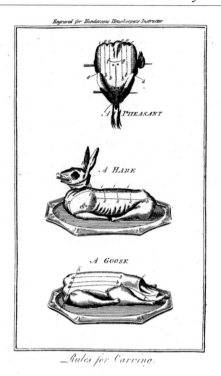

Rules for Carving.

Figure 4   Rules for Carving: an illustration from: 'The Housekeeper's Instruction or Universal Family Cook.' W. A. Henderson (ca 1800, 10th edition London: J. Stratford)

(Museum of English Rural Life)

and feelings about her possessions, especially as her record is an account and memoranda book and not a diary, yet some conclusions can be drawn. It is clear from her inventory and subsequent purchases that she was a woman who entertained, liked to be fashionable and enjoyed her creature comforts.

It must be assumed that Mary kept her furniture and farmhouse clean and tidy. She would have had at least one servant to do the work, and there is evidence that she read Hannah Glasse's recipe book, *First Catch your Hare, The Art of Cookery made plain and easy,* in which the reader is told how to clean. 'Always when you sweep a *Room,* throw a little wet Sand all over it, and that will gather up all the Flew and Dust, prevents it from rising, cleans the Boards, and saves both Bedding, Pictures, and all other Furniture from Dust and Dirt.'[13] Household servants were paid very little, but remuneration usually included board and lodging, tips from visitors, and items of clothing; Mary provided her two maids with woollen caps and aprons. Parson Woodforde gave two coloured handkerchiefs to his two Washerwomen costing 4s. 8d. and two cotton gowns for his maids of Pink & White, 17 yards costing £2 2s. The outside of the house was also given attention soon after the Bacons arrived at Aylesfield farm; Mr Turvil was paid 10s. for the garden and £1 5s. for the orchard, although there is no record of the work he did. There is no sign of an orchard at the house now, and although there is no cider recipe in Mary's 'My Book of Receipts', the necessary apples would have been grown. Turvil also did

Dressing Glasses; Scotch Carpet; Painted Floor Cloth; four Pair of Venetian Window Blinds; and Eight Day Clock; two Mahogany Knife Cases, with a complete Set of White Ivory Handled Knives and Forks; requisite Kitchen Furniture; good Iron-bound Casks, Mash Tub; Washing Ditto, and a Pair of Coolers …'.

13 Hannah Glasse, *First Catch your Hare, The Art of Cookery made plain and easy,* eds. J. Stead and P. Bain (1995). First published 1747.

some work in the yard and provided ashes for the pigs for which he was paid the not inconsiderable sum of £3 10s.

Before leaving Cliddesden the Bacons had sold a wagon (£22), a bull (£5), 'White Foot' (£12 12s.), presumably a horse, the white faced cow (£8 8s.) and the black cow (£7 10s.) to local farmers. In August, after they arrived at Aylesfield farm, there were additions to be made to the farming stock; they bought two horses, one costing 14 guineas and the other 10 guineas, a cow at 6 guineas, and a hen and ten chickens at 6 shillings. Unfortunately the more expensive of the two horses died on 18 September 1791, very soon after it was bought. Finally, in November 1791, 20 sheep at 14 shillings a head were added to the livestock. The Bacons continued to add to their stock, or to make replacements, and in May the following year bought a cow and a calf at Farnham fair (£6), 22 tegs at Overton fair[14] (£17 12s.) and two weeks later added 20 more sheep (£15 16s.) to their flock. They also kept pigs, as did most farmers, and in 1794 purchased a sow and eleven pigs for £4 12s.

Despite the fact that the Bacons kept sheep, cattle and pigs, there were still butcher's bills to pay. Beef was relatively expensive and in 1791 Mary bought a pound for 10s. 6d. Mutton was cheaper and a leg, weighing about 6 lb, or a shoulder, cost approximately 5s. The price of mutton seemed to have increased during the second half of the eighteenth century. Thomas Turner, a grocer from East Hoathly in Sussex, recorded in his *Diary*, written between 1754 and 1756, that he had only paid 1s. 7½ d. for a 6 lb leg.[15] There was a distinction made between mutton and lamb: the latter being smaller only cost 3s. 8d. for a shoulder. Mutton was Mary's choice for Christmas.

There is no record to show whether the Bacons made their own beer in Cliddesden, but they did at Aylesfield and started to brew shortly after they arrived. They were now living in a hop growing area but there is nothing to indicate in the ledger that they grew their own. They bought in the malt from several different people, measured in sacks or by the quarter. Whether the beer was entirely for use on the farm, or whether some of it was sold on, is not recorded. During 1792 brewing was done on a regular monthly basis, using a sack, or on one occasion a quarter, of malt at a time. It is difficult to know how much beer this produced but a reasonable guide is that a quarter would brew about 15 gallons of beer. A sack was slightly more than double that amount and would produce at least 30 gallons.[16]

William Bacon needed the income from his farm as, among other expenses, he

---

14 There were four fairs a year held at Overton, one of which was on 4 May, presumably the one referred to by Mary.

15 *Diary of Thomas Turner*, 19.

16 Information given by Gales' Breweries, Horndean, Hampshire. For more information about brewing methods and the Bacons' equipment, see Chapter Five.

had taxes to pay. Tithes were paid to the incumbent of Alton; this tax, a tenth of all farm produce in the parish, was the one which probably caused the most resentment. Mary recorded payment of the small tithe, '1794 the small tythe is five shillings a score for Dry sheep four shillings for a Cow two shillings for the yard.' The great tithe had to be paid on hay, corn and wood, while the small tithes covered most of the rest of the output of the farm including dairy produce and vegetables. Although originally the tithes were paid in kind, by the end of the eighteenth century they were usually paid in cash. It is possible that the great tithes were paid by the owner, in this case Richard Palmer Baker, as this was often the custom; there is no record in the accounts of this payment being made by William Bacon.

There would have been other taxes to pay too, but there is no record in the accounts. The land tax records show that William Bacon paid £3 4s. in 1800, but his later payments were exonerated under the Act of 1801; he died in 1803. According to the *Hampshire Chronicle* (26 March 1796)[17] 'Hampshire pays about 20d. to 22d. in the pound' and, like many counties, fluctuated from the standard 4s. in the pound originally set by government. Without knowing whether or not Richard Palmer Baker made a contribution, it is impossible to gain any clear idea of the size of the Bacons' holding from these figures. There was one tax which was especially sympathetic to farmers. The Window Act 1796, provided,

> That no duty shall be charged on any windows or lights in any dairies, or in any rooms or places kept and used for the sole purpose of drying and keeping cheese, or of making cheese or butter, and for no other purpose; whether the same shall be attached to, or detached from, the dwelling-house or not, and which shall be occupied by any person who shall sell, or be in any manner concerned in selling, the produce of dairies, or any kind of cheese.

The Act was very explicit as to how windows of these dairies were to be made.

> But such windows or lights must be made with splints, or wooden laths, or iron bars, and wholly without glass; also the dairies or rooms aforesaid must not be used to dwell or to sleep in; and on the doors thereto there must be painted, in large Roman black letters, of two inches in height, the words Dairy and Cheese Room, or some of them, as the case shall require: otherwise such dairies and rooms shall be charged with the duties.

Mary certainly made and sold butter at the price of 2s. 1½d. for 3 lb, but whether her dairy complied with all these above regulations must remain open to speculation.

---

17 *Hampshire Chronicle* (*H C*) was, and still is, an important provincial newspaper which covered a very large area in the eighteenth century. Its distribution ranged from Berkshire in the north, much of the west country, and the Channel Islands in the south. Comments made by its editors are therefore not necessarily confined to the smaller area of Hampshire only.

TVRX TRVYE BEVIS   **O HAMIVN**

Figure 5   *The Hampshire hog*

From Jill Rushton *Hundred Years of Progress* (Hampshire County Council, 1989) HRO

The war with France led the government to bring in further taxation and in 1796 there was an announcement that sporting dogs were to be taxed and that would include greyhounds, pointers, spaniels, lurchers and terriers; 5 shillings would be charged annually for each. Duties were payable on male servants, horses for riding or drawing, and clocks, one of which is listed in Mary's inventory. There are no records of these additional taxes in the accounts, but the entries are incomplete. One certainty is that William Bacon paid the poor rate, increased in 1793 from £4 to £4. 10s. The Assessed Tax Bill, 1798, was extremely complex and covered a long list of exemptions. For example, farms with an income of less than £70 per annum were exempt; it will never be known if the Bacons benefited as the accounts are not full enough to assess their income over any one year. Neither will it be known if they benefited from the exemptions of income tax as set out in the *Hampshire Chronicle* in November, 1798. 'Persons not possessing an annual income of 60l. (£60) to be exempted.' Although from their accounts his income appears to have exceeded this sum, William Bacons's name does not appear on the Hampshire list of those paying income tax.

William Bacon was undoubtedly a respected member of his community, a position which brought responsibilities. In 1798 he was elected an overseer of the poor. The requirement was that he had to be a substantial householder and nominations were made in Easter week or up to a month afterwards. Most parish officers served for several years at a time, but William died in 1803; his health may have started to fail by the end of his first year in office, as he did not continue after that. Helpfully,

Mary owned *The New Universal Parish Officer*[18], a book that was,

> Very proper for Attornies, Constables, Churchwardens, Justices, Overseers of the Poor, Surveyors of the highways, and all Persons in Office, who would gain a competent Knowledge of this Branch of the Law, so as to enable them to discharge their respective Duties with ease and Expedition. It is also very proper for every House-keeper and inhabitant who is desirous of being perfectly acquainted with the Laws relating to Parishes but too frequently unacquainted with some material Part of their Duty.

The duties of overseers are set out in the book and mainly concern responsibilities towards the poor of the parish. For example, they were to bind poor children apprentice, administering the money needed to do so, and they could put poor children out to sea service, paying 50s. to the master of such boys for their clothing and bedding. Another duty was to enable the building of houses for the poor on parish waste ground at the charge of the parish. Overseers also had responsibilities towards illegitimate children abandoned by their parents. Fathers could be arrested unless they gave security to their children, and their goods and chattels could be seized by the overseers if they abandoned their families and moved on elsewhere. They also had a duty to raise money to pay for a stock of flax, hemp, wool, thread, iron, among other commodities in order to make work for the poor. One of William Bacon's responsibilities as an overseer was to examine the accounts of the poor house in Alton and those for 1796 show that efforts were being made to provide the occupants with employment. Spinning jennies to spin the yarn, looms, and a carding machine were all purchased, with the result that the inmates were enabled to produce calicoes, which were then sold.

Two of the Bacon daughters were married from their new home and their mother recorded in her ledger: '1792 February the 16 Day Mary Bacon was married to William Tuersly Shalden'.[19] An announcement was made in the *Hampshire Chronicle*: 'Last week was married... Mr. Wm. Tously, of Shaldean, to Miss Mary Bacon, of Alton, in this county'.[20] The inclusion of the marriage in the local newspaper implies that this was a farming family of some stature. As well as entering the date of her daughter's wedding in her ledger, Mary included a list of all the presents she gave her at the time:

---

18 *The New Universal Parish Officer* (1769). The need for this kind of book continued and on 29 June 1794 the *Hampshire Chronicle* advertised *The new complete Parish Officer, or Perfect Guide to Church Wardens, Tithing Men, Overseers, Sidesmen, Constables, Borsholders, Headboroughs, Beadles and other parish officers of every denomination.*

19 Shalden was a small nearby village where William Tuersly (not Tously) lived.

20 *H C*, 25 February 1792.

febry 24 I Gave to my Daughter Mary tuersly a Bed a bolster & two Pillows a patch Quilt a table Cloth & three Napkins one Guinea to bye her some teaspoons a Gold ring with a Crystal Stone in it a Looking Glass Six blue & white China plates one Dozen of Common plates a Quart Cup a pint Do & /2 pint Cup three egg Glasses & a pickling Jar Blairs Sermons Book & a fender and Coal shovel a Chocolate pot & mill

October a coat for her master	2 = 2 = 0
October 20 a barrel	0 = 12 = 0 (crossed out)
a large Grate to burn wood in	1 = 11 = 6
a large Jar	2 = 0 (crossed out)
1795 a large pickling Tub	1 = 0 = 0

The list is a mixture of practical gifts together with items such as a gold ring and a chocolate pot which indicate that Mary wanted her daughter too to have a certain status in the community.

Sarah Bacon was also married from Aylesfield farm: 'Eggar, James, of Holybourne, yeoman 25, b. and Sarah Bacon, of Alton, 26 sp. At A(lton) 19 April 1803.'[21] The Eggar family were much respected in the area and it was an appropriate marriage for Sarah. The only record concerning James is of a frivolous nature. Three old manuscript ledgers record that every year from 1798, on about 11 June, the farmers of the locality held a dinner at the Hen and Chicken, a pub built in 1760 in Upper Froyle, a village not far from Aylesfield farm. They met together with the exclusive object of betting on the total amount of the autumn hop harvest, laying 5s. for each wager. Not all the bets were on the crop yield, 'Mr Andrews lays Mr. Watford foive guineas to one that he does not last all the Bets he has laid here this day' James Eggar, not yet married to Sarah, made his bets. 'Mr James Eggar, Holybourne, Mr Eggar lays Mr Page one guinea that Mr Wm Smith is nearer in the sweepstake than Mr Christmas and again, he is bet a pair of boots that the hop duty pays £150,000.'[22]

Unfortunately the *Twelve True Old Golden Rules*[23] which Mary copied into her ledger from a broadside was published too late to be given to her daughters to take into their married lives. Courtesy or conduct books such as, *Female conduct, being an essay on the art of pleasing to be practised by the Fair Sex, before and after marriage*, by Thomas Marriott, published in London in 1759, were extremely popular in the

21 *Hampshire Allegations for Marriage Licences*, Harleian Society Publications (1689–1837).
  Sarah's baptism was registered on 20 April 1775 which would make her aged 27 at the time of her marriage, a day short of her 28th birthday. It was not unusual for baptisms to take place some time after the birth, and this may have been Sarah's case.
22 HRO 12 M98/1.
23 *Twelve True Old Golden Rules* (1800).

eighteenth century and more usually found in the libraries or papers of the gentry. The rules of morality and good behaviour, especially in respect of young ladies, are also reflected in many of the contemporary novels of the period. However, not all conduct books applied to the gentry. For example, Samuel Richardson wrote *The Apprentice's Vade Mecum*, in 1733, a book of advice on morals and conduct. Mary Bacon's *Golden Rules*, judging from their content, also applied more appropriately to middle or lower class men and women. Honest men are exhorted to go to the market rather than the alehouse; gin, a drink not normally consumed by the gentry, is abhorred, industry and frugality are extolled. The class of person to whom these Rules was addressed was unlikely to have many servants – it is assumed that the wife does her own cooking. Although the title indicates twelve Rules, Mary only copied out ten of them.

Twelve True Old Golden Rules

For those who like to fare better than they now do, and at the same time to thrive and grow rich.

1   The ready penny always fetches the best bargain. He who buys upon trust, must not complain if he is cheated. The shopkeeper suspects the customer who buys on trust, and thinks that he means to cheat and never to pay; and therefore he takes good care to be before hand, and charges highly accordingly.

2   The best pennyworth is to be had where most sit together in the open market; and bargains are often cheaper in the latter end of the day. When honest men have done their work, it is better for them to go to market than to the alehouse.

3   When times are hard, why should we make them harder. Still, it is not enough to be taxed once by Government without being taxed by folly, thrice by drunkenness four times by Laziness, and so on – a good man, even in hard times will do twice as well as a bad man will in the best of times, let us all then rise up against ourselves, who thus tax and injure ourselves and we shall soon find that the times mend. Let us do good to ourselves at home, and we shall become happy in our own habitations; and learn that it is a true saying, that God helps those who help themselves.

4   Time is our estate; it is our most valuable property If we lose it, or waste it, we can never – never purchase it back again. We ought, therefore, not to have an idle hour, or throw away an idle penny. While we employ our time and our property (however small that property may be) to the best advantage, we shall find that a fortune may be made in any situation of life; and that a poor man, who once wanted assistance himself may become able to assist and relieve others

5   Industry will make a man a purse, and frugality will find him strings for

it, Neither the purse nor the strings will cost him any thing. He who has it should only draw the strings as frugality directs and he will be sure always to find an useful penny at the bottom of it the servants of industry are known by their livery; it is always whole and wholesome. Idleness travels very leisurely, and poverty soon overtakes her. Look at the ragged Slaves of idleness and judge which is the best master to serve – Industry or Idleness

6   Marriage is Honorable: and the married state when entered into with prudence, and continued in with discretion, is of all conditions of life the most happy: but to bring a wife home, before, we have made provision by our Industry and frugality, for her and our children, or to choose a wife, who has not by attention and economy on her part, proved herself fit to manage a family, is extremely imprudent and improvident. Let therefore the young prepare themselves for the married state, by treasuring up all the Surplus of their youthful earnings and they will [have] confidence and live together in comfort.

7   Of all Idolatry that ever debased any Savage and ignorant nation, the worship of the gin bottle is the most disgraceful. The Worshipper of the gin bottle becomes unfit for anything; he soon rots his liver, and ruins himself and family.

8   He who does not make his family comfortable, will himself never be happy at home; and he who is not happy at home, will never be happy any where. Charity begins at home: the Husband and Wife, who can hardly keep themselves and their Children, should not keep a dog to rob the Children of part of their food.

9   She who roasts or broils her meat, wastes a great part of it in the fire. She who boils it, loses a third of it in the water, but when the good wife stews her meat gently, thickening the liquor with a little meal, ground rice or pease and vegetables, and making it savoury with fried onions, herbs, and seasoning, she gets the good of the whole, her husband and she fares much better their, Children thrive and grow hearty and stout and their money goes twise as far.

10   When you stew or boil your meat, if you leave the vessel uncovered some of the best part goes off and is wasted in steam; and when you make the fire in a wide chimney, with a large open throat, there is at least twise as much of the heat goes up the Chimney, as ever comes into the room to warm the family.[24]

The late eighteenth century was a difficult and unnerving time in which to live. On 1 February 1793, the republican government of France declared war on Britain and Holland, a war that was to last for nine years. The invasion of Britain became a real possibility, especially in the summer of 1795 when the French were in control of the entire Channel coast. As the war progressed all fit civilian men, other than

24 Anon, *Twelve True Old Golden Rules, for those who like to fare better than they now do, and at the same time to thrive and grow rich* (1800).

clergy, had to make themselves available for enrolment in the armed services. By 14 April 1794 anxieties were rising and at a Hampshire County meeting, as reported in the Hampshire Chronicle:

> a most respectable and numerous body of gentry, clergy and freeholders assembled at the castle in this city, to take into consideration the most advisable measures for the further augmentation of the county militia, for any other purpose of defence, as may be thought most proper at the present crisis.

Farm workers left to join the militia and the navy, putting pressure on the farmers who had to produce food for an increasing number of servicemen, with a consequent decrease in their own labour force. Although the harvest of of 1794 promised to be a good one, the editor of the *Hampshire Chronicle* expressed his concern.

> But we are fearful that they (the farmers) will experience from inconvenience the ensuing harvest for want of hands, as great numbers of their servants have declined the profession of husbandry for the personal protection of the constitution and country, and have changed the round-frock for the military habit.[25]

Fortunately, he was able to report later in the summer on 28 July that 'we are happy that there appears not to be so great a scarcity of hands as it was apprehended there would be, in consequence of the number of farmers' servants promoted in the army.'

The Bacons were relatively isolated at Aylesfield farm, but they must have been aware of the general atmosphere of war and of troop movements; the militia were constantly on the move. Although the French never crossed the Channel, there were times when the threat that they would do so was all-pervading. In 1798 the danger seemed imminent but, according to the *Hampshire Chronicle*, the British people were united and preparations for an immediate invasion were well under way. On 21 April 1798 the Winchester reporter wrote, 'At this critical juncture of affairs, when a most inveterate and designing enemy is arming to invade this country, we are happy to see such unanimity in all ranks of people, both within doors and without.' Again on 28 April 1798 he wrote, 'It is said that the whole armed forces in Great Britain will be increased to 400,000 men before the first week in May. There is every reason to expect that the attempt of an invasion in this country will be an immediate one.'

In 1801 defences were strengthened again, with a probable further diminution in the size of the farmers' labouring force. The *Hampshire Chronicle* reported on 31 August 1801,

> A plan of defence upon a more extensive scale and more effectually calculated to answer every object, than any which has been proposed or adopted, is said to be nearly brought to a conclusion. It has been under the consideration of the cabinet

25 *H C* 19 May 1794.

for three weeks; and the late inspection of the coasts by the Duke of York was intimately connected with it. This new system of defence only waited his Royal Highness's sanction, to be carried into effect. According to report, all persons capable of service, from the age of 16 to 60 are to be armed with pikes in the districts along the coast most liable to any sudden descent of the enemy.

There were times when the war must have felt very near to home for the Bacons. William Tuersly of Shalden, their son-in-law, is recorded as a collector and assessor of land tax, but was also a tythingman.[26] Under the Defence of the Realm Act of 1798, parish clergy nationally were required to submit to the lord lieutenant of the county a schedule of what the parish could provide and what they would need in the event of an invasion. This had to include the number of bread ovens, oxen and other livestock, carts, a record of mills, and also those frail and elderly parishioners who would need assistance if they had to be evacuated. William Tuersly was appointed to collect this information, on behalf of the incumbent whose overall responsibility it was. The numbers under each heading which Tuersley had to record were small in relation to those for Alton North. Under Shalden, only about 2,000 animals were offered and a mere 28 wagons with 28 draught horses. The small number of three riding horses must reflect the social class of that population, indicating that there were few well-to-do farmers or gentry living in the area. Alton, a much larger parish, offered to produce 287 wagon drivers, 50 sacks of flour (280 lb each), and 1,072 loaves of bread to be furnished by the subscribers every 24 hours. In an emergency the number would be increased to 2,112. Sheep and goats were the predominant animals numbering 23,330, while 3,417 pigs were offered, 1,371 cows, 1,667 draught horses with 451 wagons, and 490 carts. There was a large army of farmers of which William Bacon was one. He may have offered stock and equipment and Mary would have baked some of the loaves in the event of invasion, but he was too old in 1799 to join the men of Alton North who agreed to serve with firelocks, felling axes, shovels, bill hooks, saws, and pick axes. However, he was not in the category of the 2,454 people incapable of removing themselves, as he was able to travel to Alton as an overseer of the poor in 1798.[27] Parson Woodforde, who lived at Weston Longeville, Norfolk, recorded in his Diary that he had to provide the names of all the people in his parish between the ages of 15 and 63. There was also a meeting held at his local inn, 'respecting a sudden Invasion from the French &c what was necessary and proper to be done on a sudden attack.'[28]

26 HRO Q22/1/2/5.
27 Anon, *Hampshire Repository*, vol I (1799) 44–7.
28 James Woodforde, *The Diary of a Country Parson: the Reverend James Woodforde, 1758–1802*, ed. J. Beresford (1924–31) 564.

Further evidence of the war was experienced by the Bacons very near to home, when French prisoners escaped to Holybourne, a village only two miles from Aylesfield farm. On 14 April 1798 the *Hampshire Chronicle* reported:

> On Saturday last General Pitt received information of some Frenchmen being seen on the London Road, supposed to have escaped from Forton Prison; a party of the Fawley light dragoons were immediately ordered by the general to go in search of them, who found four of them in a public house at Holybourne, near Alton, from whence they were brought to this city (Winchester) and lodged in the guard house belonging to the barracks; and on Monday they were safely escorted back to their old habitation by a party of the guards. Corporal Young, owing to his great exertion on this occasion, lost a very fine charger.

There were further worries for the Bacon family. Nationally, there had been six bad harvests during the 1790s, which, together with grain shortages caused by the war, resulted in the price of bread rising to an alarming level. The quartern loaf (4lb 5½oz.) cost from 6*d*. to 8*d*. from 1765 to 1794, but rose to 1*s*. 3¼*d*. in 1801. The *Hampshire Chronicle* of 28 April 1800 reported that it was 'with deep regret we notice the rapidly encreasingly high price of every article of human subsistence, particularly bread and butcher's meat, the latter of which has risen more than 20 per cent within the last month, and there is every prospect of its being considerably higher.' The editor went on to exhort his readers to encourage the breeding of pigs and not to eat any lamb in their families for some time to come. He wrote that 'this would undoubtedly encrease the stock of mutton, and consequently lower the price.' He also recommended that his readers should eat fish and plant vegetables, particularly potatoes. 'In some districts the farmers have given their labourers liberty to plant the latter root in the corners of their fields and other waste land on their estates.'

The repercussions of these shortages were felt all over the country, but for the Bacons there were further events which were too close to home for comfort. *The Hampshire Chronicle* (31 March 1800) reported that a letter, dated 7 March 1800, had been picked up in Odiham, a village where the family had relatives and which is situated only five miles from Aylesfield farm. The authors were

> threatening to set fire to the premises of all the Farmers in the different counties throughout the Kingdom who have any Wheat in their Possession, and intimating that a Society of Villains, to the number of Twenty-one, are bound to each other by Oath, and dispersed for that Purpose over the Country, who are to be allowed a Premium for every Fire that they may occasion, by some Gentlemen, by whom they profess to be employed.

Parts of the letter contained strong words of an extremely threatening nature. 'To the Damnd Eternal Fire Brands of hell Belonging Odiham and its Vicinity. In

Other Words to the Damnd Villans of Farmers that with hold the Corn that please God to send for the people of the Earth away from them'. The letter went on to say that any farmer having corn for his own profit would have it burnt to the ground:

> We know every Stack of Corn about this Country and Every Barn that have Corn Concealed in it for The Purpose of Starving the Poore But wee are Determind if there is to Be Starvation it Shall Be a General thing not a parcial one for Both Gentle and simple shall Starve if any do wee Don't Care a Dam for them fellows that Call Themselves Gentlemen Soldiers But in our opinion they Look moore Like monkeys Riding upon Bears.

The letter ends with a warning for 'your dwelling houses as well'. The *Hampshire Chronicle* gave notice, signed by the vicar of Odiham, and, among others, all the principal farmers and inhabitants of the area, that the utmost endeavours would be used to 'prevent the Execution of such nefarious designs'.

Unfortunately, history does not relate if the threats were carried out and there is no evidence that the Bacons lost their grain. Life could be pleasurable too and, although conditions could be hard, people found plenty of occasions for enjoyment during the late eighteenth-century. There were times of celebration, often national, when the church bells rang, candles were lit in the windows, bonfires ignited and fireworks set off. The bellringers at Alton were paid regularly for ringing the bells on 5 November, the anniversary of the Gunpowder Plot. God was praised for saving Parliament, and the event was made into a celebration of patriotism as the congregation sung the hymn specially set for the day, known to Mary through her book, *Hymns for Sundays*:

> Shout to the Lord, and let our joys
> Thro the whole nation run;
> Ye *British* skies, resound the noise
> Beyond the rising sun.

In the next verses, God throws vast confusion on the plots of our foes:

> Their secret fires in caverns lay,
> And we the sacrifice;
> But gloomy caverns strove in vain
> To 'scape all-searching eyes.

Fortunately, their dark designs are all revealed and their souls will 'pine with envious rage.'[29]

There were other events to celebrate. When in March 1789 the health of King

---

29 Anon, *Hymns for several Sundays and Festivals of the Year, for the Sacrament and other Public Solemnities* (c.1770) 144.

George III was restored, the nation rejoiced. The citizens of Winchester and its environs joined in and on 2 March 1789 the *Hampshire Chronicle* reported how the city was lit up for the celebrations and how all the villages in the neighbourhood were illuminated. The people of Basingstoke also rejoiced and as that town was very near to home for the Bacons, who were living in Cliddesden at the time, it is more than likely that members of the family were present. The celebrations were reported in the *Hampshire Chronicle*:

> the dawn of that day was ushered in with ringing of bells, and a song at three in the morning on the top of the Church Tower of 'God save the King' by the loyal singers of that Town, who, with the band, particularly requested the mayor, that he would permit them to join him in the general festivity, in order to testify their loyalty and attachment to the best of Kings, and their laudable desire was most readily granted. The Gentlemen of the Corporation met in the morning at the mayor's to breakfast, from then they paraded (the Mayor and aldermen in their gowns) to the Town Hall, preceded by the proper officers with a band of musick, playing, 'God save the King' and colours very elegantly painted were borne before them. At the Council room a cold collation for the company was provided, and a most respectable number of Gentlemen of the neighbourhood honoured this Meeting with their presence ... In the evening all the houses in the Town very handsomely illuminated, some were ornamented with most beautiful transparencies, particularly the Town Hall. The populace were plentifully regaled with several hogsheads of beer, and about ten pounds given in bread on that day, to the poor of the Town.[30]

There were nationwide rejoicings during the war as well. Nelson's victory at the Nile on 28 July 1798 brought hope that peace was in sight and was celebrated across the country. The *Hampshire Chronicle*, 29 October 1798, reported that 'Numerous villages near Winchester lit up bonfires, fireworks to celebrate the victory over the French at the Battle of the Nile which had just been won by Nelson.' The main occasion for rejoicing was when the agreement for setting out the preliminaries of peace in the war against France was ratified. This was signed in London on 1 October 1801 and confirmed by Napoleon four days later. The following year, on 25 March 1802, it was finally incorporated in the definitive Peace of Amiens. The news of the peace with France was taken to the provinces by mail coaches, which were decked with laurels and carried banners. Celebrations were widespread; the *Hampshire Chronicle* included a detailed description of these events in Winchester in its issue of 19 October 1801. Even if the Bacon parents declined to make the journey, it is possible that one or more of their children were there. Bells were rung; people put laurels in their hats and wore blue ribbons. The artillery fired a royal salute, 'three excellent *feu de joye*'. 'In the evening ... the market-house, the tower

---

30 *H C*, 23 March 1789.

of the cathedral, the guild-hall, the market-cross, and the inhabitants' houses in general were illuminated from top to bottom.'Then follows descriptions of various very patriotic transparencies exhibited by some of the stalwarts of the city.

> The Mayor, J. N. Silver Esq., – A large transparency representing Britannia seated in the centre, resplendent with the lion couchant at her feet, welcoming the angel of peace who is descending with the olive branch. The figure of plenty is represented with a cornucopia, which she is presenting to Britannia, under which is the motto 'The blessing of peace.' Above are geniuses, two of which are supporting a medallion of his Majesty, with the motto 'Long may he reign;' and two others with suitable emblems. In the border are introduced the harp, shamrock, roses, and thistles. On one side the eye of Providence guarding commerce, which is represented by Mercury, just alighted with a sprig of olive on our island, on which is seen wheatsheaves, bales of goods, &c. and the appropriate motto 'May commerce be diffused throughout the world.' On the other side is seen Neptune with his trident, standing on a shell, looking up with complacency on a dove descending with the olive branch; over which the motto 'Peace and plenty'.

Alderman Earle also displayed Britannia on his transparency, 'looking down with pleasure on a medallion of his Majesty'. Ceres was appropriately leaning on a cornucopia and Peace was holding a palm branch. In contrast to these patriotic depictions, Mr Marr, another citizen of Winchester, appeared to be celebrating a time of feasting, food for the body as well as the spirit. He had three transparencies, 'one lit each window; at the first opening was left, where were set two fine ribs of beef, and a girl to turn it, in imitation of roasting; the second had a large plumb pudding, and the third a gallon loaf.' The river Itchen, which runs through the city, was also lit up and a ladder fixed across the river on which candles were placed. It was a still and beautiful evening in which to terminate the celebrations with fireworks. The mayor, however, imposed some restrictions, although he clearly wanted everyone to have a good time. He ordered that no fireworks should be thrown in the streets till after nine o'clock. Alcohol was not forgotten and Sir H. Mildmay, Sir Richard Gamon and the corporation put out hogsheads of strong beer and the day closed without mishap. The celebrations in Winchester were elaborate as befitted a cathedral city, but towns such as Alton had bonfires and candles in the windows, which members of the Bacon family almost certainly enjoyed. Sadly, the peace with the French was not to last.

There were other recreational activities nearer to home. Odiham, a few miles to the north of Aylesfield farm, and where the Bacons had relatives, was the meeting place for the Odiham Society of Agriculture and Industry which held annual ploughing competitions. The prize for ploughing with oxen was considerably less than if horses were used. 'To the ploughman that ploughs one or two lands, with so many turns as shall be determined by the stewards, the best within a given time to be allowed by the stewards, the value of £12 12s. 6d.'[31] If ploughing with oxen, the winner could only expect £1. 11s. 6d.

Fairs were important business and social meeting places for farmers all over the country and may have been where Mary bought some of the tracts she copied out. She listed several of these fairs in her ledger, some of which, like East Grinstead, were a considerable distance away. If they were important enough to record, it is likely that Mary went to them. There is a mysterious little entry in her ledger, written vertically across the page: 'The wonderfull Cambridge Prophet who has been most cruelly Martyrd To be seen at –' followed by a gap. Then the passage continues,

> He is not the Wandering jew, nor an old Levite, nor St John, as some people Imagine. It seemes his generation was in the world before Adam and in the ark with Noah, and with Christ when Condemned to be crucified, The Scripture makes mention of him. He is no imposter. He knoweth not his parents, nor ever did Suck the breast of his mother. His beard is the colour of vermillion, and is seldom or ever cut. He goes barefooted like a grey friar. He wears neither hat cap, or wig. His coat is neither wove, knit spun or made with hands, neither is it silk.

Does the clue lie in 'to be seen at', followed by a gap where a name place could be filled in? Was this a handbill for some kind of sideshow at one of the country fairs, which Mary took home and copied out? The Bacons may have taken sheep or cattle to sell at the fairs and perhaps William and his shepherd joined in the competitions. In an advertisement for the Westbrook fair at Alton (*Hampshire Chronicle*, 13 April 1789), the prizes were listed and instructions given that the sheep had to be cooped by nine o'clock.

> A prize of a Gold-laced Hat, will be given to the Shepherd who scoops for sale the best score of Dorsetshire couples; and a Prize of another Gold-laced hat, to the Shepherd who scoops for sale the best score of Hampshire couples; and a Prize of a Silver-laced Hat, to the Shepherd who scoops for sale the best score of weathers. No Shepherd entitled to a Prize, unless his sheep are cooped before ten o'clock in the morning.

Other fairs the Bacons may have attended included Odiham, known for cheese, cattle and toys, and Winchester also famous for cheeses; there was a summer lamb fair at Alresford. The *Hampshire Chronicle* promised 'a great show of horned cattle' at the large fair held at Weyhill near Andover.[32] This was one of the biggest fairs in the country to which people travelled long distances, coming from 'all parts of the kingdom.' The chief purchasers of oxen were Welshmen 'for the supplies of the

---

31 *H C*, advertisements in May 1792.
32 *H C*, 18 October 1790.

counties of Suffolk and Kent, which are said to be under stocked with lean cattle from the failure of the Irish importations…'.[33] So many people attended that the cost of a bed for the night could be as much as that of a stall for a horse.

One of the main recreational pleasures for farmers was hunting. There is no record in the ledger which would indicate whether or not William Bacon hunted but most men in his position did. He may have ridden with one of the many small packs supported by country squires and well-to-do farmers. The huntsmen usually consisted of a few near neighbours of different ranks to whom the master sent notice according to his personal whim or convenience. Boundaries of each hunt were undefined and variable; each owner took his hounds wherever there seemed an opening for them and different packs jostled each other.[34] Whether or not William Bacon hunted, either on horseback, or as was often customary, on foot, it is likely that the hounds crossed his land regularly and that the hunt was a common and colourful sight. The Prince of Wales took Kempshott House, at Dummer, on a seven-year lease from 1788 as a hunting lodge, and later The Grange at Northington, also in Hampshire, visiting annually. In the eighteenth-century hunting pink was not standard dress but each hunt had its own colours. The Prince of Wales hunted with the Hampshire Hunt, the original dress of which was a blue coat with white waistcoat and yellow buttons, having the letters H H and the Prince of Wales's crest engraved on it. In 1799 the hunting dress changed to red coats in the field and blue in the evening.[35] William Chute, M.P. for Hampshire at the time, had his own hunt for which the master wore a long pink coat with powdered hair, and a pigtail tied by a black ribbon. The men wore round hats and long scarlet coats, which would lap over and defend their knees against cold or wet.[36]

It can only be speculated that life at Aylesfield farm was a mixture of anxieties and pleasures for William and Mary Bacon. The strains and stresses of war could hardly be outweighed by farmers' fairs, competitions, and the sharing in national celebrations. Farming was very hard in the eighteenth-century, not helped by the very long cold winters. Despite it all, Mary lived to be 75, a very reasonable age for a woman of her time. William Bacon died on 22 May 1803 and was buried in Cliddesden. Mary stayed in Aylesfield farm until the lease expired in 1805 when she probably went to live with or near to her daughter Sarah Eggar who lived in the nearby village of Froyle. The 1806 Land Tax assessments for Froyle record a Mrs

---

33 *H C*, 12 December 1791.
34 Stephen Terry, *The Diaries of Dummer: Reminiscences of an Old Sportsman* (London: Unicorn Press, 1934) 116.
35 *ibid.* 138.
36 *ibid.* 151.

Bacon who was assessed at 9*s*. 3½*d*.; this entry was repeated the following year.[37] By 1808 there is no further record. The property she paid the tax on was owned by a William Heath, who had some connection with a mill owned by James Eggar, her son-in-law.[38] By the end of 1807 Mary no longer had a home of her own. On 21 December of that year she recorded 'an account of my goods at Mrs Baldings' and there follows a complete list of everything she owned.[39] This was probably her last entry in her ledger. It is sad that at the end of her life she had to part with all that she possessed and no doubt cherished. The Cliddesden parish register records her burial on 30 January 1818 as Mary Bacon of Hollybourne near Alton, aged 75. It is to be hoped that her deep religious devotion held her in good stead at her death and that she anticipated going to that 'land of pure delight' which was in one of the funeral hymns in her book, *Hymns for Sundays*:

> There is a land of pure delight,
> Where saints immortal reign;
> Infinite day excludes the night,
> And pleasure banish pain.

37 HRO Q22/1/1/14/5
38 HRO 57M78/E/T371
39 For Mary Bacon's full inventory list see Appendix Five.

Chapter Three

Agriculture

PART ONE   THE LAND

MARY BACON'S LEDGER provides an unusually full insight into the life of an eighteenth-century farmer's wife. Details of stock, the weather, the care of animals, and cures for people living in or around the farm provide a picture of what life was like. Although Mary's carefully kept accounts are not as detailed as those of her uncle, Augustin Kinchin, they are still a valuable source of information as to the crops grown on the farm. Apart from one year of very full accounts recorded at Cliddesden there is little indication of overall income and expenditure. In the absence of any accurate measurement of the acreage, or consistent accounts of the turnover of crops, or the sale of livestock, it is only possible to make a rough guess at William Bacon's income, which probably varied from year to year. Nevertheless, these accounts do give some insight into eighteenth-century farming, a way of life better understood against a background of contemporary information about agriculture in the south of England as a whole.

The latter half of the eighteenth century was an important period for English agriculture during which a number of changes were made, resulting in more efficient production. Between 1750 and the 1840s, and probably before 1812, the acreage under wheat in England and Wales almost certainly doubled at the expense of rye and barley.[1] The traditional method of farming was the three-course rotation system consisting of wheat, rye or barley in the first year, beans, peas, oats or barley in the second and fallow in the third. By the end of the century the 'Norfolk' rotation, a four-crop variant, was being widely used. Wheat and barley for human consumption were grown in the first year; clover, which is nitrogen-fixing and enriches the soil, in the second, turnips both for the green tops which smothered weeds as well as for the roots which were used in animal fodder in the third, and finally clover and grass ley in the fourth. When the field lay fallow, as in the third or fourth year,

---

1   Turner, Beckett & Afton, *Farm Production in England* (2001) 18, 23.

according to the method of rotation used, it was usually left to grass and grazed, thus benefiting from dung and urine. Dung was an important product; it was often mixed with straw, ashes and other waste, and was carted regularly from the farmyard onto the fields. Further changes were made possible by improvements in making cast iron, enabling mass production of traditional farm implements, which reduced prices. In some instances progress was slow; for example, seed drills were not widely adopted prior to the 1780s. Books were produced to aid farmers and Mary herself owned *The Whole Art of Husbandry, or the Way of managing and Improving of Land*, by J. Mortimer F.R.S.[2]

One of the main products of William Bacon's land was grain, shown in the records for both farms. Although he also grew barley and oats, wheat was his principal source of income. The grain income for the Cliddesden farm for the year 1790-1 is well accounted for in the ledger. It is entered in far greater detail than any other commodity and amounted to about £573. Was this unusually careful accounting because the produce of the Cliddesden farm came under scrutiny by the landlord at the end of Bacon's lease in June 1791? He would want to know that the land had been well looked after at the end of the tenancy. After the move to Aylesfield farm in Alton, Bacon continued to grow wheat, but not in the same quantity. His total earnings for this grain in 1799, at £18 a load, amounted to £131 11s. 6d., representing 31 quarters, or approximately 7½ loads. Mary Bacon's land management manual advised that the average production of wheat was 20 or 30 bushels an acre.[3] Using this method of calculation, at 20 bushels an acre, the area given over to wheat would have been approximately 128 acres. This calculation does not allow for entries not made or for land used in the production of other grains, lying fallow or for the raising of sheep. A further difficulty arises when making any attempt to calculate the acreage given over to wheat in that the amount charged varied. The variation occurred from year to year, and also according to who the purchaser was. For example in 1799 Mr Monk bought 4½ quarters at £19 11s 6d., whereas Mr 'Eager' (Egger) got only four quarters for his £20. On the other hand, Mr Monk, who did better than Mr Eager, paid £22 for five quarters of wheat and Mr Simmons only paid £19 10s. for the same amount. Even knowledge of social relationships would not help to understand the logic of these transactions. It is possible that delivery was thrown in, or the price was less where a favour was owed, or where the purchaser was a friend. Sales of oats and barley are also recorded in the accounts, but they are too intermittent to gain any real overall picture of the amount sold.

---

2   J. Mortimer F.R.S, *The Whole Art of Husbandry, or the Way of managing and Improving of Land* (1761, 6th edition) 93.

3   *ibid.* 128.

Wheat was the usual grain used in making bread, although by 1799 barley was often substituted. The war with France caused a heavy drain on the wheat stocks, the military had to be fed, and it was difficult to boost supplies through imports. The rise in wheat prices during the 1790s is demonstrated in the accounts. In 1791 William Bacon sold 8 quarters of wheat for £21 12s., but in 1795 sold the same amount for £29 12s. The Bacons sent grain to the mill for grinding at least three times a month and the accounts for 1799 show clearly the increase in the use of barley as an alternative. The price of bread was rising rapidly and in 1800 Mary entered in her ledger, '1800 In May flower was one pound & one shilling a bushel 13 June it was 22 Shilling a bushel.' She also copied out a market report, probably from a newspaper, which shows clearly the fluctuating prices at the time.

1800 June 20

Wheat sold at Devise market at 166 shillings pr Quarter

August the 10 the prices of Corn continue to lower. At Birmingham, wheat at the last market, sold for 20 shillings per quarter less than at the market before. Pease, too, fell, 20 shillings and oats 12 shillings the best flour, which fell 15 shillings per sack, sold at from 90 shillings to 95. Oatmeal fell three pence per peck at Edinburgh, on the 5th at Haddington, wheat experienced a reduction of six shillings & 9 pence per boll at the last market, when the price was two pound six Shillings & four pence. Best oats sold at 2 pound nine shillings being 2 shillings and six pence per boll less than at the preceding market, & 2 shillings & 8 pence more than the average price of wheat. At Worcester the last market wheat fell from 18 shillings & 19 shillings to 14 shillings & 15 shillings. in consequence the price of the shilling wheaten loaf was fixed at 3 pound 11 ounces at Exeter the shilling loaf is one ounce less the price of Wheat fell to 13 Shillings the bushel. The average prices of Wheat in Yorkshire were 29 shillings per quarter than those of England & Wales the very small quantity of Wheat at Alresford on the tenth of July, was from 32 pound to 42 pound per Load. & bread was 3 shillings & one penny per gallon the next market on the seventeenth Wheat fell from 32 to 38 pound & bread to 2 shilling & 11 pence, on the 24th there were 50 sacks of wheat in the market and the price fell 22 pound to 30 pound & the bread to 2 shillings & 7 pence, on the 31 the quantity, exceeded the demand and the price fell to from 18 pound to 24 pound being a reduction from the tenth, of 18 pound or nearly one half per Load. But the most extraordinary alteration that has taken place on this, or perhaps any other occasion, has been experienced at Wincanton on the first instance, the Quarter Loaf sold at one shilling and 8 pence on the following morning at one shilling & 2 pence halfpenny, & in the evening of the same day at 9 pence halfpenny, being a reduction of ten pence halfpenny or more than one half, within 30 hours.

The storage of grain was important and judging from the numbers of rat poison recipes, these rodents were a very real menace. Did the Bacons have one of the new barns praised by Vancouver in his report for the Board of Agriculture? He wrote,

> A very excellent practice seems to be fast gaining ground in many parts of the coun-
> try, of building wheat barns, as well as corn stacks in general, upon stone stands or
> straddles. The barns thus constructed are usually of beech, elm, and fir-boards, with
> oak, beech, or elm plank, for thrashing-floors; the other part of the bottom of the
> barn may be formed of any other old and useless plank or boards.[4]

The Bacons certainly stored grain at home and also in other granaries. There are several entries for the granary at Basingstoke and it was also stored with a Mrs Tolfree
in 1791. For example, on 11 February 1791 'Shot up in the Granry at Basingsok 20
Quarters of Oats' and six more quarters were stored later. Beans and peas were
nitrogen fixing crops generally used for animal fodder. An entry in the accounts
shows 'beens' bought in quantity, a total of £60 being paid in 1791. At approximately
20s. 6d. a quarter, this was a substantial amount.

There is no evidence in the ledger of sales of wool while the Bacons were living at
Cliddesden, but with inaccurate accounts of this nature, that offers no definite proof.
It is clear, however, that William Bacon did rear sheep and produce wool at Aylesfield
farm, as shown by the accounts for 1791–2. 'Novm 16 bought twenty sheep at 14 shillings a Head Comes to £14 May 4 bought at overton 22 teegs at Sixteen Shillings a
head Comes two £17 12 0.' On 27 May the Bacons bought 20 sheep at Overton for
which they paid £15 16s. and four couples at £5 6s. According to Vancouver, wool was
'one of the most important articles in the whole catalogue of rural economics'.[5] Mary
recorded the sale of wool from 1792 to 1795, the best year being 1794 when £9 was
received for 8 tods and 25lb of wool.[6] The Bacons were lucky as wool production was
beginning to decline from 1793, due to the financial uncertainty generated by the
war with France, and there was a drop in the purchase of raw wool at country fairs.
Fortunately for the Bacons, who entered their sales in the ledger during this difficult
period, their sheep brought in a steady, though small income.

Sheep were not the only livestock kept at Aylesfield farm. Recorded in the
accounts are payments made for taking oxen into the yard during the winter, a
not uncommon practice. Turner, Becket and Afton recorded that at a farm in
Somerset in the 1750s and 1760s a farmer took into his yard cows, heifers, and oxen,
feeding them on grass for which he charged at the rate of 1s. 3d. per week; sheep
were cheaper at 3d. a week.[7] In December 1791, a few months after they arrived
at Aylesfield farm, the Bacons laid '3 score and 18 oxen' in the yard at 4d. a head.

4 Vancouver, *General View* 64.
5 *ibid.* 497.
6 A tod is approximately 28 lbs in weight.
7 Turner, Beckett, Afton, *Farm Production in England*, 59.

This was repeated in 1793 with 3 score of oxen. If it is assumed that the price is per week, then it was cheap in comparison with the Somerset farmer. One of the great advantages of wintering other people's sheep was the additional amount of dung produced, essential for the fertility of arable land. Advice given to farmers in *The Whole Art of Husbandry*, advocated the use of two yards, – one for the cattle eating hay, and one for the cattle eating straw.

> with racks and other conveniences to fodder them in; observing to feed them often, and not to give them too much at a time because when they have blown upon it they will not eat it; both your yards ought to be well sheltered, and made as dry as you can, and a good deal of straw given them to lie dry and warm in, which is a very great advantage to them and will much increase the quality of your dung.[8]

There is no evidence that the Bacons used oxen for draught or for yoke. If they had done so, they would have found advice in *The Whole Art of Husbandry*. The author advised strongly against working oxen in wet weather and recommended that 'In matching them, let them be as near as you can of one height, spirit and strength, else one will be apt to injure the other.' They were to be put to work at three years old and the farmer was encouraged to start by working them very gently. Finally, Mortimer advised that 'meat and fair words bring them sooner to the yokes than fear or blows'.[9]

There are very few entries relating to cows. They were certainly kept as Mary sold butter which would have been heavily salted. She recorded in her ledger that on 23 June 1792 she sold three pounds of butter at 2s. ½d. and entered another three and a half earlier in the month. Pigs, or 'hogs' were reared and on 23 August 1794 a record for the purchase of a sow and eleven pigs costing £4 12s. was entered in the ledger.

Although Mary wrote a very full inventory of all her worldly goods in her ledger in 1807, she did not record the contents of the farmyard as this was something she could not take with her. An advertisement in the *Hampshire Chronicle* on 17 March 1800 gives an idea of the sort of equipment the Bacons might have had:

> The stock comprises the Draught Horses and harness, six Milch Cows and ten Heifers, the principal part in Calf, one Rick of meadow hay about twenty seven tons, two narrow wheel wagons, one strong Timber Carriage with iron Arms, a capital Timber Gin – with Brass Cogs, two Dairy Carts, one roomy Pleasure Cart, with a Tilt, two Light Carts, Drags and Harrows, three double-wheeled Ploughs, two single Wheel Ditto, one Norfolk Ditto, a nine-shared Ditto, three sets of Winnowing Tackle and Winnowing machine, Heavers and Rudders, with both Articles on the husbandry Business.

8 Mortimer, *The Whole Art of Husbandry*, 233.
9 *ibid.* 229–230.

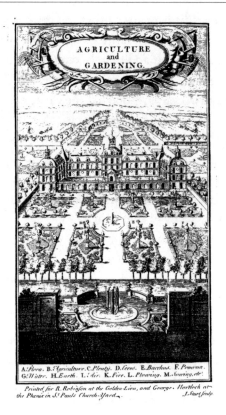
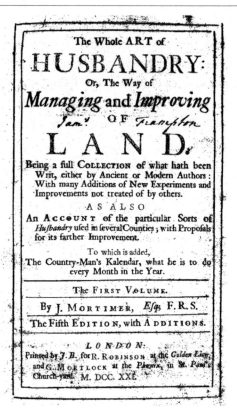

Figure 6   *'The Whole Art of Husbandry, or the Way of managing and Improving of*
Land' by John Mortimer F.R.S. (1721)   (Museum of English Rural Life)

A farm with all its workers was a community of men and women who had a wide
range of jobs to complete, often on a seasonal basis. One of the regular agricultural
reports in the *Hampshire Chronicle* gives an idea of the kind of tasks which had to
be carried out on the farm early in the year:

> Much of the leys have of course been broken and put into a state of readiness for the
> outcrops; and the stubbles are beginning to be turned down. It has likewise afforded
> an opportunity of putting the hedges into proper repair, and of cleaning and making
> up the ditches, but in the low wet districts it has been rather too open for getting the
> dung upon the grasslands ... Excepting land yet covered with turnips, in this district,
> almost every acre is prepared for receiving the seed intended to be sown thereon,
> and in dry loams some farmers have begun to drill beans.[10]

10 *H C*, 9 March 1801. It is unlikely that this agricultural report was written for this newspaper alone
   as much of the material in it was extracted from national publications. The advice was probably
   relevant over a much wider distribution area.

It was indeed late for dung which, according to Mortimer, should be spread in winter so that the showers would wash it into the ground and it would be the least exposed to the sun.[11] There are not many records in the Bacon accounts showing either the number of farm labourers employed, or the domestic servants and dairy maids, whose work was often combined. As already described in Chapter One, the farm labourers were usually employed by contract starting at Michaelmas, earning as much as £10 or as little as £2 a year. This ensured that they had completed the work of the harvest, when all available hands were needed, by the following Michaelmas when they were paid. It was usual for some domestic servants and some labourers to live in receiving full board and, in the case of women, some clothing, which would account for the very low wage. Although servants moved frequently from one job to another, they rarely went very far from their home area. There are no records as to how the Bacon children were employed but it is possible that at least one of them worked either at home, or on a local farm for a time, as this was common practice among farming families.

Farm labourers divided into two distinct categories. First there were those on annual contract, many of whom lived on the farm and could expect board and lodging as a major part of their wages, essential when some entered employment at the young age of 12. It is difficult to assess the amount paid to these workers as the sum varied according to the type of employment and rose during the century. Vancouver, writing in 1813, gave an account of the kind of work and wages expected of each category of labour:

> The wages of the head carter are about eleven guineas (per annum); that of the head carter's mate, about nine guineas. When a boy supplies this place, in driving plough and assisting to take care of the horses, his wages may be placed at *4l.* or guineas. Second carter's wages about the same with first carter's mate; his boy or assistant, the same as the other man's boy. The teams generally consist of five horses, and when the head carter's mate is not employed in helping to feed and take care of the horses, or accompanying the team on journeys upon the road, he is usually employed in thrashing or helping to dress corn, gripping, fending, or other jobs, about the farm. The thrasher receives about ten guineas per annum, and when more plough-teams are kept, the wages of the ploughmen and boys are generally regulated by their strength and qualifications, varying from *20s.* to *50s.* below the wages of the second carter and his boy. The day's work is usually performed in one journey of eight and a half or nine hours. The servants in these cases are all considered as boarding and lodging in the house.[12]

Vancouver also included the female servants in his account of wages. 'The

---

11 Mortimer, *The Whole Art of Husbandry*, 30-1.
12 Vancouver, *General View*, 381.

dairy-maid and cook's wages are about five guineas each; girls from two and a half to three guineas, with board, washing, and lodging.'[13] Second, there were those farm labourers who were paid by the day according to seasonal demand. They lived in their own cottages and were employed in such tasks as mowing grass, reaping, hedging and ditching, fencing, collecting faggots, coppice work, picking turnips and of course, the harvest. In the mid-eighteenth century, they might expect to earn on average a shilling a day except at harvest time when they were paid more. Vancouver wrote that '... cow, crow, pig, and milk-boys, procured from the adjacent villages, generally receive from 4*d.* to 6*d.* per day. The shepherd is generally a villager, who has 12*s.* per week the year round, besides perquisites, which usually attend his situation as butcher.'[14] As they worked for different people, it is very difficult to assess their overall income. Harvest time, when all available labour was needed in the fields, was a little different and the sum of 2*s.* a day was not uncommon and would probably have included food and beer. Mortimer estimated the amount to be mown. 'A man may mow an acre of meadow in a day, if it stand well and be even an acre and a half; and if the grass be thin on upland mowing grounds, then two acres.'[15] Visitors were usually generous with the tipping of domestic servants whose wages could be augmented appreciably in this way. Although Augustin Kinchin recorded the wages of his servants and labourers in detail, Mary Bacon made no such entries into her ledger.

The farm workers who lived in could expect to be reasonably fed. Charles Vancouver gave a full account of what they ate.

> The ordinary breakfast of a farm servant is bread and skimmed milk, with the remainder of what bacon was left the day before: their lunch or noonchine, consists of bread and cheese, with the small beer they take in their kegs to the field. Their dinner is usually prepared between three and four o'clock, and consists of pickled pork or bacon, with potatoes, cabbages, turnips greens and broths, seasoned to the palate with a variety of garden-stuff and pot-herbs, thickened with wheat flour. The general bread corn is wheat; the remainder of the dinner, with bread and cheese, is given to them with a pint of ale for supper, and the remnants, as before-mentioned, are eaten the next morning; this is their weekly diet, Sundays excepted, when they usually partake of whatever fresh meat may be prepared for the heads of the family.[16]

Life as a farm servant could be tough, especially in the severe winters of the eighteenth century. A dairymaid's hands would become red and sore, and her

---

13 *ibid.* 388.
14 *ibid.* 388.
15 Mortimer, *The Whole Art of Husbandry*, 30-1.
16 Vancouver, *General View*, 383.

fingers clumsy as she would be expected to milk the cows outside, whatever the weather, even in frost and snow. Dairy maids had to rise as early as 4 o'clock on summer mornings to milk the cows, after which they had to scald and scour their utensils and make butter and cheese. Sometimes they were also responsible for the marketing of the dairy produce. Everyone, whether employer or employee, had to live through the bitter cold of an eighteenth-century winter. The weather affected the whole way of life and for farmers, their very livelihood depended on it.

PART TWO THE WEATHER

The Storm

With awful gloom the heav'ns are overcast;
   The skies, relenting, pour down floods of rain;
Through bending woods resounds the hollow blast
   And torrents rush, impetuous, o'er the plain.

The mazy lightnings flash from pole to pole,
   And tip the mountains with their silver light;
While deep'ning peals of echoing thunders roll,
   And shake the guilty breast with dire affright.

Prone on the earth and shiver'd by the wind;
   The leafy monarchs of the forest lie;
While ruin'd palaces to earth consign'd,
   Awaken terror, and provoke the sigh.

Loud was the shock of elements! – Shall man,
   The pow'r that rais'd these wonders dare to scan.

The Calm

The winds are hush'd – once more the skies serene –
   The lightning spent – the roaring thunders cease,
Returning sun-beam gild the past'ral scene,
   And all around is happiness and peace.

The rain-drop quivers on the verdant spray –
   The shrubs again their lovely blooms renew –
The vocal choirs resume the broken lay –
   And nature smiles through pearly gems of dew.

Who can the pleasures of the village tell,
   When from their huts the rural tribes advance?
Who, while no curfew sounds the evening knell,
   Bespeak and bless the sons of liberty![17]

17 *H C*, 15 April 1799.

Poems were published very regularly in newspapers, this example reflecting characteristic British interest in the weather. During the eighteenth century the recording of the weather was a very common practice. Daily records were kept in diaries and regular reports published in newspapers. These were often written very dramatically, especially when the weather was extreme or caused havoc, as it often did. St. Swithin's day was taken note of, though not particularly seriously, by the editor of the *Hampshire Chronicle*, who on 28 July 1798 wrote:

> St Swithin has arrived this year with a wet jacket, but it no more follows from thence that we shall have forty days rain consecutively, than that you will die imme-diately after having cut your finger, though you must die after it. St. Swithin was a Saxon, a Prior, and a Bishop of this diocese, and put into the calendar for his extraordinary deserts:
>
> > This when Swithin from his fountain pours,
> > St. Swithin, tutelary God of Showers;
> > Beaux skip, Belles scamper, fly the cocks and hens,
> > With drooping plumage, to the sheltering pens.
> > While lo! The waddling ducks Te Deum utter
> > Clap their glad wings, and gabble through the gutter.

Each issue of the *Gentleman's Magazine* carried a digest of the previous month's weather, giving details of thermometer and barometer readings and noting levels of sunshine, rainfall etc. Weather recording was treated seriously and scientifically, and many private individuals, recording in their diaries or weather books, used rain gauges, thermometers, barometers, and hygrometers. Eliza Chute, wife of William Chute M.P., kept a yearly diary and in the printed part at the back of the book for 1790 there are rules for foretelling the alteration of the weather by the Barometer 'as laid down by Mr Halley, Mr Patrick and others.'[18] As a regular part of the weather report, outbreaks of infections, both of humans and livestock, were analysed in their relations to climate, and predictions made of likely future epidemics and seasonal health risks.[19]

The Bacons were extremely dependent on the weather throughout the whole cycle of the farming year, both in terms of the produce of their land, and because the health of their labourers and their own family was important, if that produc-tion was to be maintained. A hymn from Mary Bacon's book, *Hymns for Sundays*, charmingly links the weather with growth during the farming year.

---

18 The Diaries of Elizabeth Chute, HRO, 23M93/70/1/1–9.

19 R. Porter, 'Lay medical knowledge in the eighteenth-century: the evidence of the *Gentleman's Magazine*', *Medical History* **25** (1985) 152.

Good is the Lord, the heaven'ly king
 Who makes the earth his care;
Visits the pastures ev'ry spring,
 And bides the grass appear.

The clouds like rivers rais'd on high,
 Pour out at thy command
Their wat'ry blessings from the sky,
 To chear thy Christy land

The soft'ned ridges of the field
 Permit the corn to spring:
The vallies rich provisions yield,
 And the poor lab'rers sing

The little hills on ev'ry side,
 Rejoice at falling show'rs;
The meadows dress'd in all their pride,
 Perfume the air with flow'rs.

The barren clouds refresh'd with rain,
 Promise a joyful crop;
The parching ground looks green again,
 And raise the reapers hope.

The various months thy goodness crowns,
 How bounteous are thy ways
The bleating flocks o'erspread the downs,
 And shepherds shout thy praise.[20]

Winters were much colder in the eighteenth century than today with weeks at a time when snow lay on the ground. It was a period later labelled 'a mini-ice age' and these conditions lasted through most of William and Mary Bacon's life together, making farming very difficult at times. In 1768, three years after they were married and when they were living in Cliddesden, Gilbert White, who lived not far away in Selborne in Hampshire, wrote that between 3 and 9 January it was so cold that the meat was frozen too hard to be spitted and that several types of thrushes were frozen to death.[21] The January of 1776 was one of the coldest ever recorded in the south of England and on the 31st of the month Gilbert White measured a temperature of 0° Fahrenheit (-18°C) just before sunrise; three rivers in the area were completely frozen. The winter of 1785–6 was also very severe with snowdrifts up to 10 feet. This meant that root crops such as turnips, essential as a feed in the

20 *Hymns for Sundays and Festivals of the Year, for the Sacrament and other Public Solemnities* (c.1770) 66.
21 Gilbert White, *The Journals of Gilbert White 1784–1793*, ed. F. Greenoak (1989). Recorded in June 1790.

early months of the year, were very scarce; cattle were dying as there was insufficient straw and hay to feed them and sheep suffered from liver rot. As if to create a lull in the storms, and to have something beautiful by way of a change, weather watchers were treated to a very fine display of the Aurora Borealis in the Octobers of 1787 and 1788, which appeared to come from all quarters and formed a red centre. As it was recorded in Bristol, it is possible that the Bacons were able to see it.

Starting in 1788 Mary Bacon entered weather reports in her ledger, usually for the winter months and in note form. Whole days were left out and the records are full of spelling mistakes. As she recorded a whole winter in one long entry, unless she had a prodigious memory, it is likely that she kept her daily notes elsewhere and then copied reports for several months into her book. 1788–9 was an excessively severe winter and in most places collections were made for the relief of the poor. It was reported that the bishop of Chichester had ordered nine chaldrons of coal to be distributed among the suffering poor, on account of the inclement season. This weather was widespread over Britain with some startling results. On 19 January 1789 the editor of the *Hampshire Chronicle* reported that the carpenter and boatswain of the *Woolwich*, off Porchester, were walking the quarter deck when they saw 'a hare driving with the tide, on a large piece of ice; they immediately got into a boat and rowed after her, and instead of it being a fine hare as supposed, it proved to be a jack rabbit with one eye.' In January 1789 a man in the New Forest was found frozen to death half-way in water in a brook; he was standing straight and had been missing several days before he was found.

Not all the weather was bad, and Mary Bacon recorded that in 1790 'on the 20 June it was very hot and on the 21 first it was exceeding hot and many fainted with the heat and some Died.' The good weather was not to last and December 1790 brought some of the worst storms to be recorded in the eighteenth-century. On 22–23 December a great storm raged not only through England but also on the Continent, causing loss of life and a great deal of damage. Gilbert White, who mixed near poetry in phrases such as 'sun and clouds, sultry red even, sweet moonshine'[22] with scientifically measured temperatures and wind directions, gave a dramatic rendering. On 23 December he recorded that there was 'thunder, lightening, wind, rain, snow! Sun & wind.' His comments were, 'A severe tempest. Much damage done in and about London. Damage to some ships at Portsmouth ... Vast damage in various parts! Two men were struck dead in a wind-mill near Rooks-hill on the Sussex Downs: & on Hind-head one of the bodies on the gibbet was beaten to the ground.'[23] The Bacons would have experienced this storm and Mary recorded

22 *ibid.* June 1790.
23 *ibid.* December 1790.

it, expanding her weather report to add drama to the occasion. Her dating is inaccurate, as most reports, including that of the exact and scientific Gilbert White, recorded the storm as being at its worst on 23 December. White lived not far from the Bacons as the crow flies, and his timing of the storm should have been little different from theirs. Mary wrote in her ledger:

> December 22 in the year 1790 a Dreadful storm of thunder & Lighting with violent high winds which Done a Great Deal of Damage it blowed Down 36 Trees one after the other in Hackwood park belonging to his Grace the Duke of Bolton & many other in the Spring woods it took Part of the Pheasentry and Carried it forty yards it whent through a Window into a Room where two men Lay it tore the Curtain & Lodged between the bolster & teeck without Doing any further Damage. This storm was in most parts of the World Little or much. Read this and think how wonderful the Works of divine providence is over his Creatures. M B 1790

An article in the *Hampshire Chronicle* of 3 January 1791, taken from a London newspaper, reported the event nationally and for a second week running described the horrors and the destruction caused by the elements. It was reported that in London roofs were blown off, including that of Dolly's chop house in Paternoster Row, chimneys came down, people were killed and a great number of sparrows 'were picked up that had been killed by the lightning'. For a great part of the storm, there was 'a strong sulphurous smell' in London and 'at Hailsham a mare belonging to Mr. Goldsmith was struck blind by the lightning, which also contracted the muscles of her neck in a manner that has drawn her head on one side.' Nearer to home for the Bacons, 'the drivers on the road from Salisbury and the passengers corroborate the testimony, that the lightning was like a stream of fluid from a glasshouse furnace; and the horses were so generally terrified, that with difficulty the drivers could get them on.

After the Bacons moved to Aylesfield farm in the summer of 1791 there was no real amelioration in the weather; the winter was cold and stormy. In September there was excessive rain and the family would have joined in the prayers for fine weather said in churches all over England. One over enthusiastic parson caused some embarrassment to his congregation as he said the prayer for rain in error. The *Hampshire Chronicle*, 24 September 1792, reported that

> when the minister of a village near Warminster, Wilts, either by mistake or design, read to his congregation with great seeming devotion, the prayer of rain, directed by our Liturgy to be put up in times of great drought, although at that instant the rain was falling in torrents. The audience, who were chiefly farmers, having their crops of corn abroad, looked with consternation at each other, and some of them rose from their knees with intent to apprise the parson of his error, but were prevented by their

neighbours who whispered in their ears that it would be impious to interrupt the parson in his duty.

The winter of 1792-3 was also very cold. Parson Woodforde lived in Norfolk, not in Hampshire, but his graphic descriptions invoke a vivid picture of what it was like to be inside a freezing eighteenth-century house in winter and therefore the conditions which the Bacons had to endure. He wrote on 14 January that the milk in the dairy pans was one piece of ice and that the basins upstairs froze a few minutes after the water was put there.

Farming in the summer of 1793 was hazardous as the uncommonly hot weather proved fatal to a considerable number. Newspaper readers appear to have enjoyed disaster and the editor of the *Hampshire Chronicle*, 22 July, reported that four people died of heat at Shepton Mallet, 'a servant of farmer Grailey of Nether Lampton, near Salisbury, was suddenly taken ill while working in the field and died in about two hours. One Ridout, of Braidford, near Sherborne, was taken ill while hay-making and died soon after he was carried home.' According to the same editor, writing on 2 September, there were compensations and the fine weather 'has been very favourable to the breeding of partridges, which has given great spirits to the veteran gunner, who is impatiently awaiting the arrival next Monday, heroically to join in the general slaughter of the bloody day.' Unfortunately it rained and he reported the following week that 'the carnage among the feathered tribe was not so dreadful – Monday as expected, owing to the rain, which frightened many of our fine-weather gunners from the field, and gave the poor birds, at least, another day's respite from their deadly guns.'

January of 1794 was very cold and windy with a heavy fall of snow and high winds over England and Scotland and with several shipwrecks reported. The winter of 1794-5 was excessively severe with a great deal of damage to shipping, especially in the Irish Sea. Mary Bacon recorded in her ledger,

December 17th the frost began and the 26 of December it snow'd all Day the frost continued till the 6 of January 1795 when it thawed a little and the 7 at night freesed again and Continued frosty with snow at intervals till the 26 January when we had a great thaw which caused a flood in many parts Brother James Thorp had 57 sheep and 14 pigs and a Dog all Drowned in the morning which was a Dismal sight to see the frost still Continuing till the first of feburary when we had another thaw at night freesed again and so Continued till the 7 of February when it thawed a Little and the 8 rained all Day and the 9 rain with blustering winds and the 10 a great Deal of rain with high winds the 11 & 12 day the ploughs went and the 13 Day a very great snow with high winds the 14 it was very fine and the 15 fine and a Gentle thaw all night an the next day the 16 at night a hard frost with a Rime Continued frosty with a great Deal of snow and Blustering winds till the 21 and then a thaw which Continued with misty mornings till the 28 of February & then we had a great deal of snow and a hard frost at night the first of march it was very fine and the sun shone all Day at night a hard frost the 2 of march the wind high and it snowed all Day 4 & 5 misty the 6 & 7 misty bringin Rain the 13 snowed a Little the 14 a great Deal of Snow the 15 a fine Day and the 16 more snow rain & snow the 19 and a hard frost at night

Most work on the land must have been almost impossible and ploughing very difficult indeed. The mention that 'the ploughs went' implies that it had become such a rare occurrence that it was worth recording. The effect of this cold weather on farmers was severe and widespread. Hester Pitt, Lady Chatham, commented in a letter that 'In the spring the mortality amongst the sheep and lambs from cold and scarcity of food was very great and the deficiency of the wheat crop, the ensuing harvest was such as had not been experienced for several years before.'[24] Cold summer weather followed, with frosts in June, devastating for the newly shorn sheep, thousands of which died. The winter of 1796–7 was also very cold and the *Hampshire Chronicle* dramatically reported the story of an old woman who was seized by a fit, half upset a pail of water and her body was frozen to the floor; she died.

The winter of 1798–9 was equally long and harsh. Local landowners were not without charity and the *Hampshire Chronicle* recorded that in December 1798,

Because of the inclement weather, bread and soup were distributed to the poor in Winchester at 12 noon every day. The receipt for the soup is given for 400 quarts. Beef 50 lbs, ox cheeks and legs of beef 5; rice 30 lbs, peas 25 quts, black pepper 5¼ oz, Cayenne ½ oz, ground ginger 2 oz, onions 13 lbs, salt 7½ lbs, with celery, leeks , carrots, dried mint etc.'

The precise quantity of a number of spices may be indicative of their importance in eighteenth-century cooking. It is certainly a nourishing stew and two years later £200 was raised by subscription in Andover to pay for the distribution of soup for the poor. The weather in February 1799 was even worse. In London the Thames was frozen over at Execution Dock and it was difficult for carriages to make their way in the streets. Snow drifts on the Isle of Wight were so deep that carriages had to be dug out. Mary Bacon entered a lengthy record of the weather during this long hard winter.

In the year 1798 Account of the Weather
Novemr 14 fine day & frost at night Continued frosty till the 19 then high Winds with snow all Day with a frost at night. 20 a fine day a frost at night Continued frosty till the 22 snow at night the 23 thawed the 24 a little snow hard frost at night

24 V. Birdwood, ed., *So Dearly loved, So Much Admired, Letters to Hester Pitt, Lady Chatham from her relations and friends 1744–1801* (1994) 169.

the 25 a storm of snow & hard frost at night the 26 27 Dark foggy wether till the 9 of December then a hard frost and so Continued with high Wind till the 16 then a wet Day with a fog not much alteration till the 23 & then a hard frost and the 25 snowed all day the frost stil Continued with a sharp frost and a rhime the first of January 1799 Lighting at night the 3 & 4 frost with Great Rhimes then open weather till the 27 rained all Day a Little snow at night still frosty 29 a Deep snow and Continued frosty with Rhimes, till the first of feburary then a thaw frost at night 2 of feburary snowed all Day the 3 Sun shined all day the 4 a Rhime Continued frosty with snow at intervals the 9 a thaw the 10 rain the 11 snow a frost at night and very high Winds 12 a fine day but high winds the 13 a thaw with dark foggy Weather and so Continued till the 17 then a fine day the 18 & 19 mist with rain the 20 then fine open Weather till the 5 of March the High Winds with frost the 7 snowed all day the 8 a deep snow and still Continued with frost the 9 snowed all day the 10 the sun shined all day the 11 a Rhime the 12 a fine Day the 13 snow and Rain all the afternoon with Blustering winds all night and a hard frost the 14 high freesing winds the 15.

Bad conditions continued into the summer and heavy rains in August, together with cold easterly winds, reduced the summer fallows and turnip fields into a mire, half rotted a great part of the hay, stopped the growth of the second share of clover and badly affected the corn and wheat. The following winter was not much better and Poole Harbour froze over. Mary continued to record the weather during the winter of 1799–1800 in much the same way as the example given above. It is difficult for those living in the present day to appreciate the discomforts of an eighteenth-century winter but her detailed daily records give a strong indication of what it was like. It affected a farmer's whole way of life, causing personal discomfort and ill-health, failure of crops and diseases in animals increasing the work of a wife whose duty it was to care for those around her and for the welfare of the stock on the farm.

Chapter Four

The farmer's wife

ALTHOUGH THE BACONS were not wealthy, they could have afforded the services of a veterinary surgeon. Whether or not they did (and nothing is shown in the accounts), it is clear from the number of recipes which Mary entered into her ledger that she was well equipped to deal with the majority of diseases affecting livestock. Many of the cures are marked as her own, and she collected others from friends and relatives. She was not alone in these skills; amateur veterinary practices were widespread and prescriptions for animal cures abounded in the eighteenth-century. Many of the diaries, widely used at the time, had lengthy information sections printed at the beginning and the end, some of which included remedies for animals. Elizabeth (Eliza) Chute, wife of William Chute M.P. of the Vyne in Hampshire, filled in her small, neat, leather-bound diary on a daily basis over many years. At the printed end of one of them is a draconian remedy, 'Cure for the Rot in Sheep.'[1]

> Take a handful or two of common salt, which put in the sheep's mouth, and hold until all is dissolved. A gentleman in Cambridgeshire has served several so, that were apparently rotten; they afterwards thrived exceedingly, and their wool looked more lively than before. A pound of salt is sufficient for three sheep.

Most medicinal remedies, both for animals and for humans, contained a high proportion of herbs, roots, bark and berries. Although some ingredients were limited in which diseases they would cure, the majority were multi-purpose.

Cows

There is clear evidence that the Bacons kept cows, both from the number of recipes used to cure these animals in 'My Book of Receipts', and from Mary's entries in her ledger of sales of butter, but unfortunately there is no indication of the specific breed or breeds. According to Charles Vancouver, a number of breeds of cattle were

---

1 Chute Diaries, 1790.

'indiscriminately met with' in the region, including the Sussex, Suffolk, Leicester, Hereford, Glamorgan, North and South Devon, and Norman breeds, the latter being preferred for the dairy.[2] Horned cattle were common in the eighteenth-century, although they were never referred to in Mary Bacon's ledger.

The herbs, spices and other ingredients used are as varied as the illnesses each medicine was purported to cure. A list of herbs and berries commonly used for cattle included bayberries, turmeric, and aniseed. Celandine, which sounds appropriate for a cow, was also believed to have suitable medicinal properties. According to Culpeper's *Complete Herbal and English Physician*, first published in 1653, 'the herb or root boiled in white wine, and drank, a few aniseeds being boiled therewith, opens obstructions of the liver and gall, helps the yellow jaundice …'.[3] Mary Bacon used both celandine and aniseed for cattle, sometimes mixing them with alcohol, adding rum to celandine and warm ale to aniseed. Pepper and mustard were said to sooth the internal workings of a cow, but it takes an act of faith and some imagination to believe that hog dung had medicinal properties and made the animal feel better. Nevertheless, it was used by Mary to cure urinary infections.

A Cow that hath the red water

Take a handfull of Hog Dung half a pint of Rennet half a pint of Brine a handful of mustard Seed Bruised Simmer it together and Give it the Cow and let her Stand two hours without meat If one Drink fails Stop one Day & Give her another in the morning

Fortunately for the cows, such draconian remedies were not always necessary and the following extract from the printed end of one of Eliza Chute's diaries indicates that sometimes good husbandry – and patience – were enough.

An infallible Method of cure for the Gripes in Horses and Horned cattle

As soon as you perceive the first symptoms of that disorder, fold a large sack or coarse sheet in four, let it remain sometime in boiling water; then carry the vessel near the animal, and clap the sheet or sack on his loins, covering it over with a warm blanket. The animal must be kept in a close place, and safe from any cold air. The pain is removed in less than eight minutes and you are certain of the cure being completed when the animal stales. [4]

Mary Bacon's cures are not so simple and must have been very time-consuming both to make and to administer. It is not always clear to the modern reader exactly what ailment she hoped to cure; it must be assumed that making a cow clean is a

---

2   Vancouver, *General View*, 352.
3   Nicholas Culpeper, *Complete Herbal and English Physician*, ed. C. Hedley (1997) 49. First published in 1653.
4   Chute Diaries, 1790.

reference to a stomach disorder.

A Drench[5] to make a Cow Clean

Take one ounce of Long peper half a ounce of the grains of Paridee[6], beat them fine & boile it in a quart of ale, then stir a quarter of a pound of treacle, give it Luke Warm Let the Cow fast two hours after give her some Warm Water M Bacon

To make a Cow Clean

take a quart of ivy berries a little sprig of savin[7] 2 or three blades of long peper, boil all this in a quart of new milk; a little while, then strain it of and stir the turmerick in and Give it the Cow luke warm [8]

To make a Cow clean

one ounce of Bayberries one ounce of turmerick one ounce of marden seed[9] one ounce of fennigreek[10] one ounce of vinery ounce of Coriander seed

Bayberry was one of the more common ingredients used in Mary Bacon's veterinary remedies. Culpeper gave a long list of diseases cured by these berries and included among the many complaints and conditions for which they were efficacious, 'the poison of venomous creatures and the stings of wasps and bees', 'speedy delivery in childbirth', 'all cold and rheumatic distillations from the brain to the eyes, lungs, or other parts … consumption, old coughs, shortness of breath and thin rheums'. Most aches and pains were also relieved by bayberries and they also had properties which 'expel wind and provoke urine', diseases of the bladder and stopping of urine'.[11] Although it is difficult to understand how the same berry could both provoke and stop urine, no doubt it had some effect on cows as Mary used it for curing jaundice or 'the yellows', mixing it with turmerick, caman seed and aniseed.

A Drench for a Cow that has the yellows

Take one ounce of bayberry one ounce of Carnan[12] seed one Ounce of Turmerick one Ounce of Anniseed. To make two Doses to be giving three days apart in Warm Ale

---

5 Drench: a dose often given to an animal forcibly, through a drenching horn. Mary Bacon does not always make it clear what the 'drench' is actually intended to cure. Some of the ingredients, such as feverfew, cured worms and it is possible that some of the doses were given for infestations of this nature.

6 Paradise.

7 Juniperus Sabina.

8 In the margin: 'Farmer Bennet gave it me'.

9 I have not been able to trace 'marden seed'.

10 Probably Fenugreek.

11 Culpeper, *Complete Herbal* 13, 14.

12 Caman seed. I have not been able to identify this ingredient.

Alcohol was frequently given to ailing animals; Mary preferred rum, adding a pint of rum and milk and an ounce of bark to a handful of celandine as a drink for a cow. To make another similar drink she added feverfew,[13] ginger, cloves, rue and horehound to two quarts of ale. In a third she mixed ale with rue, camomile, wormwood, and honey '& bake a bit of bread and put in it and beat it two pieces with a spoon and give it altogether two the Cow Luke Warm'.

Sore or infected udders had to be attended to and Mary included two recipes for this complaint, the first for a fomentation. To make this she mixed camomile, marshmallows, rue, a little hemlock and some soft soap, then boiled all the ingredients in two quarts of milk for a quarter of an hour before fomenting the udder 'as hot as you can beare your hands in it' A simpler cure using milk and celandine was probably equally effective.

Mary Bacon did not include any cures for oxen in her book, but they were probably the same as for cows. This exclusion is surprising as these animals were commonly used in farm work; a number of them were stabled in the Bacons' yard during the winter for other farmers. A cure for the twist in oxen was not included in her receipt book but had an operation been necessary, Mary would have had to ensure the sobriety of her husband. The *Hampshire Chronicle* editor wrote about the twist in an article and noted that, 'The unskilled performance of a necessary operation[14] upon them when calves is the cause of this disorder...' Then follows a description of the operation that the farmer needs to witness in order to perform it. Finally there is the warning, 'persons in liquor should never be employed in this business, on the performance of which the future health and value of the beast so materially depends.'[15] It is possible that William Bacon had to perform operations on greedy cows, as reported in the *Hampshire Chronicle*.

> A few days since a cow, that was swollen, or as is more commonly expressed, blowed, by feeding too greedily on hay, was opened by a farmer in the neighbourhood, who took from her what her excessive feeding had produced, which he caused to be measured, and found to be two bushels. The animal was however relieved by the operation, and is now a fair way of recovery.[16]

13 A plant from the aster family.
14 It may be assumed that this is castration.
15 *H C*, 1 December 1788.
16 *H C*, 28 January 1797.

Sheep

The accounts in the ledger show that William Bacon farmed sheep at Aylesfield farm, since his land was well situated on top of the downs for rearing this kind of livestock, but do not indicate the breed. Vancouver asserted that Hampshire had no established breed, but that there were several alternatives: 'In the woodland district of this county (Hampshire) the heath sheep and Old Hampshire, or the native Wilts breed, were those formerly the most prevalent, but which in many places are now found to have given way to a cross of the New Leicester upon the native speckled-face Berkshire and Old Wiltshire breeds.'[17] Sheep farming had its hazards, and losses could be severe. Turnips were grown as food for animals and a bad winter could ruin the crop with disastrous results. On 16 May 1791, just before the Bacons moved to Aylesfield farm, the *Hampshire Chronicle* reported that 'The sheep in Hampshire and many other counties have been materially injured by a too forward spring. Turnips, which form their chief sustenance, have run to seed too soon this year, that many sheep and an infinite number of lambs have died in consequence.' Scab could be a problem and the *Hampshire Chronicle* reported on 17 February 1794 that 'the western flocks are much tainted with the scab, and the South Downs have had more unsound flocks this winter than they have known for many years before.'

Sheep are vulnerable animals, prone to disease, and Mary Bacon included a number of cures in her 'Receipt Book.' In particular, aniseed, bayberries and elecampane were general elixirs and were used indeterminately in either cows or sheep, and for differing complaints. Mary wrote down the ingredients for the remedies, but also described the management of the animals during their period of treatment. Unlike cows, lambs were to be bled, appropriately under the tail if the complaint was red water. As with cows, care was taken to give sheep medicine which was of blood heat. The red water in sheep, which presumably referred to blood in the urine, seems to have been a common complaint, as it was with cattle. There were a number of ingredients in Mary Bacon's cure:

> Powder of Liquorish one ounce Elicompane Turmarick Grains of Paradice Diapente[18] Annisseed Longpepper Boldarmanack[19] bayberys of each one ounce. Boil it all together in Chamberly and give it them Blood Warm three spoonfulls to a Lamb and bleed them in the vain in the under side of the tail and pen them up all night and give it them in the morning fasting this is a Drench for four Score.

17 Vancouver, *General View*, 365.
18 Grains of Paradice: grains of paradise have long been used as a spice and traditionally as a medicine. *Encyclopedia Brittannica Online* (http://library.eb.co.uk): Diapente: a medicine composed of five ingredients.
19 Boldarmanack: I have been unable to trace this ingredient.

Mange was another common ailment, found in sheep, but also in other farm animals. Mary had a cure for that as well.

Three pound of tobacco Dust will make two quarts with Brine boylle it till one part in three is boyled away Take a halfpenny worth of Stone brimstone one pennyworth of Blew Vitterel a Little Tar the Vitorel[20] may be put into a bottle with Spring Water and that will serve three times

Rot in sheep was a common problem and it was thought that as many as a million animals a year died of it in Britain. The *Hampshire Repository*, a record book covering a wide range of subjects and first published in 1799, described rot as a fluke worm, lodging in the liver or blood vessels.[21] This complaint was of grave concern to farmers and when the *Repository* recommended Fleet's Restorative, a lively exchange of letters followed. Most cures were homemade and are to be found in notebooks and diaries of the period; the following is by an anonymous farmer: 'Take a pint of White wine Vinegar Four ounces of Verdue grew[22] two oz of blue Vitriol Quarter of a pint of spirits of turpentine All these mixed together let it boyle Over a gentle fire about ten minutes Pare the foot as far as it is hollow Anointe it with the above when Cold' [23] Mary Bacon had her own remedies and may have consulted her manual which was listed among her books, *The Whole Art of Husbandry or The Way of Managing and Improving of Land*.[24] This recommended mashing malt as for beer and then boiling shepherd's purse, sage, plantain, pennyroyal, wormwood, bloodwort in the liquid; they were all herbs which she used frequently in her own recipes. The method which she recorded in 'My Recipe Book' was extremely simple and contains good advice.

To prevent the rot in sheep

Bruise a quantity of rue Leaves well and press out the juice to which add an equal weight of Salt When Sheep are in Danger of being rotten give them a table Spoonfull of this mixture once a week It should always be given to new bought sheep it will keep them well if they are in danger if not it will do them no harm the adviser of this remedy recommends also the sheering of sheep so early as may the new wool has then to get an head so as to secure the sheep from the attack of the fly, and they will be effectually preserved from taking Cold, by washing them with sea water or brine made of Salt and Soft water if it can be had, this washing also

20 Vitterel/vitorel: an example of how haphazard spelling could be.
21 Anon, *Hampshire Repository*, vol. 2 (1799) 279.
22 Nehemiah Grew was an English botanist and it is possible that 'verdue grew' was a plant named by or after him.
23 HRO 3M51/607.
24 Mortimer, *The Whole Art of Husbandry*

greatly preserves them from the gripes the Scab the red water the rot and many other Disorders

Horses

J. Mortimer, the author of *The Whole Art of Husbandry,* was of the opinion that horses were the 'most necessary and useful beasts on a farm.' Their importance is also reflected in the Schedule return figures for Alton: 1,667 draught horses alone were to be offered by the parish in the event of an emergency caused by an invasion from France. Mortimer went on to advise making 'your mares as tame as you can; it is better to keep them to a gentle, easy work, such as ploughing an hour or two in a day than to have them wild,' and advocated that 'fifty acres of fallow land, is as much work as can be well managed by a team of five horses.'[25] Soon after arriving at Aylesfield farm, Mary recorded the purchase of horses in her ledger. Unlike her uncle's record of horses bought at the Rugby horse fair, she gave few details or names, but made an entry that on 19 May 1793 'Smiler brought a mare colt'. It is likely that the Bacons' horses were mostly working animals and may have looked like Vancouver's unflattering description of them:

> Although it is necessary in most parts of this county to have strong teams for carrying out the crop, performing long and heavy journeys upon the road, and for hauling chalk, marl, clay, &c. &c. nearer home, yet among the larger sort of horses generally through the country, there is by far too much bone, and being often in low condition, they have too frequently a coarse, heavy, and uncomfortable appearance.

Horses were valuable and useful animals, and great care had to be taken of them if they were to be maintained in good health. According to the *Compleat Horseman: or Perfect Farrier,* another of Mary's books, this was not always the case. 'Among all the Creatures, there is none which yields more Profit and Pleasure to man than the Horse; yet oftentimes, for want of Skill to ride him, or through negligence in his Diet or Dressing, or by Watering him unseasonably, or any other Accident, he becomes unserviceable.'[26] The fact that horses needed a great deal of care is reflected in the high proportion of cures concerning them recorded in 'My Book of Receipts'.

Mary Bacon would have administered her medicines to the Bacons' horses in three principal ways, by drenching horn, by pills and by a 'clyster'. The use of a drenching horn was common practice among those treating both cattle and horses, and it is likely that Mary was thoroughly conversant with this method. Instructions

---

25 *ibid.* 93, 208-9.

26 Sieur de Sollysell, *Compleat Horseman: or Perfect Farrier,* abridged from the Folio done into English by Sir William Hope, 4th edition (1729) 1.

for making pills were given in the *Compleat Horseman or Perfect Farrier*, they were
to be washed down with wine:

> In making of Pills, after you have broken and beaten your Drugs coarsely, mix the
> Composition with two Pounds of fresh Lard, or for want of it, the like quantity of
> fresh Butter; and having beaten and mixt it well together in a Mortar, make pills
> about the bigness of small tennis-Balls, and when the Horse has swallow'd them,
> give him, in a Horn, some White-Wine to carry them down to his Stomack, and to
> take away the Bitterness from his Mouth. If it be for a Drench, you are also to beat
> them coarsely, and either to mix them with a Decoction or with wine, and letting it
> infuse about a quarter of an hour, give it to the Horse early in the Morning, with a
> Horn, after he has been tied up two Hours to the Rack.

After giving him a decoction, 'rinse the Horn with the remainder of the decoction, or with wine, and make him swallow it; after which wash his mouth with
a little Wine, to take away the bad Relish.'[27] Mary used pills in curing urinary
disorders in horses mixing 'four ounces of Castilesope four ounces of Rosin two
ounces Gumgyacum[28] two ounces of Nitre if two thick mix a Little Honny with
it'. A 'clyster', the third method of administering medicines to a horse, was a kind
of enema, usually inserted by means of a pipe and bag into the anus of the animal.
The recommended amount of liquid was a quart, or at the most three pints, and the
treatment was to be repeated often.[29] The ingredients in a clyster varied as it could
be used for both purging and nourishment, and commonly contained purging salts
or greasy broth accordingly.

Some of the ingredients put into a drenching horn, a pill, or a clyster, would
appear lethal to modern equestrians and it is difficult to know how horses survived
some of the concoctions. Quicksilver sounds particularly poisonous and was used
by Mary as, 'the last Expedmt for ye farcy Take three or fore Ounces of quicksilver
pour It into a Horses Nostrills his head being tyed up To the rack it will imediately
run through him'. She was more generous with her dosage of quicksilver when
compared with the much smaller quantity recommended in another eighteenth-
century recipe.: 'then take your Drenching Horn & yr first Hornfull put in one
ounce of fine Quicksilver give this in a morn fasting and keep yr Horse three hours
after without meat and give him no water till the next Day.'[30] Other ingredients
used by Mary Bacon, which would now be considered poisonous, included myrrh,

---

27 de Sollysell, *Compleat Horseman: or Perfect Farrier*, 125.

28 *Enc.Brit*: genus Guaiacum.

29 Among Mary's listed books is the title, *Every Man's Ready Companion*. She was not always
   accurate as to titles and this is probably *Every Young Man's Companion*, by W. Gordon (1759) This
   book contains a section on farriery in which advice is given on the use of clysters.

30 HRO 5M50/2244

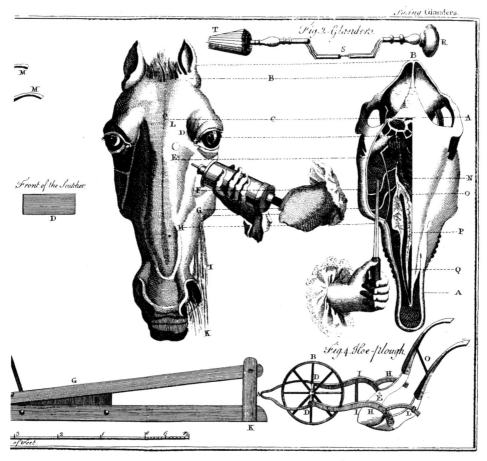

Figure 7 Treating the glanders. Note the woman's hand & cuff administering the dose.
From R Baldwin et al. *The Complete Farmer: or a general dictionary of husbandry
by a society gentleman.* (1769) (Museum of English Rural Life)

turpentine and vitriol.

Sometimes good preventative medicine was used and equine pick-me-ups were given. How else may 'A Recipe for a Rising Drink' be interpreted? '3oz of Black Rossam 1 oz of brimstones 1 Quart of Blacksmith's forge water Lukewarm wash it down with Ale'.[31] Was there iron in the blacksmith's forge water? – a good tonic for the blood? It sounds like a witch's brew, as indeed do many of these 'cures'. Hares and witches go together and a cure for 'A Haemorrhagy' or 'a Flux of Blood at the Nose or Mouth' sounds like a potion: 'Take a Hare Kill'd in March, flay her, and without larding prepare her for the Spit, but do not put her upon it; then dry her in an Oven, so that the whole flesh may be reduc'd to powder, which, if blown

31 From a small, hand-written notebook marked 'Receipts' HRO 3M51/607.

plentifully into the Horse's Nose, will effectually staunch the Blood'.[32]

Further illnesses and conditions of horses treated by Mary Bacon cover a very wide range of ailments from digestive disorders, injuries, through to the dreaded 'staggers', which was all too often lethal. In the following recipes it may be assumed that 'fret' refers to a digestive disorder rather than to a nervous irritation, as this complaint is put in the context of colic or gripes in the *Compleat Horseman*.[33]

a excellent Drench for the fret in a horse

Take two ounces of Cassteel Sope, slice it and put it in a pint of warm Ale, one ounce of the Oyle of turpentine, a quarter of a ounce of the Oyle of Amber, mix it all together and give it to the Horse, Cloath the Horse if he is warm

For a horse in the fret

A halfpennyworth peper pownded a halfpennyworth of Ginger pownded a halfpennyworth of mustard seed pounded Boile it in a Quart of Drink Give it the horse Blood warm

Mary included several recipes for staggers in her book, usually referred to as either 'sleepy staggers' or 'mad staggers'. The 'yallows' or 'yellows' appear to have been connected with this complaint and, although it is likely to refer to jaundice, I have not been able to establish this conclusively. The *Compleat Horseman* offers the following definition of the affliction:

In the Stavers or Staggers, a Horse loses the use of his Senses he reels and staggers, as if he were Drunke; beats his Head against the Walls and manger with extream Violence, and lies down and rises with greater fury than in the Cholick. The Causes of this Distemper, are hard riding or labour in hot weather, noisome smells in the Stable, long Races ... excessive eating and above all a redundancy of hot and sharp Humors in the stomach.[34]

There were innumerable cures for this complaint, but none as strange as a very simple remedy for a horse with the staggers from William Marshall:

In the livery stables in London, He-Goats are kept for preserving the health of the horses, and it is a popular opinion that they keep off the Staggers. Whether it is their odour, or anything else, that prevents this fatal disorder, the correspondent

---

32 de Sollysell, *Compleat Horseman*, 247.

33 Fret: alternatively, the *OED* gives the definition as a fretting sore or a canker.

34 de Sollysell, *Compleat Horseman*, 259. *Enc. Brit.* gives the explanation: symptom of several unrelated animal diseases, in which the affected animal walks with an unsteady, staggering gait and seems to be blind. The many possible causes include poisoning from ingesting plants containing a high level of selenium or from ingesting grasses infected with the fungal disease known as ergot. Magnesium or calcium deficiency may also cause blind staggers, as may inflammation of the brain (encephalitis) or of the brain coverings (meningitis).

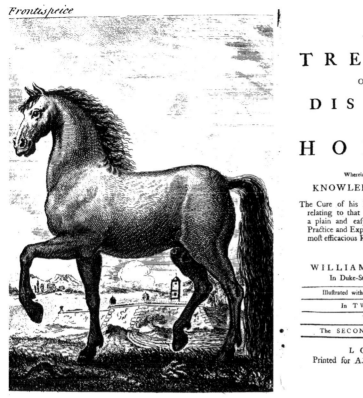

Frontispeice

A NEW

TREATISE

ON THE

DISEASES

OF

HORSES:

Wherein what is neceffary to the
KNOWLEDGE of a HORSE,

The Cure of his DISEASES, and other Matters relating to that Subject, are fully difcuffed, in a plain and eafy Manner, from many Years Practice and Experience. With the cheapeft and moft efficacious Remedies.

B Y
WILLIAM GIBSON, Surgeon,
In Duke-Street, Grofvenor-Square.

Illuftrated with Thirty-two COPPER-PLATES.

In TWO VOLUMES.

V O L. I.

The SECOND EDITION, corrected.

L O N D O N:
Printed for A. MILLAR, in the Strand.
MDCCLIV.

Figure 8   A New Treatise on the Diseases of Horses. William Gibson (1754)

(Museum of English Rural Life)

cannot say; but he thinks that it is his duty to inform readers the following fact. About sixteen years since, a Mr. William Pacey lost several horses from the staggers. He was advised by a friend, whose experience had led him to believe that he had benefited much by what he had recommended, to keep a He-Goat in his stables. He got one, and had not for many years another instance of that disorder. While the goat lived, his horses were free from the staggers; the goat dying, his horses again became afflicted with this alarming disorder. He procured another goat, (which is still living) and has not since had an instance of the staggers. He has seldom less than twenty horses in his stables.[35]

Mary Bacon had her own cures for the staggers, the first of which must have been a favourite of her husband as she wrote his name at the end of it:

35 William Marshall, *The Rural Economy of Glocestershire* (2005) 174. First published 1789.

To Cure the yallows or Staggers

Take one ounce of Venus treacle in a pint of new milk Stir it together till it is all Desolved and half a pound of Common Treacle and Two ounces of Turmerrick & one ounce of Dyapenty and a Little Saffron Squeezed through a fine rag Bleeding & Roweling[36] Will be proper in 24 hours after Give one ounce of Dyapenty one ounce of turmerrick one ounce of Elicompane put in a Quart of warm Ale Dr Ramtoms Drench Wm Bacon

For the mad Staggers

Take away three quarts of Blood the first time and every four or six hours take one or two quarts more as the horse can bear it. Take Saltpetre & Castile Soap of each two ounces, Virgin Snake Root[37], Contrayerva Root Assafoetida[38], Valerian Root, of each half a ounce, Opium Camphor, Barbadoes[39] Aloes, of each two Drams, put them in a mortar, & mix them well with a pint of warm water, for a Drink give one every night & morning, or till the madness abates, give a Clyster every Day of three Quarts of Greasy Broth with two ounces of purging Salts, offer him warm water every two or three hours. When a horse recovers a fit of the Staggers & Does not feed give one or two of these Drinks in a morning fasting. Take true Diapenta four ounces, Elixir of Vitroal half an ounce, Saffron, one Dram, Coarse sugar four ounces Good Ale, one quart, made warm & mixed, A mesh of malt or boiled barley, at this time would Do well Rowels are good in both the yellows & Staggers, but in the mad Stagers, three or four should be put in, one in the forehead, & the others in the belly or thighs as the farrier pleases, they should be soaked in warm yellow Basilicon, with a little powdered flies mixed to bring on an immediate Discharge

Mary Bacon had a number of recipes for alleviating conditions in the feet and legs of a horse, the particularly vulnerable parts of the animal. Some of them are relatively simple, 'To Draw a pain out of the foot thats nailed bound four ounces of Soft Sope four ounces of elder ointment two ounces of the Spirits of turpentine Dress the foot every Day Give the Phisic first'. Other recipes are more complicated and give a treatment plan for the animal in some detail. 'A Recipe for a horse that have bad Legs that Breaks out behind' gives the ingredients for a poultice, describes the making of it, followed by a drink to be given the following day:

Take two ounces of Honey two ounces of Lard two ounces of horse turpentine two ounces of Rockallom this is to make a poultis & and its to Lay on 48 hours, To make a ointment to dress it with afterwards two ounces of Honey two ounces of

---

36 Rowelling: *OED* gives a late seventeenth century definition: Rowelling of Horses is putting of Hair Rings through the Horse skin to draw out Corruption.

37 Virgin snake root: snakeroot is a group of plants mostly growing in North America. It has not been possible to establish exactly which member of the family this one is.

38 Assafoetida: asafoetida, a resinous gum. *OED*.

39 Barbadoes: this is more likely to be Barbados tar, than Barbados sugar.

Verdigrease (tryed Wm Bacon junr)

How to make the above poultis put the Honey and horse turpentine lard in a pipkin or skillet and simmer it together then thicken it with flower then put it on a thick Rag and mix the Rockallom in it if the allom is not Deaded put it on a hot fetter before you mix it (tried WB jun⁴⁰)

This Drink is to be give to the Horse the next Day after the poultis is Laid in one ounce of flour of Brimstone one ounce of Nitre once ounce of black Rosin in a pint of warm Ale you must mix the Rosin in a Little cold Ale first as it will not mix in any thing warm the Nitre and brimstone will mix in the warm ale if you think it proper to give him another Drink stop one Day between

Horses, like sheep, could be affected by the mange and tobacco dust was also used to cure them:

For the mainge in a horse

Take two Gallons of Soap Lees two handfulls of Broom, Sulphor, & Allom, & white Eleber, & Tobacco Dust, of each one pound & of Green Coperas⁴¹ half a pound, all these must be powdered & add to it one pint of Oile of Turpentine, when Boiled. if Soap Lees, Cannot be got you may add to it Brine or Chamberlie or both of them into it or you may add all these in it.

In another recipe for the same complaint white mercury, black brimstone, turpentine, green broom and green ash wood were boiled with the tobacco. It was to be dressed 'as hot as you can.' Another of the many conditions affecting horses was a spavin, or a swelling on the hoof. It is difficult to know whether the condition or the remedy was more painful for the horse. 'Take of yellow asnick & Sprits of vitrol three pennyworth of Each to take a vain from a Horses Leg when a blood Spavin put it in a spoon and touch the vain with your finger two or three times in one place and it will eat of the vain in a Day or two'. A similar affliction was the 'grease', a disease in horses' heels, in which both honey and turpentine was used. 'a Quarter of a pound of Honny one ounce of burnt Allom two ounces of Lard two ounces of horse turpentine a Quart of milk & flower Sufficient to make it into a poultice boil them all together after it is well wash it over with Gypsyacum'. A cankered foot could be troublesome. First a salve had to be made, then 'Pare the foot out Clean Dip towl in the butter of Antimony then Dip it in the powders & press it well on the foot till the fowl Criveses are Covered all over then take the shoe & wedge it Down as tite as possible & bind it with some List of rope yarn'.

Horses' backs were vulnerable too, but Mary Bacon had no specific recipe for strains and stresses in this area other than 'a green ointment'. She would have

---

40 The Bacons' son was also William.
41 I have not been able to trace 'green coperas'; it might refer either to copper or to dried copra.

done well to have collected one from a recipe book dated c.1708. This involved sending 'the shaveing of the flesh side of the sheep's skin' from London, presumably to Hampshire:

> Mr Thomas goats of Hackney his Recipe for a horses strain of the back sinews. Take halfe a pint of wine vinegar the bigness of an egg of Deer suet or if it cannot be had so much soap set them on the fire till the suet or soap be melted then add a quantity of the shaveing of the flesh side of a sheep's skin (which I believe I must send on munday from London to make it thick as a poultice). Stirring all together apply it warm (not hot) to the weak part having first drawn on an old stocking over his leg & then put the poultice in & apply it to the grieved part & let it lye on 48 hours, & then repeat it again if there be occasion.[42]

It must be assumed that many of these cures worked, as horses were valuable animals and were not to be killed off lightly by poor veterinary practice, whether professional or lay.

Pigs

There is only one recipe for a cure for pigs in 'My Book of Receipts', which is surprising as they were important animals on a farm, providing bacon and pickled pork, the principal source of meat for farm workers and servants. The Bacons certainly kept these animals, as there is an entry in the ledger in August 1794, recording that Mary bought a sow and eleven pigs for £4 12s. Exactly what these pigs looked like is open to speculation. It is likely that they bore some resemblance to the Hampshire native hog, which according to Vancouver was:

> a coarse, raw boned, flat-sided animal, agreeing in no respect with the idea entertained of it in other parts of the kingdom: the great number fed for a few weeks in the close of autumn, upon the mast which the forest and other woodlands produce, in the county, and the excellent mode of curing hog-meat practised by the house-keepers, have contributed in a far greater degree to establish that superiority ascribed to Hampshire bacon, than any inherent excellence in its native breed of hogs. Very few, however, of the genuine native hog are to be met with, the common stock being either the native Berkshire breed, or a considerable predominance of that blood in the native swine of the country.[43]

In this context, 'hog' is used with a collective connotation, but at a time when there was considerable differentiation between kinds of pigs and their culinary usage, it could also refer to a castrated male, or an animal which had been 'gelt'. Young 'shoots' (swine of nine months) were considered best for pork, those of one

---

42 Heathcote papers, HRO, 63M84/235.
43 Vancouver, *General View*, 378.

to one-and-a-half years for bacon. A porker, a young fattened hog, weighed a great deal less than a bacon pig. Eliza Chute recorded in her Diary for 1797,

seven Porkers at 5d per lb	10	12	11
Five Bacons at 6d per lb	27	3	0

making the approximate weight of a porker 73 lb, and a bacon pig 217 lb. Mary Bacon does not state the purpose of her one cure for pigs. She used oil of earthworms to ease strains in horses, and presumably pigs can also suffer from aches and pains. In order to 'anoint a hog' she combined 'two pennyworth of Dyathe 2 pennyworth of the oyle of wormes and a bit of hogs Lard about as big as an Egg to be Simmered together'.

Dogs and cats

Dogs and cats are the common domestic animals frequenting every farmyard, yet Mary Bacon did not write out any cures for them in her ledger. Cats have been traditionally tolerated as vermin exterminators in farmyards, demanding a minimum of attention, but she might have been expected to have taken more care of the dogs on the farm. Dogs are liable to a number of canine diseases and are frequently bitten by other animals in fights. At a time when rabies was widespread in Britain, every effort had to be made to prevent and cure this killer disease. There is an example of a cure for a dog bitten by a rabid animal, given in a veterinary manual found in the Hampshire Record Office, and it contains some of the herbs Mary might have used:

> Two ounces of Pullapochen (Polypodium),[44] hart strong, madenhair, Deadman's thomb, Plantenay (Plantain), and one ounce and a half of hollebone (Hellibore). 'boyle them in 2 quarts of Skim mealk or whey. Boyle then a quarter of (anouer?) with half a pound of brakle (?) Put in the same quantatay of butter Give to each dog a point (pint) and to any Stronger beast a quart all but what Wasteth in boyleing wash all the Roots clean.[45]

The spelling leaves much to be desired, but it is given as it is because of the soft echoes of Hampshire accent, which can just be heard. Sometimes there appears to be no rhyme or reason in the ingredients of eighteenth-century herbal remedies. One herb is used for many different ailments and for each illness there are a number of different combinations of a wide variety of herbs. This is the case in cures for bites of mad dogs. The recipe given in *The Art of Cookery made Plain and Easy*, by Hannah Glasse, is quite different from the one above:

44 Polypodium: member of a fern family.
45 HRO 5 M50/2245.

For the Bite of a mad Dog for either Man or Beast; Take six Ounces of Rue, clean picked and bruised; four Ounces of Garlick, peeled and bruised; four Ounces of Venice Treacle, and four Ounces of filed Pewter, or scraped Tin. Boil these in two Quarts of the best Ale, in a Pan covered close over a gentle fire, for the Space of an hour, then strain the ingredients from the Liquor. Give eight or nine Spoonfuls of it warm to a Man, or a Woman, three Mornings fasting; eight or nine Spoonfuls is sufficient for the strongest; a lesser Quantity to those younger, or of a weaker Constitution, as you may judge of their Strength. Ten or twelve Spoonfuls for a Horse, or a Bullock; three, four, or five to a Sheep, Hog or Dog. This must be given within nine Days after the Bit; it seldom fails in Man or Beast.[46]

A very common remedy for rabies in humans, although an unlikely cure, was sea bathing; it is difficult to envisage this treatment being used in animals.

Rat catching

No farm is complete without its resident rats and no matter how competent the farmyard cats are they will always need human assistance. In the eighteenth century, farmers were left to their own devices unless they could afford to purchase ready-made concoctions such as Dutch Paste. This was a popular remedy and was frequently advertised in newspapers. Rats were everywhere, but 'This valuable composition being of so enticing a nature, draws them from different parts of a house, warehouse, farmer's premises, outbuildings or a ship, to eat it, which instantly kills them.'[47] To authenticate the fact, the advertiser referred the public to the author of a letter which he has received: 'My kitchen and cellar being infested with Rats, I used your Dutch Paste, which has entirely cleared my house and given me much satisfaction. Price 30s. a dozen.'

There were many and varied methods of destroying these unhealthy pests and remedies were common. Sometimes the rats were tempted with delicious ingredients. Claver Morris, in his diary noted that on 25 July 1726, 'I pounded 27 Drams of Maccaroons & with it mix'd 4 Scruples of white Arsnic powder'd, & with Brandy made a Paste for the Ratts.' On 29 July in the same year, he was unlucky and a very unfortunate accident occurred:

On Thursday night I mixd with the Fowles-Meat a Fortieth part of White Arsnick, on a large Tile, & yesterday morning it was all eaten up; & this day in the Forenoon, 5 or 6 Pullets, out of Ten died: I suppose they pick'd up some of the barley-Meal which was mix'd (as above) with the Ratts-Bane; Though I cannot imagine how

46 Glasse, *First catch your Hare*, 166.
47 *H C*, 10 December 1788.

they could, being confined in the two partitions of their Coop.[48]

Another remedy, invented by a miller in Hampshire, whose property was infested by rats, was widely sold all over the county. An assurance was given that no cats would touch it. Following the use of this remedy, there were no further holes gnawed through the miller's sacks. Unfortunately, the mixture was also used to destroy water rats, which were numerous at the time and which are now subject to conservation programmes. Rats were a nuisance in the Bacons' farmyard and Mary included several recipes for killing them in the 'My Book of Receipts' section of her ledger:

To Catch Rats

in some convenient place feed the rats with the following food take one pound of flower three ounces of treacle & six Drops of oyl of Carryway seeds mix them well together & add to it one pound of fine Crumbs of bread touching it with your finger as Little as possible Let them be fed for some time to make the place and food familiar to them you must Likewise Put some of the food into the traps fastning it up some time that it may not fall Down to Catch them after they have been thus fed for about ten days Let them have no food but in the traps Still fastned up till you begin Catching them when you begin Catching Amend the traps Constantly & take out one by one as fast as they are Catch by no means suffering any to remain in the traps when you are weary of Catching fastning up the traps as before & Let them feed unmolested as before till you begin Catching again you must Scent the traps with four Drops of oyl of Rhodiam[49] & a very little musk & a Little oyl of Anniseed if you would kill them Leve out the Bread & put in some poison.

A premium of five guineas was Latley (given) by the Dublin Society for the following recipt to kill rats. Take one Quart of Oatmeal four Drops of oil of rhodium, one Grain of musk & two nuts of nuxvomica powdered, mix the whole together & place it where the rats frequent Continue to Do so while they eat it & it will soon Destroy them

Rats were not the only wildlife to face destruction in the eighteenth-century. When Mary was a child, she may have been taught that nearly all wildlife was considered as vermin and should, therefore, be destroyed. An advertisement in the *Salisbury Journal* in 1756 gives a good indication of the contemporary attitude of farmers. It is difficult to believe that any wildlife survived such potential destruction:

A NEW EDITION OF / VERMIN-KILLER / BEING

A complete and Necessary Family-Book shewing

---

48 Claver Morris, *The Diary of a West Country Physician* (ed. E. Hobhouse 1934) 135.
49 Rhodium: one of the platinum metals.

A ready way to destroy Adders, Badgers, Birds of all Sorts, Caterpillars, Earwigs, Flies, Fish, Foxes, Frogs, Gnats, Mice, Otters, Polecats, Rabbits, Rats, Snakes, Scorpions, Snails, Spiders, Toads, Wasps, Weasels, Wants or Moles, Worms in Houses and Gardens, Buggs, Lice, Fleas etc…with many curious Secrets in Art and Nature Printed W. Owen, London.

Curing animals and keeping down the vermin was only one of the responsibilities of a farmer's wife. A farm, with its servants, labourers, and in many cases, their families, was a community in itself and a good wife would have concerns about their welfare. Mary Bacon was an amateur veterinary practitioner but she was also a herbalist ready to cure those she employed, as well as her friends and neighbours.

Chapter Five

The physician

A WOMAN OF MANY parts, Mary Bacon cured not only the animals on the farm, but her friends, servants and neighbours as well. Approximately a third of 'My Book of Receipts', a large section of the ledger, is devoted to remedies for a wide range of human ailments. The lay practice of medicine was not unusual in the eighteenth century when life was precarious and when there was a keen interest in remedies of all kinds. It was an age when health was poor, boils and ulcers could last for weeks and become infected, malarial mosquitoes invested swampy areas, rabies was relatively common, and the serious diseases such as measles, smallpox and tuberculosis took a heavy toll on the population. For those who could read, there was a wealth of information about illnesses and their cures in newspapers, almanacs, journals, and books such as John Wesley's *Primitive Physick*[1] and William Buchan's *Domestic Medicine.*[2] The *Gentleman's Magazine* contained numerous medical insertions and listed eleven physic books in one advertisement alone, in 1736. These included *A History of Plants growing about Paris. With their uses in Physick and a Mechanical Account of the Operation of Medicines,* a treatise on rheumatism, an essay on sickness and health, *Experienced Measures on how to manage the Small-Pox,* a critical essay on fevers, and a practical dispensatory.[3] The *Hampshire Chronicle,* on one single day in 1792, included advertisements for: *A certain cure for corns; The British Ointment for Corns; The Cardiac and Nervous Tincture; Johnson's Asthmatic Candy; Jackson's Patent Ointment for the Itch; Jackson's Patent Tincture for the Rheumatism, Gravel Stone, Bruises, Sprains;* and *Dr. Watson's Balsam of Amber, for Coughs, Asthmas, Difficulty of Breathing, Whooping cough, Spitting of Blood.*[4] The editor of the *Hampshire Chronicle* was well aware of the importance of health. When the summer of 1793 was very hot, he exhorted his readers to beware of the consequences of the heat,

1 John Wesley, *Primitive Physick: or an Easy and Natural Method of Curing most Diseases* (1759).
2 William Buchan, *Domestic Medicine* (1769).
3 R. Porter, 'Lay medical knowledge in the eighteenth century', *Medical History*, 29 (1985) 140.
4 *H C*, 6 February 1792.

A CAUTION The ill consequence which arises from the indiscretion of drinking cold liquors when in a great perspiration is too obvious to require the least proof. During the present fervent season, it is strongly recommended to those who are much exposed to the rays of the sun in the open fields, &c., as well as the soldier on his march, to avoid, as much as possible, the free use of cold liquors; the evils which often attend them may, however, in a great measure be corrected, by adding a small quantity of ginger, powdered, to their drinks, whether cyder, beer or water. It will also be of infinite service to put two ounces of powdered ginger, or more, into a hogshead of cyder for common use, which will prevent those very unpleasant complaints in the stomack which that beveridge too frequently occasions.[5]

Interest in disease was not confined to concerns for family and friends. George III suffered from a long and difficult illness which included manic phases; daily reports of his condition were given in the *Gentleman's Magazine*, as they were in the London and provincial newspapers. They were detailed, enlarging on the kind of night the king had, and how he was in the morning. This concern over the king's welfare was partly due to the general interest in health, but 'Farmer George' was popular with his people as evidenced by the rejoicings which occurred when he recovered. Not only disease, but death and the way of dying was of interest to the eighteenth-century reader. Although the *Hampshire Chronicle* included short death notices, few details were given of the illness to which the person had succumbed. However, if an accident had occurred, then the manner of death was reported in full, and sometimes highly dramatically. Later in the century the *Gentleman's Magazine* gave greater emphasis in obituaries to the last moments of the deceased; the way of dying was more important than the actual illness itself.[6] In eighteenth-century literature, heroines sometimes took a very long time to die. The most dramatic example is to be found in Samuel Richardson's *Clarissa* where the heroine took three months and 413 pages to expire.[7] Mary Bacon, in attending the sick while dispensing her medicines, may well have had more experience of death than most.

For a farmer's wife both convenience and cost must have been motives in providing lay medicine to her family, farm workers, other servants, and friends. She commented on more than one occasion that she had cured people with a given remedy and it is likely that her ministrations included those poorer members of the community who lived in her neighbourhood. Aylesfield farm was isolated and it would have taken time, which in busy periods of the year could be ill afforded, to send for the local physician or surgeon. Few labourers would have been able to

5 *H C*, 22 July 1793.
6 Porter, *Medical History*, 157.
7 Samuel Richardson, *Clarissa*, 1747–8 (Penguin Classics, 1985) 1013–1426.

pay for professional help. A rough guide to costs can be found in Thomas Turner's diary for 1756 in which he noted that he paid 5s. to his physician for 'opening one of my temple arteries'; in 1760 he paid 2 guineas to Dr Poole for treating his wife. A few days later he paid Dr Poole 10s. 6d. and made the comment, 'Really a fine thing it is to be a physician who can charge just as they please and not be culpable according to any human law.'[8] The *Gentleman's Magazine* published a table entitled 'Pharmacopoeia Empirica, or the List of Nostrums and Empirics'.[9] This shows the price of various remedies and where they could be purchased in London. The cost of drops for rheumatism was 3s. 6d. a bottle or, from another pharmacy, 20s. a box. To cure most itches was cheaper at 1s. or 2s. a bottle or phial, while an electuary[10] for a cough could be purchased at 1s. a pot; a remedy for gout was 5s. a dose. Although Mary had to buy many of the ingredients she used, her treatments must have been much cheaper. She may have agreed with John Wesley, who was very much against apothecaries and doctors whom he thought were in it for gain. He believed that experience, common sense and the common interest of mankind were important. His intention in his book, *Primitive Physick*, which Mary owned, was to set down safe, cheap, and easy medicine, 'easy to be known, easy to be procured, and easy to be applied by plain unlettered Men'.[11] It must be supposed from the long list of ingredients both gathered from nature and bought from her local pharmacist that Mary took her practice of medicine very seriously. It is easy to envisage her rows of little pots, jars, and bottles sealed with a cork or a hog's bladder, on her larder shelf, ready for use.

A reading of eighteenth-century cures can be very confusing, as it seems at times as though almost any ingredient could cure almost any illness. Another of Mary's books, Culpeper's *Complete Herbal and English Physician*,[12] gives an indication of this. The book was advertised in newspapers and the remedies used throughout the eighteenth century. The properties of ivy serve as an example. The flowers help the 'bloody-flux',[13] and, if outwardly applied, are helpful to the nerves and sinews. The yellow berries are good against jaundice, preserve from drunkenness and help 'those that spit blood'. The white berries kill worms. The berries also prevent the plague, 'break the stone, provoke urine, and women's courses … Fresh leaves of ivy, boiled in vinegar, and applied warm to the sides of those that are troubled with the spleen,

8 *Diary of Thomas Turner*, 72, 213–4.
9 Porter, *Medical History*, 166–168.
10 Electuary: medicinal ingredients mixed together to form a paste and sweetened with sugar or honey.
11 Wesley, *Primitive Physic*, xxxiv.
12 Culpeper, *Complete Herbal*.
13 Bloody flux: dysentery.

stitch in the sides, so give much ease.' The leaves are also good for headaches, treat 'old filthy ulcers' – and 'stench therein'. They quickly heal green wounds as well as burns, scalds, or 'salt phlegm or humours in other parts of the body.' The juice of the berries or leaves clears the head from catarrh as well as sores in the ears. Continual drinking from a cup made of ivy will help those who are troubled with the spleen. Finally, a hangover is alleviated by putting a handful of ivy leaves, bruised and boiled, into some wine.[14] The apparent ability to cure all manner of diseases by one remedy alone is reflected in newspaper advertisements. Dr Brodrum's Botanical Syrup, advertised in the *Hampshire Chronicle* during 1798 is an example of this, and its success was announced 'with infinite pleasure'. This remedy was said to cure 'Evils, Cancers, Leprosy, scrophulous Complaints, extracts Mercury out of the system, though ever so subtilely situated, and even in cases where salivation has failed of cure in the most inveterate venereal complaints'. Further on in the same advertisement, which is more than half a column in length, Dr Brodrum went on to recommend the Botanical Syrup to those 'Ladies and Gentlemen bordering on the state of Matrimony (prior to their appearance before the Altar of Hymen), who are in the smallest degree apprehensive of the system not being entirely sound or subject to relaxation of the solids.' What exactly is meant in the latter half of this sentence may well be left to the imagination.

Some cures demanded an act of faith and with so many ingredients sounding poisonous and improbable, psychological factors must have played a large part in a patient's ability to get better. Parson Woodforde was given an unlikely remedy for cramp by his brother, who recommended that he should take a roll of brimstone sewn up in fine linen to bed with him. Perhaps he was able to relax and drop off to sleep because his brother had been sympathetic. It is clear that an interest in medical cures was widespread; it was not uncommon for laymen to dispense cures regularly to their family, friends and servants. Judging from the large number of recipes and occasional comments that she had cured a number of people with a certain remedy, Mary Bacon certainly took her role of amateur herbalist-cum-physician very seriously and probably had a reputation in this respect among her immediate community. Most of her cures were no doubt her own, but a number of her recipes were given to her by friends and relatives. She covered a range of illnesses, although there are a few glaring omissions. It was an age when the dreaded smallpox was common. The disease frequently resulted in death or severe disfiguration; the vaccine had only recently been introduced and was still viewed with mistrust by many people. There were religious scruples, and debate as to whether it was right to inflict illness on a child unnecessarily by vaccination, together with a general mistrust of something

14 Culpeper, *Complete Herbal*, 81.

new. Even if she disapproved of vaccination, it is surprising that Mary did not include a remedy among her cures, if only to alleviate the symptoms. Measles was a killer disease and this is also excluded. It may be that these diseases were more serious than the run of the mill ailments which she treated, and that in those cases, a medical practitioner would have been called in. This is borne out by Roy Porter's comments on a certain visible pattern in the characteristic ailments for which relief was sought by readers of the *Gentleman's Magazine*.[15] He found relatively few requests for treatments for the main killer complaints such as consumption, child-bed and infant fevers, madness or cancers. He concluded that readers were inured to living with or dying of these serious conditions, or they would expect to receive treatment from physicians and surgeons. Readers did not mention venereal disease, and neither did Mary. In both cases, it was probably from modesty.

Many of the ingredients used by Mary

A
COLLECTION
O F
RECEIPTS.

1. *Abortion, (to prevent).*

1. USE daily a Decoction of *Lignum Guaiacum.*

2. *For an Ague.* *

2. Go into the *Cold Bath* juſt before the Cold Fit.
3. Or, take a Handful of *Groundſell*, ſhred it ſmall, put it into a Paper Bag, four Inches ſquare, pricking that Side which is to be next the Skin full of Holes. Cover this with a thin Linnen,
C 3 and

* An *Ague* is, An Intermitting Fever, each Fit of which is preceded by a cold Shivering and goes off in a Sweat.

Figure 9 A page from 'Primitive Physic: or an easy and natural method of curing most diseases' by John Wesley (1761), a book in Mary Bacon's collection.

(Chawton House Library)

Bacon would be unpalatable, bitter and seemingly poisonous to us today. She was not without humour and one particularly bitter remedy has a little sketch beside it in the margin of someone vomiting. Powdered flies, oil of swallows, and oil of worms, the formula for which is given below, were all in regular use. Some of the components of recipes such as red lead, oil of turpentine and elixir of vitriol sound very poisonous to us today, whereas others such as Calcined Magnesia alba, presumably similar to Milk of Magnesia, and also used by Mary for bowel problems, are very familiar.

Although many of the ingredients would obviously have to be purchased in a pharmacy, Mary Bacon was well placed to gather most of the plant material herself as Aylesfield farm was near to downland and a wood was close to the house. She did not own *The Useful Family Herbal* by John Hill[16] as it was not included in her

15 Porter, *Medical History*, 150.
16 John Hill, *The Useful Family Herbal* (1754) .

list of books, but had she read it she would have found that it gave comprehensive advice on the opening page.

> The Useful Family Herbal or An Account of all those English plants which are remarkable for their Virtues and of the drugs which are produced by Vegetables of other Countries. Contents include: Directions for gathering and preserving roots, Herbs, Flowers and Seeds; Recipes for making from them distilled Water, Conserves, Syrups, and other Forms, proper to be in readiness, and for keeping, all the year. The ways of making up Electuaries, Julips, Draughts, and the other common forms of Remedies; together with Cautions in the giving them. The whole intended for the use of families and of the Instruction of those who are desirous of relieving the distressed sick.

Mary Bacon would have produced some ingredients herself; for example, she kept bees and would therefore have provided her own honey. Judging by her uneven spelling and grammar, she wrote down most of her recipes from memory, but there are a few which have obviously been copied out.

THE RECIPES

The ague

There has been some speculation as to the exact definition of an ague. It is sometimes referred to as a fit of shivering, with 'flu-like' symptoms, but the *Oxford English Dictionary* defines it as malarial fever with hot, cold, and sweating stages. John Wesley in *Primitive Physick*, described it as 'An Intermitting Fever, each Fit of which is preceded by a cold Shivering and goes off in a Sweat.' His cure sounds a little unlikely; he advocated putting groundsel in a paper bag with the sides pricked, which was then put next to the skin and worn on the pit of the stomach.[17] Mary Bacon's recipes were more complicated. [18]

A Cure for an ague

> Take one Large Nutmeg & two small ones, take their weight in Rock Allom[19] grate the Nutmegs and beat & Search the Allom, then mix them well together & divide them into three equal doses or parts, take one in a Glass of warm Clarret & fast after it, eat neither Milk nor Cheese, take it on the well Day, and continue taking till the three Papers are taken but only on the Well days keep it Down if you can, if it purges two or three times so much the better.

---

17 Wesley, *Primitive Physic*, 29.

18 Many of Mary Bacon's ingredients are traceable but due to her spelling and use of local names it has not always been possible to identify everything she used in her recipes. Modern equivalents are given where possible.

19 Rock or Roche Alum prepared from the alum stone from Italy.

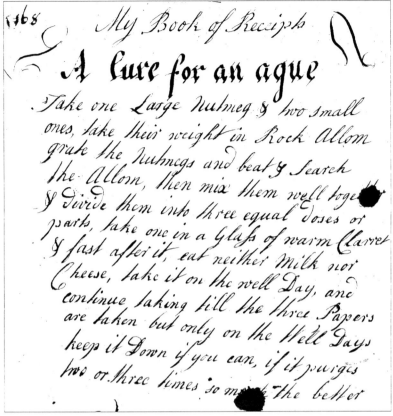

Figure 10   A Cure for an Ague from Mary Bacon's 'My Book of Receipts'.

(HRO 28M82/F1)

A Certain Cure for an Ague

Take one ounce of the Best Bark two ounces of the Syrop of maiden hair and one ounce of Honny mix it together in half a pint of Sage tea give it at 3 times the one part as soon as the fit is over, another part about six hours after and the other about 8 hours after that all this must be Given again in 6 Days after[20]

Another for a Ague

Take 40 Grains of snake Root powder 80 Grains of the Salts of wormwood half a ounce of Best bark put it in half a pint of port wine or Gin to be taken every three hours

It will never be known whether or not Mary Bacon and Jane Austen met. The Austens knew the Terry family, meeting them at balls, and Mary's grandmother was a Terry. But there may be another connection. It is possible that the cure for the ague which Mrs. Norris gave to the gardener in *Mansfield Park*, was the same as Mary Bacon's own remedy which was to be placed next to the 'shurt'. Mrs. Norris

20 In the margin: 'I have cured Agues with this Recipe'.

met the gardener,

> with whom she had made a most satisfactory acquaintance, for she had set him right
> as to his grandson's illness, convinced him that it was an ague, and promised him a
> charm for it; and he, in return, had shown her all his choicest nursery of plants, and
> actually presented her with a very curious specimen of heath.[21]

This does not prove that the two women met, but that they may have both known
the same local charm for a common ailment:[22]

For the Ague

When Jesus saw the Cross whereon his body was to be Crucified his body did shake
then the Jews said art thou troubled with an Ague or shaking he said I have no ague
nor shaking but whomsoever keepeth this in mind or in Writeing shall never be
troubled with any ague or shakeing So the Lord Jesus help thy Servant who puteth
his trust in thee Amen & Amen

Digestive problems

For the Bowels Stomach & Bloody Flux

Take Calcined Magnesia alba, half a drachm, Turkey Rhubarb twelve grains Ginger
Grated Six grains to be taken in a large tea cup full of pepermint water when going
to bed it seldom fails the first time taking but if it should repeat the next night but
one

Rhubarb was a favourite remedy of Parson Woodforde who recorded that he took
a little in the evening before going to bed, 'being rather dull and melancholy'.[23] He
also used it as a cure for violent pains in the stomach and mixed it with ginger, again
taking it at night.[24] More cures for stomach problems might have been expected in
an eighteenth-century book, but Mary only recorded this one. Although hygiene
showed some improvement during the course of the century, it was still far removed
from twentieth-century standards.

Recipes for surfeit water abounded in the eighteenth century, and were used for
general indigestion – or overeating. The well known cookery writer, Hannah Glasse,
some of whose food recipes Mary copied, made surfeit water using 27 ingredients
plus brandy. Mary used fewer ingredients, but also included brandy.

To make surfeit water

Take some redweeds and mallard flowers Coriander and Angelica balm and mint
penyroyal and hyssop put it into a pan boile the water and put to it Let it Stand
twenty four hours then strain it of and put Sugar as you think fit and some Brandy

21 Jane Austen, *Mansfield Park* (Clarendon Press edition, 1949) 104.
22 Brian Southam, 'The charm of Mrs. Norris', *Jane Austen Society Report*, 2002.
23 Woodforde, *The Diary of a Country Parson*, 345.
24 *ibid.* 369.

To make Surfit Water

Take Corriander Seeds, Anisseed, Sweet fennel seed, Pioney Roots of each 2 ounces Liquorish roots four ounces & Redweeds one Bushell, British brandy two Gallons bruise the seeds in a Morter, the roots must be Sliced very thin & Let them Steep for 8 or 9 Days Stiring them once a day Add one pound of Lent figs[25] & one pound of Reasons you may Distill from it afterwards if you Please take one ounce of Turkey Rhubarb two Drams of Safforn one ounce of Cardaman seeds & a pint of the Best Brandy Let it Steep for ten days then Strain it of and put it in a Clean bottle

Another way to make Surfeit Water

one ounce of Colander [coriander?] seeds one ounce of Sweet Anniseeds one ounce of Carraway seed one ounce of Stick Lycorice one pound of Lentfigs sufficient for one Gallon of brandy

Ointments

Ointments and salves for cuts and muscular strains and stresses would have been vital to any amateur herbalist or physician connected with farming, where such injuries were commonplace. It was important to cure quickly as labourers were required back on the farm, especially at harvest time when men, women and children were all needed to bring in the crop. This was particularly true in the 1790s when more and more men were joining the militia and there was a consequent shortage of labour on the land. Augustin Kinchin recorded in his part of the ledger that one of his labourers had broken his hip joint. He rarely entered individual events of this kind, an indication that this injury must have been of some importance. Mary Bacon had a number of recipes for this group of incapacitating ailments. In her cure for stiff joints,

> Take four Ounces of Neats Foot Oil[26] one Ounce of Spirit of Sal Ammonia, and rub the Parts three or four Times a Day wearing some Flanell for stiff Joints of any kind

To make an Ointment

> Three pound of Lard will take one handfull of wormwood one of Stiningnettles one of mallards one of Elder Leves one of night Shade Cut it all small and boil it in the Lard some time and make it up for use

Oil of earthworms would now be considered an unlikely ingredient but it was commonly used to treat horses as well as humans. A recipe for it is given in *The Compleat Horseman or Perfect Farrier*, a very popular manual of the period. Mary had a similar

25 In mediaeval times dried figs were popular during the Lenten fast and became known as 'Lent figs'.
26 Pale yellow fatty oil made by boiling the feet (excluding hooves), skin, and shinbones of cattle and used chiefly for dressing and waterproofing leather and as a lubricant. *Enc. Brit.*

title included in her book list, *The English Horseman and Complete Farrier* and it is
possible that this was the same book.

> Take a sufficient quantity of worms, wash 'em, and leave 'em in clean Water six
> Hours, that they may cast forth their Filth; then put 'em in an Earthen Pot, with so
> much Oil Olive, as may rise the breadth of two Fingers above them, the Pot remain-
> ing half empty. Cover the Pot, and lute the Junctures with Clay mixt with Hair or
> Saddle Stuffings; then bury it in warm Horse Dung; and after it has stood there
> three Days and three Nights, take it out; and as soon as 'tis cold, uncover it, taking
> care to avoid the noisome Smell and strain out the Oil … [27]

Mary's recipe for 'How to make medison for any green wound' includes oil of earthworms as well as oil of swallows in the list of ingredients.

> Take a quarter of a pint of Sallat oyl & and two ounces of red Lid[28] one pennyworth
> of burgomy[29] pitch one pennyworth of beeswax one pennyworth of Camphire one
> pennyworth of Deaclum and one pennyworth of oyle of worms & one pennyworth
> of oyle of Swallows three pennyworth of oyle of Spike put the oyle of Swallows &
> the oyle of wormes both in one Glass put the red Lid & the Sallad oyle together
> & boile it till it is black then put in the burgundy pitch then the beeswax then the
> Camphire then the Deaclium then the oyle of Swallows & then the oyle of worms
> then the oyle of Spike[30] and let it boile a little while

The making of ointments appears to have been one of Mary Bacon's most important pharmaceutical skills as she copied a long list into her ledger. One, marked in
the margin as 'a very good one', was given to her by a George Taylor and could be
kept for seven years.

> Take the tops of Lavender Wormwood Southernwood Camimoil, Red sage walnut
> leaves the youngest you can get two handfulls of each some Hysop some Bay Leaves,
> tutsen Leaves, pound them all Together & put in as much very good Sallat oyle as
> will wet it well, then put into a pewter bason and Cover it very Close, & Let it stand
> three weeks or a month, then put it into a skillet and set on a gentle fire, and Let it
> boile half an hour, then Strayn it and Put it into Gallipots, and it will keep Good
> seven years you must make it in May

Mary Bacon used a very wide variety of plants in her ointment recipes, many
of which could be gathered near the farmhouse. Elder was commonly used and
red sage, plantain, celandine, hemlock, shepherd's purse, dock, and parsley were
frequently used in the recipes. Some ingredients are difficult to trace as 'affsmart',

27 de Sollysell, *Compleat Horseman* 264–5.
28 Lid: lead.
29 Burgundy pitch and other resin products are obtained from the silver fir.
30 Spike oil, or spike lavender oil, is distilled from an inferior grade of lavender having grayer leaves.
    Enc. Brit.

'tutson', 'sedwell' 'singreen', 'featherfew', either because of her spelling or because of local dialect names. Others are impossible to guess: what, for example, is 'house Green'? Butter and beeswax were commonly used and the resulting ointments were probably soothing and even curative. Gathering or in some cases, purchasing, all the ingredients must have been very time consuming especially when a number of plants were used, as in the recipes for green oil, or green ointment.

> Take of Lavender cotton, Featherfew, Camomile Parsley, Southernwood[31], Roman wormwood, Smallage[32], Marygold Leaves Rosemary tops Hyssop, green Sage, Single Mallows; Rue, Lavenderspike, St Johns wort of each these Herbs two large handfuls After you have shred, or cut them as small as you Can takeing none but the fine green Leaves and tender tops, five Large handfuls of red rosebuds, after you have Shaken out the Seeds from them and Cut them as small as you Can then take one Gallon of the best Sallad Oil one Gallon of the best French Brandy Stiring it well together, then put in all your Herbs, & Let them steep in it ten Days well stirring them when you first put them in and every Day till you Boile it Boile it over a clear soft fire till all the juice be out of the Herbs & it looks green, then Strain it into an Earthen Pan, take the Clear for your own use, the Bottom is good for All sort of Cattle, a spoonfull taken Night and Morning is very good for Asthma, or at any time for any Person to take when troubled with Shortness of breath it is good likewise for inward or outward Bruises for Strains, for inflamations, and for any Swellings whatsoever

To make Green Ointment

> One handfull of Pilewort[33] one handful of Sedwell[34] one of Ground Ivy one of Plantiny one of Singreen, one of St Johnswort a large Handfull of each after they are shred very small, and two Large handfuls of Adderstongue And one Large handfull of Elder flowers boil them in a Pound of Butter wherein is no Salt till the juice of the Herbs be out and it looks green then Strain it out & let it Stand till it is Cold then put it up for use. The Pilewort and Seedwell are in perfection before the other herbs are therefore I Boil them in the Butter first and then the other herbs when they are in their perfection and then the Elderflowers It is good to cure any Sting whatsoever, both in Man and Beast, and take away any inflamation especially if a Fever should fix in any part of the Body & for burns and green wounds

To make Elder Ointment

> Take of Celandine, Centuary Cleavers[35] Clownswound – Wort Marshmallows,

---

31 A shrubby wormwood.
32 Smallage: a wild celery.
33 Pile wort: lesser celandine.
34 Sedwell, seedwell: speedwell?
35 Cleavers: a native annual with a small white flower, found in fields and hedgerows. There is a long tradition for its use in the treatment of tumours and ulcers.

Southernwood Adderstoungue Plantine Bugle Singreen, Dwarf Elder, Alheal, Woundwort, Tutsar or Park Leaves Woodsorrell, mild Arefenart Bayberries, Beech leaves One Blade Alcost or Balsam herb is called Costmary[36], take of these herbs two Large handfulls of each, after they are Cut Small & four pound of fresh butter without Salt, put the butter in a kettle over the fire & melt it first then put in your herbs & boile it one hour & half then Strain it of Let it Stand a little, then pour the Clear into a fresh pot and the squeezeing of your herbs & the other in a pot by it self if you Cannot get butter put a pound & half of Lard to your two pound of butter I Do

To stop any humour in the Leg

Take two ounces of white Coperrass one ounce of bold almanack two ounces of oak Bark a small piece of Allom, a Little Roach allom Put it into a Quart of Spring water in a Bottle and shake twice a Day

There are occasional names in the margin beside recipes and it may be assumed that these indicated gifts of favoured remedies to Mary Bacon. There is only one example of a remedy being purchased. It is 'an Excellent Recipe for a Bad Leg' and Mary has recorded that 'My Husband gave five shillings for it'. The amount appears excessive for what must have been a single sheet of paper and there is nothing unusual in the ingredients used. It is therefore possible that William Bacon gave his wife a book of cures, much more likely at the price of five shillings and that it included:

Take four ounces of the oil of olives two ounces of white Lead four ounces of Linseed oyle two ounce of Black Pitch four ounces of Deer suet four ounces of Beeswax four ounces of Lapis Calamineras[37] when prepared, melt it all with the oyle, and as soon as the mixture begins to Congeal Sprinkle in the Calamineras and Stir it well till the Coret [Cover?] is quite Cold

When Mary gave the recipe for making an ointment, she sometimes included instructions, such as 'Lay on your Plege upon the wound wash it well with Water; round the Plege spread your Plaister very thin Bind it tight with a flannel Roler If the wound is foule put in some Rossim pownded if the medson Cannot be made use Turner Cerate'.[38]

A further use of ointments was in the alleviation of burns, the ingredients of which were sometimes very simple, but cures could also consist of a very long list of plant material. The first recipe is marked as being 'mothers own medson 1781' and

36 Costmary: an aromatic herb. It was sometimes referred to as Alecost as it was used for flavouring ale.

37 *Lapis Calamineras*: a mixture of zinc oxide with a small amount of ferric oxide used in lotions, liniments, and ointments. *Enc. Brit.*

38 Cerate: an unctuous preparation for external use consisting of wax or resin or spermaceti mixed with oil, lard, and medicinal ingredients. *Enc. Brit.*

'can be made any time of the year.' It consisted of a quarter of a pound of red lead, two ounces of Beeswax, two ounces of Rosin, half a pound of lard, and threepenny worth of oil which was ground up and mixed together. The second recipe involved considerable plant gathering and is assigned to William Bacon junr.

> Hogs lard 2 ounces beeswax Do Dear Suet, 3 pennyworth of Sweet oyle, Singreen, Groundivy, torchwort[39], Sedwell Leaves, Shipsdung, plantony Leaves Adderstongue, fox Gloves, Leaves, inner peel of elder, inner peel of Elm, & elder tops, Chickweed of each one handfull, if you Cannot get Dear Suet you must have mutten kidney Suet it is a very good recipe for anything

For irritations

In an age when people were riddled with body lice, skin irritation was a common complaint. Mary Bacon had only a few recipes for this affliction and perhaps being rubbed with the cream 'warm by the fire' was the most efficacious cure. There are hints throughout these recipes that Mary took care of her patients, both human and animal, an aid in itself to recovery.

> Take a Quarter of a pound of White Eliber[40] Bruised & Boiled in three Pints of Coletrough water till it is but a quart then add half a ounce of Saltpetre & a quarter of a Pint of Vinegar

For the itch

> Take half a pint of Cream and make it very Sower & then get 2 ounces of White Eleber powder & simmer it together And let the party be rubed with it warm by the fire

For the itch

> White Halebar root powdered two ounces Crued Sal ammoniac two Drams flower of Brimstone 3 ounce Lard one Pound – use the Quantity of a nutmeg twise a day

To Cure the Itch

> two ounces of Lard one handful of Dock roots one ounce of Sulfer of Ives Simmer up the lard of Docks together then Strain it of & Stir the Sulpher in anoint all over & wear your shirt a month

Aches and pains

A cold, damp, draughty, unheated farmhouse together with freezing winters and hard, heavy manual labour could cause all manner of aches and pains. It is not surprising that Mary Bacon included a number of cures for rheumatism in her book, but although they might have helped to alleviate the pain, they were unlikely to

39 Torchwort: the common mullein. The stalks used to be dipped in suet and used for torches.
40 Eliber, Halebar are difficult to trace, but may be the same: Hellebore is a possibility.

cure it. It is difficult to understand how mountain wine and whale oil could give much relief or that the uncooked yolk of an egg could alleviate the pain. As with Culpeper, almost anything was expected to cure, some ingredients may have genuinely provided relief whereas others constituted an act of faith.

For the Rhuematism
Take the Oyle of Spike four pennyworth Spirits of wine and Camphire two pennyworth Sweet oyl one pennyworth rub the part aflicted

For the Rheumatism
Two table Spoonfulls of Sweet oyle the same Quantity of Water twenty five Drops of hartshorn Sweeten these with the best sugar this Quantity to be taken at twise and repeated morning & evening shake the bottle when you use it

For the Rhuematism
Take a spoonful of train oyl[41] and a Gill of mountain wine to be take twise a Day A excellent Remidy for the Rheumatism or any thing that is Connected Take the yolk of a new Laid egg and beat it well then mix in four ounces Of Cold Water put it in a vial and Shake it well together and it is fit for use

For the Rhuematism
Take five ounces of Stone brimstone Reduce it to a fine powder divide it, into 14 equal parts and take one part every morning fasting in spring water this receipt came from a worthy Clergyman he said it had to his certain experience, a very good effect, upon great numbers of people that made use of it an approved cure for the Rhuematism

A further recipe for rheumatism offers much more to the sufferer and appears to be an alleviation of old age.

Take four handfulls of red sage beat it in a Stone morter like sauce put it into a quart of red wine, and let it stand three or four days close stopped, shaking it twice or thrice, then let it stand and settle, and the next day in the morning take of the sage wine three spoonfulls, and of running Water one spoonful fasting after it one hour or better, use this from michalmas to the end of march: it will cure any aches or humours in the joints, dry rheums, keep of all diseases to the fourth degree it helps the Dead palsy, and convulsions in the sinews, sharpens the memory and from the beginning of taking, it will keep the body mild, strengthen nature, till the fulness of your day be finished, nothing will be changed in your strength, except the change of the hair, it will keep your teeth sound that were not corrupted before, it will keep you from the gout, the dropsy, or any swellings of the joints or body

Gout
It is to be hoped that Mary Bacon's cure for gout did not take as long as the one used

41 Whale blubber oil.

by the Duke of Portland referred to in the *Diary of Thomas Turner*. This included the tops and leaves of gentian root, ground pine and centaury and could take up to two years to take effect. It also required some mental discipline as the sufferer had to fast for one and a half hours after taking the medicine. The ingredients were made into a powder, a dram of which was taken 'every morning, fasting, in a cup of wine and water, broth, tea or any other vehicle you like best; keep fasting an hour and half after it; continue this for three months without interruption.'[42] Mary Bacon only had one recipe for the gout; she used mugwort, or common wormwood, and boiled it in salad oil.

Coughs, colds and sore throats

Colds were common in the eighteenth century and could easily become feverish. Mary Bacon's cures for colds, and the sore throats and coughs that went with them, were soothing as she used sugar, honey, liquorice, oil, rum and lemon as her main ingredients. She apparently thought 'For a Cold Greatly recommended' was an almost infallible remedy.

> Take a Large teacup full of linseed, two pennyworth of Stick Liquorice, and a quarter of a pound of Sun raisins, Put these into two Quarts of soft water, and let it Simmer over a slow fire till it is reduced to one, then add to it a quarter of a pound of brown Sugar Candy pounded, a table spoonfull of old Rum And a table spoonfull of the best white wine vinegar or lemmon Juice, Note the Rum and vinegar are best to be added only to the quantity you are going immediately to take for if it is put into the whole, it is apt in a Little time to grow flat, Drink half a pint at going to bed, and take a little when the Cough is troublesome, this Receipt generally Cures the worst of Colds in two or three Days and if taken in time may be said to be almost an infalliable remedy it is a most Sovereign and balsamic Cordial for the Lungs without the opening qualities which endanger fresh Colds in going out. It has been known to Cure Colds that have been almost settled in Consumptions in Less than three weeks

There are a number of cures in the ledger for a cough. A favourite, which Mary described as 'an excellent Recipe', was as follows:

> Take of Linseed, Stick liquorice, & brown Sugar Candy each two ounces to which add half a Pound of Sun Rasins Split Boile it all together in three quarts of Spring water till it comes two Quarts Take of the above Liquor, every night at going to bed half a pint & in it a Large Spoonfull of Rum use the Same every morning fasting the Liquorice must be Sliced very thin

Another included horehound, a plant also used in the cure of asthma, recommended by a correspondent to the *Gentleman's Magazine*, who in his turn, got it from

42 *Diary of Thomas Turner*, 106–7.

Culpeper. 'From the experience I have had of it on myself, in my own family, and others, I am sure that I am justified in thus recommending it, as well as Culpeper, from whom I originally had it, and whom others will do well to consult.'[43]

> Hyssop Horehound french barly of each one one handful aniseed Garlick Elicompane[44] roots of each one Pennyworth Lickerish roots two pennyworth Lent figs one pennyworth Boil these in three pints of spring water boil it two one pint then boile it up to a Syrup with a pound of Coarse Sugar take a Spoonful night & morning

Tuberculosis was very common in the eighteenth century; Mary Bacon's alleviation 'For a consumtive cough or Tissicke' was relatively simple compared with many of her recipes. She took the same weight of Aniseed water and of honey, simmered them together and then added some white bread until it was quite thick. The sufferer was then instructed to take the quantity of a nutmeg every day both night and morning.

'To cure a Quinse or sore throat' is an interesting example of the use of amber, which was occasionally used as an ingredient in food and drink. The French sometimes added it to drinking chocolate. As amber was smoked in this recipe, it is unlikely that Mary confused it with 'ambergrease', a product of the sperm whale, as that would have melted and possibly caught fire. Her instructions were to 'Take two penny worth of Mastick[45] & two pennyworth of amber Strow it over a Chafindish of Coals put a tunnel over it. Suck the smoak through the tunnel Drink a Little pennyroyal tea then go to bed'. In another cure for a sore throat she used figs, lemons and sugar concocting a soothing gargle.

> Take half a pound of figs, put them into a quart of spring water and Let them simmer over a slow fire till better than one half is wasted in the mean time take a Large Lemon cut it into Slices and between every Slice put some brown Sugar Candy & Let it stand before the fire to roast then strain the figs & squeese them through a coarse cloth put the Juice of the Lemmon into it & Let the person gargle his throat with it warm

If the sore throat was very bad 40 drops of oil of roses mixed with tincture of myrrh was to be put into the ears, which were then stopped up with some fine wool. Friar's Balsam, known to medical practitioners for 600 years, was also used by Mary Bacon and has an unusual and very slow cooking method.

43 Porter, *Medical History*, 150.
44 Elicompane: elecampane, or Horse-heal is a perennial composite plant.
45 Mastick: an evergreen shrub.

Take of Benjamin three ounces heapatick[46] Alloes half a ounce, Balsam of tolu[47] two ounces, two pints of Double rectified Spirits of Wine put it all into a Large Glass bottle and put it in sand in an Iron pot & simmer it over a very Gentle fire 24 hours, not hardly Blood warm the next Day it will be fit for use

Mary's descendants through her daughter Sarah may have found some of these recipes for coughs too complicated and the ingredients difficult to find, as none of them is included in a little undated book among the Eggar family papers. Instead, there is a very easy to make, simple, and soothing remedy which is potentially very effective. It consists of 2 ounces of liquorice, a quarter of a pound of blackcurrant jelly, a wine glass of olive oil and another of rum. It makes a quart and a half and a wine glassful is given night and morning.[48]

Piles and constipation

Piles was another complaint treated by the author of the Eggar family notebook in a simple way, using beeswax, salad oil, and honey.[49] Mary Bacon's recipes were more complicated. She advocated the use of 'hogs lard' mixed with cork burnt to ashes and added in the margin, 'I have cured myself and many people'. May seemed to have been a preferred month for making medicines and is mentioned several times in the recipes as in the case of another cure for piles.

Take the inner green Bark of Elder fresh gathered three Handfulls, of the green tops two Handfulls, bruise them well in a morter together, & boile the juice in half a pint of good Cream, till it turns to an oile use it according to discretion this is recommen'd as an excellent oil for the piles and to be made in the May month

As demonstrated, anything went in eighteenth-century medicine, professional or lay, and John Wesley advocated warm treacle, leeks fried in butter, tobacco leaf and flower of brimstone for this painful complaint. Constipation was another condition cured by Mary Bacon. 'Where persons are subject to be Costive take of the Lenitive Electurary[50] an ounce and Half flowers of sulphur three drams Syrup of violets Enough to make an Electuary it is to be taken at discretion'.

Face – eyes and teeth

Mary Bacon had her own poultice for eyes, although she did not indicate the particular condition she used it for, only that it was intended for a child.

---

46 Heapatick: it is very unlikely that this refers to liver; it is probably the plant *hepatica*.
47 Balsam of tolu: taken from a South American tree by making cuts in the bark and a known cure for colds.
48 Eggar family documents. HRO 28M82/F2.
49 *ibid.*
50 Lenitive electuary: kept in most apothacaries' shops, containing senna and coriander.

Take a Little singreen & bruise it & a few Rose Leaves & boile it in water & put a few Crums of white bread in it & put it in a bag and put it on when going to bed and take it off in the morning before the Child is up you must let it be Cold before you put it on Do not make it thick as you do any other poultice but Let the moist come through the bag a little.

Her cure for toothache is similar to the charm quoted above as a cure for the ague. It too, needed to be carried on the person of the sufferer. Both remedies may have derived from the same source and were almost certainly used locally. Because of the mistakes in the spelling, it is unlikely that this recipe was copied but was collected by Mary Bacon from an oral source.

> Jesus Christ Came to peter as he stood at the Gate of Jerusalem & said peter why Standest thou hear, Lord said he my tooth ake therefore said he I will heal thee therefore he said he or she that shall Cause this Words to be Carried with them shall never be troubled with the tooth ake any more Jesus Christ help me and Deliver me from pain

Epilepsy and trembling

Epilepsy has been known in earliest medical writings; fortunately by the late eighteenth century it was no longer associated with witches with the dire consequences which that entailed. Mary Bacon's recipe for a cure is long, needing an amount of preparation and giving careful directions.

> Take the powder of Misletoe one ounce Assafoetida[51] a Dram syrup of Pioneys a sufficient quantity to make an Electuary take the quantity of a Nutmeg first in the Morning, at five in the Afternoon and last at Night and Drink after each Dose a Draught of the following Infusion

> Take of the whole Plant Leaves Beries Small twigs & Large ones grosly bruised in a Mortar, four ounces of the flowers of Red pioneys one handfull, boiling Water a full Quart, infuse in a pot Close Stopt by the fire-side for two Hours then Strain it out & Sweeten it with 2 ounces of the Syrup of Pioneys

> Misletoe generally keeps the Body open, but when it does not do it, it is necessary once in three or four Days to give some very Gentle Lenitive Medicine: but never any Strong Purge which always Does Mischief in Epileptical Cases

William Bacon had his own cure for 'the falling sickness' or epilepsy, in which he used leaves and berries of mistletoe growing on oak. The resulting concoction had to be taken 'three days before and after the full of the moon'. If a child had a fit, 'Take sixpenny worth of Arsafadato[52] root a Dozen of eggshells two Spoonfulls of

---

51 *Assafoetida: asafoetida*, a resinous gum with the smell of garlic
52 Arsafadato: almost certainly refers to asafoetida.

1 The parchment-over-
boards binding of Mary
Bacon's ledger.
(HRO 28M82/F1)

2 ABOVE The will of James Kinchin, Mary's father. (HRO 1748B/63/1)

3 RIGHT A coloured map of Woodmancott area showing Augustus Kinchin's house—above the centre and slightly to the left, marked by three 'A's.
(*By kind permission of the Warden and Scholars of Winchester College*)

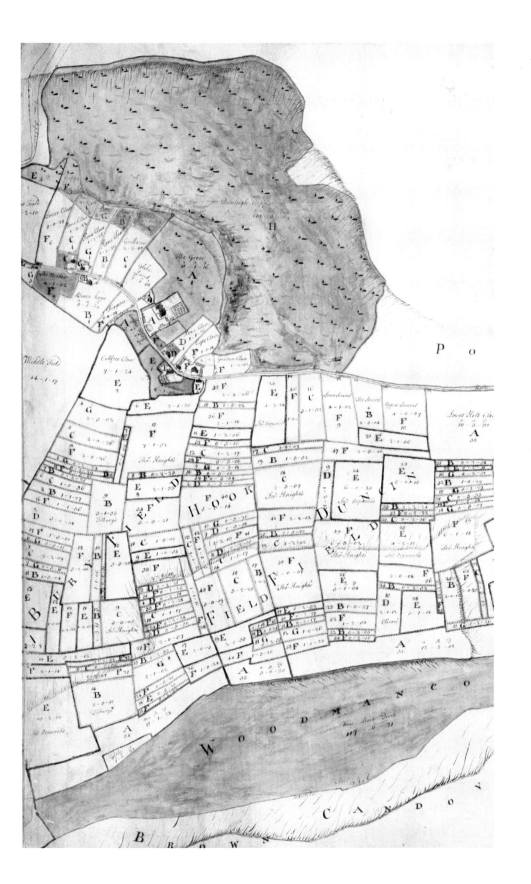

Aylesfield Farm

4 ABOVE General view from the
  front (Author)
5 RIGHT The front path
6 BELOW Seen from the East.
    (By kind permission of Tim and
        Gillian Bannerman)

7 *The Golden Pot* The public house on the junction of the main road to Alton near
Aylesfield farm. (Author)

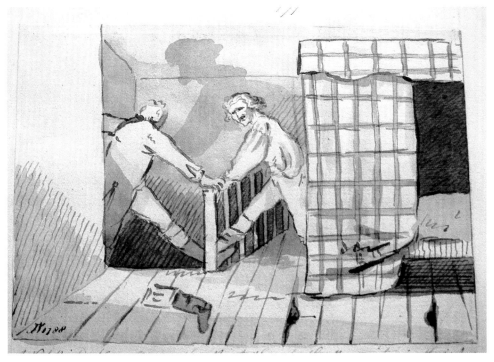

8 *J. N. (John Nixon) and Richard N pulling off their boots through the banisters in
their room at Shanklin, Isle of Wight. (J N 1788).* Note late eighteenth-century
styles of bed hanging. (By permission of the Trustees of Carisbrooke Castle Museum)

9 Alton Workhouse (1793) In 1798 William Bacon was examining its accounts in his office as overseer of the poor for the parish. (Author)

10 The nave and gallery of Dummer Church, where Mary worshipped as a child before they moved to Aylesfield. (Author)

West Indian Islands.				
Islands	Len	Brd	Chief towns	Belonging to
Jamaica	140	60	Kingston	Great Britain
Barbadoes	21	14	Bridgetown	Ditto
St. Christopher	20	7	Basse-terre	Ditto
Antigua	20	20	St. John's	Ditto
Nevis and Montserrat	each of these is 18 circumfer		Charles-town Plymouth	Ditto Ditto
Barbuda	20	12		Ditto
Anguilla	30	10		Ditto
Dominica	28	13		Ditto
S. Vincent	24	18	Kingston	Ditto
Granada	30	15	St. George's	Ditto
Tobago	32	9		Ditto
Cuba	700	70	Havannah	Spain
Hispaniola	450	150	St. Domingo	Ditto and France
Portorico	100	40	Porto Rico	Spain
Trinidad	90	60		Ditto
Margarita	40	24		Ditto
Martinico	60	30	St. Peter's	France
Guadaloupe	45	38	Basse-terre	Ditto
St. Lucia	23	12		Ditto
St. Bartholom'w Deseada, and Maragalante	all of them inconsider-able			Ditto Ditto Ditto
St. Eustatia	29	circ	The Bay	Dutch
Curaçao	30	10		
St. Thomas	15	circ		Denmark
St. Croix	30	10	Basse-end	Ditto
American Islands				Great Britain
Newfoundland	350	200	Placentia	Great Britain
Cape Briton	100	80	Louisburgh	Ditto
St. Johns	60	30	Charlotte town	Ditto

11 Mary's tabulation of facts about the West Indies in her ledger in the style of an almanac, copied from an unknown source.

(HRO 28M82/F1)

December
21:
1807 this is account of my Goods at M'^s Baldings
three feather Beds & three bolsters
one bedstead with red and white check furniture
one bedstead with patch furniture
one Clock a Larg looking Glass in a brown frame
a Weather Glass, a looking Glass with two drawers
in a mahogony frame, a book stand
two small Looking Glasses, a dressing Glass
a Japan tea board & two waiters, a tea chest and
a Mahogony tea board, one beaurow
Six Stained Chairs, Six ashe Chairs two arm Chairs
two Chairs with roded bottoms, one Chair with a list bottom
a Childs Chair a old Low Chair,
a Mahogony teatable, another teatable one Coffee mill
a Square Dineing table, one spice box
one pair of brass candle stick

12 Mary Bacon's inventory *see* Appendix Five.
   'December 21, 1807 This is account of my Goods at Mrs Baldings'

(HRO 28M82/F1)

Soot of the ovens mouth Steep it in half a pint of Brandy Dry the eggshells in the oven and powdered Steep it twenty four hour and give a Child half a Large spoonful every morning fasting'. Mary herself appears to have suffered from some kind of trembling as she indicated her own use in the following remedy.

> One ounce of Succotrine Aloes[53] two Pennyworth of Winter Bark A pint of Mountain Wine half a Pint of Double Distilled Annis seed Water put altogether in a bottel and take one Large Spoonful a going to bed for three nights runing it is a excellent remidy for tremblings and many other Complaints it is what I takes myself

Miscellaneous

Mary Bacon provided cures for most ailments or medical conditions in 'My Book of Receipts', although for some she recorded only one or two remedies. A few of the cures have names appended in the margin, including her own, indicating ones that she favoured. Lavender, valerian, carraway and peppermint water were mixed together and given for fainting; she had her own cure for rickets in children for which she advocated

> a Gallon of snails in the Maymonth and Bake them in an Earthen Pot with a Large quantity of Cammomile and Rub the Child with it Morning and Evening.

> Beeswax, rosin and lard were simmered together to relieve chilblains.

Rabies

It is surprising that in an age when rabies was fairly common and cures were advertised in local newspapers, a farmer's wife with the range of cures which Mary Bacon had, did not include a remedy for this fatal disease. Roy Porter, in his examination of the *Gentleman's Magazine*, found that great space was given over to the bites of mad dogs. He suggested that because of the horrifying nature of the symptoms and the certainty of death, correspondents wished to venture another hopeful cure.[54] Eliza Chute's diary of 1790, in the printed section at the back, has an article on Canine Madness in which there is a description of the symptoms. This is followed by,

> It is now universally admitted, that cutting out or cauterising the part bitten, as soon as possible, is the only certain cure to be depended on; and the speedy healing up of a bite by the same dog has proved fatal, while no injury has followed where the wound has been for some time kept open.

Hannah Glasse in *The Art of Cookery, made Plain and Easy*, advocated a very strenuous cure, which, considering the hydrophobic element of the disease, must have

---

53 *Aloe succotrina*: used in medicinal cures.
54 Porter, *Medical History*, 151.

been very difficult to follow:

> Let the Patient be blooded at the Arm nine or ten Ounces. Take of the Herb, called
> in Latin, Licken Cinereus Terrestris; in English, Ash-coloured Ground Liverwort;
> cleaned, dried, and powdered, half an Ounce. Of black Pepper powdered, two
> Drachms. Mix these well together, and divide the Powder into four Doses; one of
> which must be taken every Morning fasting, for four Mornings successively, in half
> a Pint of Cow's milk warm. After these four doses are taken, the Patient must go
> into the cold Bath, or a cold Spring, or River, every Morning fasting for a Month:
> He must be dipt all over, but not stay in (with his head above Water) longer than
> half a minute, if the Water be very cold. After this he must go in three times a Week
> for a Fortnight longer.'[55]

The least likely cure of all is the one advertised in the *Hampshire Chronicle* on 11
August 1794, 'a course of sea bathing at Brighton for people bitten by mad dogs.'
Even if Mary Bacon had no cure for rabies, together with small pox, measles
and malaria, she served her family and community well and whether or not they
were effective, provided a wide range of remedies incorporating a large number of
ingredients.

55 Glasse, *First catch your Hare*, 5.

Chapter Six

The kitchen

MARY BACON'S FATHER, James Kinchin, did not die a rich man. His will indicated that there would be very little left after his debts and funeral expenses had been paid, and that household property would have to be sold. His position as a grocer[1] was below that of his father, Augustin Kinchin, gent. and although the number of servants he and his wife employed is not recorded, theirs would have been a much smaller household. Despite the fact that his financial position was not very solid at the time of his death, he is likely to have employed at least one servant to help in the kitchen. His wife, Sarah, would not only have supervised the cooking, but would have done much of the work herself. Did she, like many women of her day, read books such as *The Good Housewife or Cookery Reformed*, advertised in the *Salisbury Journal*, which she might have seen when visiting her brother-in-law Augustin Kinchin?[2] His house had been advertised in that newspaper and it is likely that it was the one which he paid the newsman regularly for. It may have been in those early days in Dummer that the seeds of Mary's preoccupation with recipes were sown. A substantial part of her ledger is devoted to 'My Book of Receipts', each item carefully entered, headed in larger black writing, full of spelling errors and virtually no punctuation; at least a third of the recipes are for cooking.

Not only did Mary's enthusiasm for cooking grow from her early home environment, but the practice of the culinary arts *per se* was spreading down the social scale. Advertisements for cookery books and instruction books for the housewife, advertised in newspapers, indicate an interest in the culinary arts by increasingly literate middle-class women. During the eighteenth century over 300 books on food and cooking were published, many of which went into several editions. Had Mary read the *Hampshire Chronicle* on 3 January 1791 she would have seen an

---

1 An eighteenth-century 'grocer' dealt in a wide range of goods which could include textiles. It is not known exactly which retail commodities James Kinchin traded in.
2 *Salisbury Journal*, 1 August 1757.

advertisement for

Housekeeper's Instructor: or Universal Family Cook. Containing proper directions for dressing all kinds of Butcher's meat, Poultry, Game, Fish etc. Also the Method of preparing Soups, Hashes and Made-Dishes. With the whole Art of Confectionary, Pickling etc. Likewise the making and keeping in perfection British Wines; and proper Rules for brewing Malt-liquor etc. By William Augustus Henderson, who made the Culinary Art his study for forty Years.

The most popular of these books was *First Catch your Hare, The Art of Cookery made Plain and Easy* (1747) by Hannah Glasse, who also wrote *The Compleat Confectioner* (1742) and *The Servant's Directory* (1760). Seventeen were published between 1747 and 1803, emphasising both an increasing interest in cooking and a growing demand for books of this kind from women, many of whom came from the 'middling' ranks of society. Women from the aristocracy and gentry needed to know how to run their houses, but were not required to have an intimate knowledge of culinary method. Glasse made it clear that her work was not aimed at the upper classes. 'If I have not wrote in the high, polite Stile, I hope I shall be forgiven; for my Intention is to instruct the lower Sort, and therefore must treat them in their own Way.'[3] There was a growing reaction during the eighteenth century against complicated French recipes and Hannah Glasse's book reflects the simplicity which was now preferred. *The Art of Cookery made Plain and Easy* does not appear in Mary's list of books, but she drew on it heavily, copying from it, and found in it a perfect source for recipes. Food may have been simple, but it was certainly served in quantity, both in the households of the gentry and aristocracy, and also those of the middle classes. Thomas Turner was a shopkeeper, a man of quite ordinary means. An extract from his *Diary* for 1759 is a good illustration of the sort of meal those in his position were indulging in. It was for fourteen people. 'Thurs. 4 Jan …. About 7.30 I walked up to Tho. Fuller's, where I supped on 2 roasted rabbits, a cold giblet pie, some cold goose, a neck of veal roasted and tarts', and again on 16th January, he dined out and 'supped on some boiled chicken, cold turkey minced, a shoulder of mutton roasted, a cold chine, a cold ham, tarts'.[4]

Although some of Mary Bacon's recipes contain herbs, they rarely include vegetables, either as ingredients or as dishes on their own. The most common vegetables in the eighteenth century were roots such as carrots, turnips and parsnips, and also onions and cabbage. A. M. W. Stirling, editor of the diaries of Stephen Terry, a member of Mary's extended family through her Terry grandmother, wrote that:

In those days (late eighteenth and early nineteenth centuries) all vegetables were

3 Glasse, *First Catch your Hare*, xviii.
4 *Diary of Thomas Turner*, 171–2.

less plentiful and less widely used. In regard to potatoes, in Hampshire there was an impression that they could only be eaten with roast meat; and it is on record that when Mrs. Austen at Steventon regaled a parishioner with them at the Parsonage, and advised the woman to plant some in her own garden, she was met by the horrified rejoinder: 'No, no! They are all very well for you gentry, but they must be terribly *costly to rear!*'[5]

Some of the plants used in food cookery were added to tea to make it go further, as it was expensive. Because of its price, tea was usually drunk very weak, and often without milk, although sugar was added. Cheaper tea such as Bohea, produced by adding in sloe, liquorice, ash or elder leaves, or even used tealeaves, was sold for as little as 2*s*. 6*d*. as opposed to the 16*s*. to 18*s*. a pound which was charged for better brands.[6] There were inevitably caveats about drinking tea and, according to John Wesley, both tea and coffee were harmful to persons with weak nerves.[7]

It is clear from Mary's recipes that she preferred cooking cakes and puddings, even when it meant beating for an hour with 'your hand or a great wooden spoon'. Sugar was now cheap and plentiful and recipes for a variety of sweet and savoury rich puddings abounded. There are no recipes for fish in her book other than eels and fish sauce, and no mention of oysters which were very plentiful. They were transported inland in barrels, and were eaten in great numbers. Mary largely ignored meat recipes but would have roasted and boiled joints. As a busy farmer's wife she would have had little time to try out more elaborate sauces and dressings for meat, despite all the invitations in newspaper advertisements to buy books and magazines with culinary instructions. However, there is a record in the ledger accounts showing that she bought a 6lb leg of mutton. Did she follow the timing given by Hannah Glasse, who wrote in *The Art of Cooking made Plain and Easy*: 'A Leg of Mutton of six Pounds will take an Hour at a quick Fire; if frosty Weather an Hour and a Quarter; nine Pounds, an Hour and a Half; a Leg of twelve Pounds will take two Hours; if frosty, two Hours and a Half …'. There is no mention of beef in Mary Bacon's recipe book, but ox beef, cow beef or bull beef were all consumed and, as with all meat, the prudent housewife had to take good care that it was fresh. By 1801, however, with a nation bedevilled by the shortages of war, meat had become a luxury. The *Hampshire Chronicle* commented that 'Butcher's meat we are sorry to say, is getting up in price to a degree that must shortly prohibit the use of it at the tables of all but such as are possessed of fortunes, or very lucrative professions'.[8]

5   Stephen Terry of Dummer, *The Diaries of Dummer, Reminiscences of an Old Sportsman*, ed. A. M. W. Stirling (1934) 134–5.

6   I. Collins, *Jane Austen, the Parson's daughter* (1998) 215.

7   John Wesley, *Primitive Physic* (1759). Taken from edition of 1843, xii.

8   *H C*, 2 March 1801.

There are some interesting ingredients in Mary Bacon's recipes and her two meat recipes, both of which are for veal, include anchovies. These little fish were salty, as are the ones used today, and would have been kept in brine, possibly in small barrels. Among the Eggar family papers, dating from *c.*1825, there is a recipe for walnut catchup, in which anchovies are used.[9] Mary also added a sprinkling of Seville orange juice to her veal recipe and seems to have bought this fruit in quantity as she used Sevilles in orange wine.

Where was all this cooking done? The room to the left of the front door in Aylesfield farm was almost certainly the kitchen. The inventory which Mary Bacon wrote when she left the farm gives a full description of every piece of furniture and equipment which she possessed, including what she had in her kitchen. Jennifer Stead gives a good description of the fireplace in an eighteenth-century kitchen.

> By 1700 the usual form of grate was a large oblong basket on four legs, fastened to the chimney back with tie bars, ideal for roasting large joints of meat. The spits were rested on hooks on the two front legs and were usually turned mechanically by a clockwork spit jack, then later in the century, by a smoke jack sited inside the chimney and operated by the heat of the fire. The fire could be made smaller by winding adjustable sides of 'cheeks' inwards by a rack and pinion mechanism. Supports of the pans, called trivets, fastened to the cheek tops, could swing out over the fire.[10]

Mary Bacon's inventory, contains a long list of cooking utensils and includes the equipment used for the spit and the fireplace.[11] Some of the fireplace equipment listed was for the parlour and it is not always possible to establish in which room each item was placed. For example, a fire pan could have been used in either. Over the kitchen fire was 'a Cottrell a Crane & four hooks', a Cottrell being 'a trammel, crane or bar from which a pot or kettle is hung over the fire'.[12] The bar jutted out from a wall bracket, which was often decorated with wrought iron work. From this bar cooking pots were suspended on iron rings, which are also listed in the inventory. The Bacons had a crane with which to operate the spit, and a trivet, defined as an 'iron tripod or bracket for kettles etc. to stand on'.[13] In both the kitchen and the parlour fireplace was a pair of 'angers', a local dialect word for anjur-dogs or andirons, which were placed at the side of the hearth to support the logs and sometimes had hooks for the spit to run on.[14] Further details about the hearth furnishings are itemised and the inventory includes a kitchen fire-pan, tongs, gridiron or griddle,

9 Eggar family documents, HRO 28M82/F2.

10 J. Stead, *Food and Cooking in Eighteenth-century Britain* (1985) 7.

11 Mary Bacon's inventory: *see* Appendix Five.

12 *Oxford English Dictionary.*

13 *ibid.*

14 W. H. Long, *A Dictionary of the Isle of Wight Dialect* (1886).

two bellows and a fender.

In addition, a broiling tin and dripping pan were used to catch the juices from roasting meat. Dripping pans of the period were usually rectangular in shape and sometimes had a straining pan for the juices. The only saucepan listed was made of copper and therefore would have been lined with tin as copper, though a good conductor of heat, was thought to be poisonous. For boiling, there was an iron pot, an oval boiler and a little boiler. The iron pot, used for boiling joints of meat and puddings, was probably large, might have had three small feet, and would have hung over the fire on a hook. There is a distinction between a pot and a boiler: the latter had a lid.

Mary had a dozen skewers and one large skewer for meat, all of which were made of iron, and a bodkin for trussing or sewing a joint. The safe mentioned in the inventory would have been a meat safe, made of metal, kept in the larder where it was cooler. When the cooking temperature needed careful regulation, Mary had a chaffing-dish, which she would have used for making stews and sauces when a lower heat was required. These were small dishes of charcoal set on a metal stand and were placed on the floor of the hearth. They could be used to cook slowly, or to reheat. She also had a Dutch oven, commonly made of tin. The open side of the oven was put in front of the direct heat and the food, as it was cooking, could be viewed from an opening in the back.

Equipment used to prepare Mary's cakes and puddings is well documented in her inventory. Flour was kept in a flour box, generally made of wood, often pine. These boxes were usually quite large in order to accommodate the vast amount of flour used in the making of bread, cakes and puddings. A brass mortar and pestle was kept for grinding up the spices, which were contained in a spice box. Sometimes these boxes had little pockets and were lockable. Pepper, another spice (Mary seemed fond of Jamaica pepper), was kept in a pepper castor, which was a big shaker usually made of steel.

A cleaver for meat is listed, as well as a chopping knife with a steel to sharpen it, for all those many herbal ingredients which went into Mary's remedies for sick humans and animals. She had a pair of steel sugar nippers to cut bits from her cone of sugar, commonly known as a 'loaf', although she did use sugar in lump form as well. Lump sugar was not cut into little cubes as it is today, but consisted of small pieces broken off the loaf with a sugar hatchet, which Mary possessed. A basket for bread and a bread grater was also listed, no doubt useful in making puddings, and a toasting fork for toast.

On the outside western end of Aylesfield farm is the outline of a gable indicating that there was a further room or rooms extending from the kitchen on the ground floor. As there are no early plans of the house, the exact nature of this extension is very difficult to establish. In some farms a room of this kind was used both as a malt house and a laundry room, as well as containing an oven for baking. It is also possible that this was where the dairy was situated, although this small, but essential room where food had to be kept cool, generally faced north and the floor level was often lower than that in the rest of the house. For some reason, Mary did not record the contents of her dairy in her otherwise comprehensive inventory, but they were probably very similar to those listed in the inventory of Richard Clary, a yeoman of Writtle in Essex, appraised 1693/4. 'In the dairy: 1 little table, 1 form, 1 cheese press, 1 milk stand, 1 churn & staff, 6 shelves, 6 cheese moulds, 5 cheese breads, 3 milk pans, 2 trays, 1 hand dish, 1 frying pan, 2 sieves, 5 pots, 1 pan, 1 butter basket, and other implements.'[15] Farm labourers and servants ate cheese once, if not twice a day and with the amount consumed it was only prudent to make it on the farm.

Equipment for washing is also included in the inventory, but whether this was to be found in the kitchen or in a separate laundry room must be left to speculation. The two clothes horses listed would have been put in front of the kitchen fire with a drip box underneath, but the washtub may have been elsewhere. Four flat irons were kept on a stand ready to use when the washing was dry. The iron candlesticks on the list were for use in the kitchen together with snuffers to extinguish the candles. There are two puzzling items in the kitchen part of the inventory, but by considering them together, the problem may be solved. 'My Granary' could refer to some kind of container for bread or grain, or alternatively it could relate to 'graains', which were the remains of malt after brewing used to feed the pigs.[16] A third explanation is that it is a reference to a 'grainer', a tool used for taking the hair off skins. Also included in the inventory are 'clams' which commonly refer to the stacks in which bricks are built within a kiln. Alternatively, a local dialect definition gives a clam as a kind of vice or wooden pincers, used by shoemakers and saddlers to hold the leather between their knees when sewing.[17] Augustin Kinchin used the skins from his horses when they died. Did the Bacons have some similar use for skins from their animals and was this the context in which to put 'My Granary' and clams?

The Bacons brewed their own beer and the quantity indicates that this was both for their use and for their farm and house servants to consume on a daily basis. They lived in a hop-growing area of which the centre was Farnham, an important market

15 P. Edwards, *Farming: Sources for Local Historians* (1991) Table 1: Farm and Processing Equipment in the Inventory of Richard Clary, *Yeoman*, of Writtle (Essex), Appraised 14 February 1693/4.

16 Long, *A Dictionary of the Isle of Wight Dialect*.

17 *ibid*.

for hops and within reasonable distance of Alton. 1801, when the Bacons were still living at Aylesfield farm, was a particularly good year, as the *Hampshire Chronicle* reported[18]:

> We learn from Farnham that the shew of hops in that neighbourhood is more plentiful this year than has been remembered by the oldest person living; there not being the least appearance of insect, but health and plenty prevailing in every garden. The picking will commence generally on Tuesday and it is supposed that there will be eight thousand pickers required.

The beer was put to ferment in iron-bound barrels containing 30 gallons, 16 gallons, 10 gallons, 8 gallons, 6 gallons, and half a hogshead, all of which are listed in the inventory. A hogshead was 52½ gallons, which adds another 26¼ gallons, making a total of 96¼ gallons of beer. Further evidence that the Bacons brewed their own beer is shown by the inclusion in the inventory of 'a stand for the mash tub', a 'tun bowl hop strainer', a 'huckmuck with stick & plug', and a 'mash Stirrer'. The mash tub was made of wood and was similar to a half barrel with stays and hoops. The barley, malt and hops were mixed up in it and left to ferment. The huckmuck was a strainer used in the brewing of beer. After a period of very hard work, during which the mash was processed, the 'wort' drawn off and boiled with the hops, cooled and yeast added, the resulting brew was left to ferment for about seven days and then the process was complete. Finally the fermented liquid was strained and the 'mash' or the husk which remained was given to the pigs. The hops would then have been used for manure.

What did Mary Bacon produce in this well equipped kitchen? 'My Book of Receipts' contains a quantity of recipes, some of her own, some collected from friends, and many copied from Hannah Glasse, *First Catch your Hare, The Art of Cooking made Plain and Easy.* Eighteenth-century culinary measurements were not exactly equivalent to those of today. Jennifer Stead in *Food and Cooking in Eighteenth-Century Britain,* gives a useful list for readers wishing to try some of these recipes. Not all the measurements occur in Mary Bacon's recipe book. The size and weight of loaves is useful when considering bread shortages.[19]

Spoonful = approximately a modern standard tablespoon
Teaspoon = bigger than a modern teaspoon (heaped teaspoon)
a 'glass' = approximately 4 fl. oz.
Pint = 16 fl. oz   Stone = (for weighing meat) 8 lb
Peck of flour = 2 gallons or 14 lb
Eggs were about the modern size 4 (small)

---

18 *H C* 31 August 1801.
19 See Chapter Two.

Peck loaf = 17 lb 6 oz
Half peck loaf = 8 lb 11 oz
Quatern loaf = 4 lb 5 oz
Penny white loaf = approximately 6 oz
Penny brown loaf = approximately three times heavier – about 1 lb

Chickens were smaller in general and would have taken less time to cook. A large hen's egg in eighteenth-century terms was probably equivalent to a small one today.[20]

THE RECIPES

Meat dishes

The Bacons farmed pigs and it seems that, whatever the breed of the pig, the local method of preserving it was very good. Charles Vancouver reported that, '… the excellent mode of curing hog-meat practised by the house-keepers, have contributed in a far greater degree to establish that superiority ascribed to Hampshire bacon, than any inherent excellence in its native breed of hogs.'[21] It may be assumed that Mary Bacon's recipe was a local one.

To pickel Hams

Take a pail of water five pounds of common salt three pounds of brown sugar and three quarters of a pound of Salt petre mix it together and, put in your hams let them lay a month or six weeks turning them every day then Let them be dryed for one month this pickel afterwards will be very fine for chines without any addition of salt this quantity will take two hams

In the next two recipes anchovies are used. Mary used anchovies in several recipes, but there is no means of knowing whether she prepared them herself for preserving, or whether this was a commodity she was able to buy. If she bought fresh sprats, although this is unlikely, given the distance from Alton to the sea, and then preserved them as anchovies, she may have used a similar method to Hannah Glasse:

To a Peck of Sprats, two Pounds of common Salt, a quarter of a Pound of Bay-salt, four Pounds of Salt-petre, two Ounces of Salprunella, twopenny-worth of Cochineal, pound all in a Mortar, put them in a Stone-pot, a Row of Sprats, and a Layer of your Compound, and so on to the Top alternately. Press them hard down, and cover them close, and let them stand six Months, and they will be fit for Use. Observe that your Sprats be very fresh, and don't wash nor wipe them, but just take

20 Stead, *Food and Cooking*, 27–28.
21 Vancouver, Charles, *General View*, 378.

them as they come out of the Water.[22]

Butter was the most common fat used in cooking and, as Mary made it and sold it herself, it was always available.[23] The method of mixing flour and butter to make a ball, a *beurre manie*, is usually connected with French recipes but was probably taken by Mary from the pages of Hannah Glasse.

To fry veal cutlets

Cut a neck of veal into steaks, and fry them in butter, and having made a strong broth of the Scrag-end, boiled with two anchovies, some nutmeg, some lemon peel, and parsley, shred very small and browned with a Little burnt butter, put the Cutlets and a glass of White wine into this Liquor Toss them up together, thicken with a bit of butter rolled in flour, and dish all together Squeeze a Seville orange over, and strew as much salt on as shall give a relish[24]

To fry mutton Cutlets

Take a handful of grated bread, a little thyme & parsley & lemon peel cut very small, with some nutmeg, peper, & salt take a loin of mutton cut it into steaks and let them be well beaten take the yolks of two eggs and rub the steaks all over, Strew on the grated bread with these ingredients mixed together, for the sauce, take gravy with a spoonful or two of Claret and a Little anchovy

Although Mary covered a wide range of foods in her recipe book, there is one grave omission in the meat section. There are no recipes for poultry and it is difficult to believe that chickens, and on special occasions geese, were not produced at the Bacons' table. If they did eat a goose, it was probably stuffed with quite a sweet, rich mixture which may have contained apples, plums, or even potatoes.

Fish dishes

To Collor elts

Take a good Eal and Cut it Down the Belly & take the back bone out and cut off the head make a sesoning with Parsely & time & Lemmon peel a Little nutmeg peper & salt boile it a hour then put for Pickle the Liquor it was boiled in And a Quarter of a pint of Vinegar and a handfull of Salt put the Eel in to the Liquor Cold

To collar is a culinary term, little used today, which indicates that the meat or fish is to be tied up into a roll. Hannah Glasse made the method very clear, although she used slightly different ingredients from Mary Bacon.

Take your Eel and cut it open, take out the Bones, and cut off the head and Tail, and

---

22 Glasse, *First Catch your Hare*, 155.

23 The farming accounts record that on 23 June 1792 Mary Bacon sold three pounds of butter at 2s. 1½d., (or at 8½d. per lb.).

24 I have cooked this recipe, using two tinned anchovies and stock cube; it is delicious.

lay the Eel flat on the Dresser, and thread some Sage as fine as possible, and mix it with black Pepper beat grated Nutmeg and Salt, and lay it all over the Eel, and role it up hard in little Cloths, and tye both Ends tight; then set over the Fire some Water, with Pepper and Salt, five or six Cloves, three or four Blades of Mace, a Bay-leaf or two, boil it Bones, Head, and Tail well together; then take out your Heads and Tails, and put in your Eels, and let them boil till they are tender; then take them out and boil the Liquor longer, till you think there is enough to cover them. Take it off, and when cold, pour it over the Eels, and cover it close; don't take off the Cloths till you use them.[25]

On the whole, Mary Bacon was a simple cook but her fish sauce is quite complicated to make and not in keeping with new ideas of simplicity in cooking. It is the only sauce recipe in her book and uses anchovies, an increasingly common ingredient.

Fish in gravy sauce

Take one quart of Port wine /2 a pint of vinegar /2 pound anchovies unwashed with the Pickel a quarter of an ounce of mace a quarter of an ounce of Cloves 3 or four peices of Ginger a stick of horseradish half a table spoonful of whole pepper a quarter of a pint of walnut pickel a quarter of a pint of mushroom pickel a little lemon Peel winter savory and thyme two or three Onions and some shalots stew it all over the fire for an hour then strain it through a seive and bottle it when Cold

Horseradish, shallots, and walnuts were also used in a recipe for fish sauce found in the Eggar family documents.

Vegetable dishes

There are a few entries in the ledger which are not in Mary Bacon's hand; the following recipe for cucumbers is one of them. It is possible that a member of the family or a friend contributed it, but there is no reason to believe that Mary would not have cooked the dish herself. The recipe is almost identical to the one in *First Catch your Hare, The Art of Cookery, made Plain and Easy* with the exception that port wine is used instead of claret, and mushroom liquor in place of mushroom pickle. Hannah Glasse herself took it from *The Compleat Housewife*, by Eliza Smith, and Mary's original source was probably Glasse.[26] Many of the recipes in *First Catch your Hare* were taken from other books.

To Stew Cucumbers

Pare twelve Cucumbers and Slice them as thick as a crown-piece put them to drain, and then lay them in a coarse cloth till they are dry, fleur them, and fry them brown

25 Glasse, *First Catch your Hare*, 116.
26 *ibid.* 56.

in butter, put out the fat, then put to them some gravy, a Little port Wine, some peper Cloves and mace, let them Stew a little: then roll a bit a butter in flour, and toss them up Season with salt: you may add a little mushroom liquor[27]

Puddings

One of the most essential pieces of equipment in an eighteenth-century kitchen was a pudding cloth, as boiling was the most common method of cooking this category of food. Cloths were usually made of white cotton or muslin folded to make them double. A useful description of how to deal with a pudding cloth is given by Jennifer Stead, who includes a recipe which can be used to practice on.

> Pudding using 2 oz. plain flour, ¼ tsp salt, 3 eggs, 8 fl. oz milk or single cream. For this size of pudding make an 18 inch square pudding cloth of white cotton or doubled muslin. Boil a large pan of water and put an old plate in the bottom. Drop the pudding cloth in briefly, lift it up with a wooden spoon and let it drape over the spoon handle. Place across a pan to drip. Have ready a piece of string. Sift the flour and salt into a bowl. In another bowl beat the eggs well. Add the flour and salt and milk and beat it to make a thin batter. Squeeze out the pudding cloth, lay it on the table and sprinkle well with flour. Gently shake off the excess. To support the cloth while filling it, lay it in a pan of boiling water, which must cover the pudding at all times. Cover the pan, leaving a small gap, and boil for 30 minutes. Lift the pudding out and dip briefly into cold water then loosen the cloth. Place in a colander, untie the string and peel back the cloth. Place a heated dish over the pudding, reverse the colander, and gently peel away the rest of the cloth. Serve at once with meat, or as a dessert with hot wine sauce. [28]

The hot wine sauce is very simple to make. 8 fluid ounces (225ml) of wine is mixed with 2 ounces (50g) of butter and 1¼ ounces caster sugar. Mary Bacon wrote out a number of recipes using a pudding cloth of which the following is an example: 'Take a pint of new milk mix with it six eggs well beaten, two spoonfuls of flour half a nutmeg grated, a little salt and sugar put this mixture into a Cloth or bag, put it into boiling water and half a hour will boil it serve it up with melted butter'

The Bacon family must have enjoyed eating custard pudding as virtually the same recipe is given three times. In the first two Mary used six eggs, cream, flour, nutmeg and sugar. The third is more complicated and is almost identical to one given by Hannah Glasse.[29]

27 This recipe is in a different hand. Note the spelling of flour – fleur – and the use of the colon, neither of which are habitually used by Mary Bacon.
28 Stead, *Food and Cooking*, 29. Taken from *The Experienced English Housekeeper*, Elizabeth Raffald, 1782, 8th edition.
29 Glasse, *First Catch your Hare*, 108.

108

Mary Bacon's World

To boile a Custard Pudding

Take a pint of Cream, out of which take two or three Spoonfulls, and mix with a Spoonful of fine flour, Set the rest to Boil, When it is boiled, take it of, and Stir in the Cold Cream, & flour very well, when it is Cold beat up five yolks & two whites of eggs Stir in a Little Salt and some nutmeg & two or three Spoonfuls of Sack[30] Sweeten to your palate, butter a wooden bowl, & pour it in, tie a Cloth over it & boile it half an hour, when it is enough, untie the Cloth, turn the pudding out into your Dish & pour melted butter over it.'

Hannah Glasse cautioned care in the melting of butter advising, 'let your Sauce-pan be well tinn'd, take a Spoonful of cold Water, a little Dust of Flour, and your Butter cut to Pieces.' The cook was to be sure to keep shaking the pan 'one one way for fear it should oil; when it is all melted, let it boil, and it will be smooth and fine. A silver Pan is best, if you have one.'[31] Rice, too, was used in puddings and was flavoured with nutmeg, sugar, and finished with melted butter poured over it. In one of Mary Bacon's versions Hannah Glasse was the obvious inspiration. The following recipe is almost identical to her 'Cheap Plain Rice Pudding' except that Mary added a little wine to her sauce.[32]

To make a rice pudding

Take what rice you think proper, tie it Loose in a Cloth, and boile it an hour, then take it up and untie it, grate a good Deal of nutmeg in, Stir in a good piece of butter, and Sweeten to your palate, tie it up close boil it an hour more, then take it up and turn it into your Dish melt butter with a little Sugar and a little white wine for sauce or melted butter

Another recipe taken directly from Hannah Glasse was for a baked bread pudding,

Take the Crumb of a penny Loaf,[33] as much of flower the yolks of four eggs the whites only of two a tea Spoonfull of ginger half a pound of raisins stoned half a pound of Currants Clean washed and picked a little salt and sugar to your palate mix first the Bread and flower then the eggs and as much milk as will make it Like a good batter then the fruit butter the Dish pour it in and bake it

There is mention of an orchard at Aylesfield farm but Mary Bacon did not include any recipes containing apples and pears in her ledger.

Cakes

Mary Bacon's cake recipes emphasise the time and hard labour needed in this sec-

---

30 Sack was a dry, amber coloured wine which was exported from the Canaries and Spain.

31 Glasse, *First Catch your Hare*, 5.

32 *ibid.* III.

33 A penny loaf was about five ounces but it is difficult to assess with accuracy as the price of bread fluctuated in the 1790s.

tion of cookery; instructions for making a pound cake include beating the ingredients for an hour. A labour of love to make, the recipe has William Bacon's name beside it in the margin, indicating that it was a favourite of his. It was taken from Hannah Glasse's book.

> Take a Pound of Butter, beat it in an earthen pan with your hand one way, till it is Like a fine thick Cream, then have ready twelve eggs, but half the whites, beat them well and beat them up with the butter, a pound of flour beat in it, a pound of Sugar, & a few Carraways, Beat it all well together for an hour with your hand or a great wooden Spoon butter a pan and put it in, and then Bake it an hour in a quick Oven, for Change you may put in a pound of Currants Clean washed and picked.

A very similar recipe, also from Hannah Glasse, is to make 'Little fine Cakes'.

> One pound of butter beaten to Cream a pound & a quarter of flower a pound of fine sugar beat fine a pound of currants clean washed and pickled Six eggs two wites left out beat them fine mix the flower Sugar and eggs by degrees into the batter beat it well with both hands either make it into little Cakes or bake it in one

The quantities used in a 'pretty cake' and the 'icing for a great cake' which follows indicate that this was baked for a special occasion, or at least for a gathering of a number of people.

To make a pretty cake

Take five pounds of flower well Dried one pound of Sugar, half a ounce of mace as much nutmeg, beat your Spice very fine mix the Sugar and Spice in the flower take twenty two eggs Leave out Six Whites beat them, put a pint of Ale yeast[34] and the eggs in the flower, take two pounds and a half of fresh butter a pint and a half of Cream Set the Cream and butter over the fire till the butter is melted Let it stand till it is blood warm before you put it into the flower Set it an hour by the fire to rise then put in Seven pounds of Currants which must be plumped in half a pint of brandy and three quarters of a pound of Candied peel it must be an hour and a Quarter in the oven you must put two pound of Chopped Rasins in the Flower and a Quarter of a pint of Sack or a little brandy when you put the Currants in bake it in a hoop

To ice a great Cake

Take the Whites of twenty four eggs and a pound of Double-refined Sugar beat and Sifted fine mix both together in Deep earthen pan and with a wisk whisk it well for two or three hours together till it looks white and thick then with a thin broad board or bunch of feathers Spread it all over the top and sides of the Cake set it at a proper distance before a good Clear fire and keep turning it continually for fear of its Changing Coulor, but a cool oven is best and an hour will harden it, you may perfume the icing with what perfume you please.

---

34 Ale yeast: the froth taken from the top of the ale while it is fermenting.

Not all Mary Bacon's cake recipes are as complicated as in the making of a very large cake and would merit baking today with very few adaptations.

To make Ginger Bread

Take half a pound of brown sugar a pound & half of Treacle, two eggs beaten One Ounce of Ginger beaten & sifted of Mace, Cloves & Nutmeg all together half an ounce beaten very fine, Coriander seeds or Carraway seeds, of each half an Ounce two Pounds of butter melted, mix all these together with as much flower as will knead it into a pretty stiff paste, then roll it out & cut it into what form you please Bake it in a quick Oven on tin plates a Little time will Bake it

To make Cheesecakes

Take two quarts of milk and turn it with rennet Break the Curd and run it Dry then rub it till its to pieces put six eggs & half a nutmeg & some Lemon peel and Sweeten it to your taste put in half a pint of Cream three Spoonfulls of Wine and a bit of Butter on top of each

To make Buns

Take two pounds of fine flower a pint of Ale yeast put a Little sack in the yeast and three eggs beaten knead all these together with a little warm milk, a Little nutmeg & a little salt and Lay it before the fire till it rises very light then knead in a pound of fresh butter a pound of caraway Comfits and bake them in a quick oven in what shape you please on flowered paper

A Rice cake (*written in a different hand*)

6 oz Ground Rice 6 oz fine flour ½ lb lump sugar 9 eggs take half the whites the peel of one Lemon mix it well together & beat it one hour. Bake it in a quick oven 2/4 of an hour

Mary Bacon, being a farmer's wife, was in charge of her own poultry and would have had little trouble in making sure that all the eggs she used in baking were fresh. If in any doubt, she might have followed the advice given by Hannah Glasse. 'Eggs hold the great End to your Tongue, if it feels warm, be sure it's new; if cold, it is bad, and so in Proportion to the heat and cold, so is the Goodness of the Egg. This way you never can be deceived.' And if the hens were laying well, and Mary wished to keep the eggs, Glasse's advice was to 'pitch them all with the small End downwards in fine Wood-Ashes, and they will keep some Months.'[35] Unfortunately, as with all these recipes, it is impossible to know the exact temperature of the oven.

35 Glasse, *First Catch your Hare*, 161.

DRINKS

Mary Bacon's uncle, Augustin Kinchin, ordered his wine on a regular basis as can be seen from his accounts;[36] it probably came from France. As there is almost no mention of purchases of alcohol in Mary's accounts, it is not possible to assess either the quantity or the quality of the wines they bought. Sack, white wine, port wine, claret, and brandy are all mentioned in the recipes, but how much of these the Bacons actually drank as opposed to their own homemade wines is impossible to determine. There are no recipes for spirits in 'My Book of Receipts' but there is a pewter still in the inventory. Towards the end of the century, because of the war with France, French wines were expensive and the government was encouraging production of wine and brandy at home. Alternatively, stills were sometimes needed in the making of ingredients for herbal remedies and Mary may have used hers in this way. Wine was made in quantity and with great variation at Aylesfield farm. A large amount could have been made from the following recipes, with instructions for ten gallons at a time; the Bacon family must have drunk it on a very regular basis. Wine would not have been given to servants, who drank either ale or cider. Most wines had to be left for at least a year or more to ferment and there is no indication of how often each recipe was made. Although instructions for the making of a number of different wines are included in Hannah Glasse's *First Catch your Hare, The Art of Cookery made Plain and Easy*, none of them equate sufficiently with those from Mary's recipe book to believe that she either adapted or copied them. The closest equivalent is in the instructions for the making of raison wine in which Glasse describes graphically the moment when the liquid must be stopped, 'let it stand till it has done hissing, or making the least Noise; then stop it close …'. Her recipe finishes with a final refinement, 'when you use it, rack it off into a Decanter' but a decanter was not one of the many items in Mary Bacon's inventory.[37] She had several recipes for raison wine and like other contemporary wine makers used Malaga raisins.

To make Rasins wine

Half a Hundreds of Rasins to ten Gallons of Water Let them be in the Water three or more Weeks and Stir them well Every day then strain them off & press them Let the Liquor stand till it is settled then put it in the Vessel

To make Raisin Wine

Take fifty pounds of malaga Raisons Chop them when Picked Clean from the stalks and put them into a tub Pour on them eight Gallons of Boiling hot Water wine measure and Stir well it together, Let it be Stired twise Every day and When it Rises to a great head Like Barm Let it be prest off put in a Cask and a month after

36 See Chapter One
37 Glasse, *First Catch your Hare*, 147.

put into it one bottle of brandy
[margin: Mary Bacon a good way]

Mrs. Bacon's currant wine

Gather your Currants when Dry then squeese them, and to a quart of Juice put two quarts of Cold Water, and three pound and half of Sixpenny Sugar, Let it Stand four Days and Stir it once a day and skim it then put it into your Barrel and not Stop it Down till it done hyssing.

Other recipes also add brandy, white wine, sack, or rum.

Mary made mead, as did Parson Woodforde, who wrote on 20 October 1794 that he was busy for the most part of the afternoon making mead wine. He used 14 lb of honey to which he added four gallons of water and boiled the liquid for more than an hour with ginger and two handfuls of dried elderflower. This was then cooled in a tub and, when it was almost cold, he put in a large gravy spoonful of fresh yeast, keeping it warm in the kitchen over night.[38] Mary did not put elder flowers in her mead, but she instructed that it should be worked like elder wine. There is a very simple recipe for mead in the Eggar family documents which consists of 5 lb of honey to one gallon of water. The liquid is boiled, skimmed, cooled, put into a cask, stopped down after a week and then left to stand for a year. Mead was also said to have medicinal uses and is included in a poem entitled 'Recipe for Asthma' in the *Gentleman's Magazine*, in 1751.[39]

> Now as to liquor, why, indeed
> What I advise, I send you, mead.
> Glasses of this t'extinguish drought,
> Take three with water, three without.

Mary Bacon had her own recipe and as she kept bees, it would have been an inexpensive drink to make.

Take your combs and break them as small as you can into a Strainer then Let them Stand till they are run quite dry, then wash your Combs as Clean as you can and Strain them drye then make your Mead rise an egg about the width of a half Crown Cold put it into a brass kittle or furnace and boil it about a hour keep it Skimd all the while then Let it stand four days and put it into your vessel you may put three pound & half to a Gallon, I always runs any honny & put in spice as I Likes & the above is as I orders my Combs You must work it as you do elder wine

Among the Eggar family papers, probably dating from around 1825, is a recipe for orange wine. It is tempting to imagine that Mary's daughter Sarah, who married James Eggar, inherited some of her mother's recipes, but there are sufficient differ-

38 Woodforde, *The Diary of a Country Parson*, 471.
39 R. Porter, *Medical History*, 145.

ences to discount the possibility in this case. Mary made a far greater quantity than that specified in the Eggar recipe; she used whites of eggs and 2 lb of lump sugar to one gallon, rather than to three. She also specified that Seville oranges were to be used, the same variety of orange recommended in her recipe for veal cutlets. It was a long and laborious process and this wine was not ready to drink for eighteen months.

To make Orange Wine

Take ten Gallons of Water, 20 pounds of Lump Sugar, & the Whites of Six eggs well beaten Stir them well together & as it heats take off the Scum as Long as any will rise Let it boile threequarters of an Hour, Take Eighty Sevill Oranges, pare them thin put the peels in a tub pour the Liquor hot upon them, cover them Close Down, & Let it Stand till near Cold, Squeese the Oranges free from seeds then put four Quarts of Juice into the above Liquor then put ten spoonfulls of new Ale yeast into it Let it Stand till the yeast begins to fall then take it off Take out the Peels & barrel the wine adding two Quarts brandy to every ten Gallons Let it Stand twelve or eighteen months as the Sweetness goes off before it is bottled & will keep many years, if the above is intended to be Drank in 3 six or nine months 24 pound of Sugar 70 Oranges & 3[?]quarts of Juice is sufficient but no Less brandy

Shrub, a drink which originated in the West Country, was often referred to in eighteenth- and early nineteenth-century documents and recipe books. As a soft drink it was frequently flavoured with berry fruits and taken as a cordial. It was also made with alcohol, the method used by Mary Bacon.

To make shrub

Pare six lemons or more according to their goodness very thin pull of the white then Slise the lemons into a China bowl, with the juice of two oranges and all the peel of the lemons pour one quart of Brandy one quart of rum over them let them stand close covered two days then put a pound & a quarter of good lump sugar into a pint of water set it over the fire till it boils, then skim it pour one quart of Brandy one of quart of rum over them let then stand close covered two days then put a pound & a quarter of good lump sugar into a pint of water set it over the fire till it boils, them skim it and when Cold put it to the fruit and Spirits with a quart of lisbon wine, then strain it through a jelly bag and bottle it

Clearly, Mary's recipe did not get passed down to her descendents as the ingredients for making shrub found in the Eggar family papers are different and contain less citrus fruit. Instead, white currants were used and were strained through a jelly bag with rum rather than brandy.[40]

Two further wines made by Mary Bacon were parsnip wine and ginger wine. It

40 Eggar family papers. HRO 28M82/F2.

must be assumed that the recipe for the former was given to her as it is written in a different hand.

To make parsnip wine

Wash them clean pare them & cut them in thin slices, boil four gallons of Parsnips to ten of water & three pounds of sugar to every gallon of liquor When they are perfectly soft drain the liquor from them, when nearly cold put in a little new yeast let it stand ten days in an open vessel stir it frequently then put it into your cask & when it has done fomenting bung it down close

To make Ginger Wine

Take 10 gallons of water and 24 pounds of Lump Sugar, Boil it & take off the scum then add 10 oz of the best Ginger bruised with the rinds of 8 lemons and 2 China oranges, Boil these ingredients ½ an hour, When nearly cold put the whole into a 12 Gallon cask together with the Lemon and Orange juice, Then add 4 lbs of the best sun Raisins bruised & six table spoonful of yeast. Stir the whole trice a day for 10 days Then add 1 gallon of Brandy, or 2 Quarts of Port Wine

Mary Bacon did not make primrose or cowslip wine. Primroses still grow round Woodmancott and cowslips would have flourished on the downs where Augustin Kinchin pastured his sheep. The Bacons were principally arable farmers in Cliddesden and there may not have been a sufficient quantity of flowers on their land, but Aylesfield farm is situated in an area of downland where they should be found in abundance. Another wine which Mary may have made, but did not include a recipe for, was local 'hedgepick' wine. Seemingly it was formerly held in good repute among village women because of its astringent qualities. A correspondence, in *Hampshire Notes and Queries* in 1889, discussed the exact wild fruit described by the word 'hedgepick'.[41] The first writer was of the opinion that it meant sloes, but a second disputed this. He wrote that he did not think that the majority of Hampshire folk considered 'hedgepick' identical with the sloe. Unfortunately, he did not identify the exact species, although he commented that it was smaller than the sloe. Although Mary did not make wine from it, it is likely that many of her neighbours did.

VINEGARS AND PICKLES

Raw green sauces and mashed herbs and vinegar were replaced by pickles, ketchups, and later in the eighteenth century, bottled sauces. These were imitated and by the end of the century produced commercially.[42] Although Mary was still making vinegar, she was modern in her use of ketchups and pickles which were usually stored

41 *Hampshire Notes and Queries*, 1889, Vol. IV, 14.
42 Stead, *Food and Cooking*, 19, 23.

in stone jars or bottles and were covered first with a bladder to seal them and then with leather to give overall protection. John Wesley warned against eating pickles and smoked or salted food as he considered them unwholesome. As for strong liquors – they were slow poison![43] Gooseberry vinegar appears to have been a favourite of the Bacons as two recipes are included in 'My Book of Receipts'.

> Boile four gallons of Water one hour scum it well, Let it stand till quiet Cold, then take one Gallon of ripe Goosberries, bruise them well and put to them three Gallons of the Water Stir it together, and let it stand 24 Hours, then Strain it through a Canvas bag, Put to every Gallon of this Liquor, one pound of powder Sugar, let it stand 24 hours Longer, or till the Sugar is Quite dissolved, Strain it though flannel Barrel it and Let it Stand in the Sun

Another way to make Goosbery vinegar

> Take Goosberys when Quite ripe and bruise them then to every Gallon of bruised Goosberys put three Gallons of Cold Water and Stir it well together and let it stand in the tub four & twenty hours then strain it through a Sive and put to the Liquor one pound of powder sugar to every Gallon of Liquor then Let it stand 24 hours Longer and Skim it well and put it in the Barrell, Let It stand a week before you stop it Down

A further recipe for vinegar was taken from Hannah Glasse. Mrs Glasse's tubs are iron-hooped 'and well painted, fixed in a Place where the Sun has full power'. The vinegar is to be kept in 'little Stone-Bottles'.[44] Mary Bacon used a painted cask which could be placed in the sun for a few months before bottling the vinegar.

> An excellent way to make vinegar by which a Person has acquired a good fortune Put a pound of Coarse Sugar to every Gallon of Water, Let it boile & keep Scumming it as Long as any Scum will arise it must afterwards be put in tubs to cool like Beer & when it is Cold as Beer to Work, toast a large piece of Bread and rub it all over with yeast put this into a Stout Iron bound painted cask, which must be Set in the Sun and in Such a place, as it Can remain in if made in March it will be fit for use in July it will best to draw it off into bottles & keep it for use this is the Strongest of Vinegar and will Do very well for pickling, with a third part of Cold spring Water to it and be full sour enough, it will likewise when used alone keep most sort of Pickles without boiling nor indeed do I ever use it hot unless with my green pickles.

Making ketchup was a quicker process and was made of both black and Jamaica pepper, an anchovy, and some cloves and mace.

Pickling fruit and vegetables was an essential part of housekeeping, utilising the produce of the garden and the surrounding hedgerows. The Bacons must have had

43 Wesley, *Primitive Medicine*, xix.
44 Glasse, *First Catch your Hare*, 157.

a walnut tree in their garden or orchard, otherwise the nuts could not have been collected at exactly the right time. The following recipe was probably for the young, white walnuts, as they would still have been a little soft, whereas black walnuts were those that were fully ripe.

To Pickle walnuts

Gather your Walnuts when a pin will go through them Let them Lay nine Days in salty Water Changeing them Every other Day then take them out and Laid in a Cloth and Wiped Dry then put them in your Pickell pot and add to them Vinegar two or three quarts as wanted then boil your Vinegar up with 2 ounces of Ginger one ounce of Long peper[45] Some black peper a few Cloves Eight or ten Bays Leaves one pint of mustard seed boil your vinegar three times every other Day the Last time make your Vinegar Boil and put your wallnuts in and Let them boil up two or three Minuets

The following recipe for pickling barberries, which Mary copied from Hannah Glasse, has an interesting error which Jennifer Stead pointed out in her introductory essay to *First Catch your Hare, The Art of Cookery made Plain and Easy*. She reminded the reader that fennel has a flavour very unlikely to blend with barberries and discovered that Hannah Glasse took this recipe from either Eliza Smith's *The Compleat Housewife*, (1728)[46] and or from *The Whole Duty of a Woman* (1737)[47] both of which had in their instructions: 'boil a piece of Flannel in the Liquor and put over them, and cover the Glass with Leather'. It is to be hoped that Mary realised Hannah Glasse's error and did not taint her barberries with fennel. The glasses she used to store the pickled fruit would have been quite small probably containing about four fluid ounces.

To pickle Barberies[48]

Take of White wine Vinegar and Water of each an equal Quantity to every Quart of this Liquor put in half a pound of Six penny Sugar then pick the worst of your Barberries and put into this Liquor and the Best into glasses, then boil your pickle with the worst of your barberries, and Skim it very Clean, Boil it till it looks of a fine Colour then Let it stand to be Cold before you Strain then Strain it through a Cloth wringing it to get all the colour you can from the barberries. Let it stand to cool and Settle then pour it Clear into the glasses in a little of the pickle, boil a little fennel when Cold put a little bit at the top of the pot or glass and cover it close with a bladder and Lether to every half pound of sugar put a quarter of a pound of white salt'

45 Long pepper: a pepper of South Asian origin with a slightly sweet flavour.
46 E-S, *The Compleat Housewife: or Accomplished gentlewoman's companion* (1728).
47 A Lady, *The whole duty of a woman: or a guide to the female sex* (1695).
48 A yellow flowered shrub with oblong red berries.

Mushrooms, being seasonal, needed to be preserved. They were sometimes grown in hot beds but would have been easy enough to gather from the countryside near Aylesfield farm in the autumn. Parson Woodforde noted on 13 November 1798 that he bought a 'Quart Bottle of nice Mushrooms of Mrs Nutter paid 0.0.6.' and 'to a Quart Bottle of Mushroom Catchup 0. 3.' Mary Bacon's recipe 'to pickle mushrooms brown' was relatively easy to make. The mushrooms were to be rubbed with a piece of new flannel and put in a saucepan with pepper, salt, cloves, and mace. Then 'stew them till the juice is quite dried away then put a small quantity of vinegar and let that dry away also, then cover them with a quarter of a pint of vinegar and let the vinegar boil about five minutes'.

PRESERVES

There is only one recipe for jam in 'My Book of Receipts', copied almost exactly from Hannah Glasse who, in addition, used a pint of currant jelly when making raspberry jam. To make this 'giam' it was necessary to bruise a quart of the fruit and then boil for five or six minutes, then 'pour into your gallipots[49], paper as you Do the Currant Jelly and keep it for use, they will keep for two or three years'. There is no mention of sugar.

MISCELLANEOUS

William Bacon kept pigs and while his wife pickled the hams, she also made brawn from the heads which were slit down the middle and then boiled for three hours. The bones were then removed and the meat and fat mixed together with pepper, salt, and ginger. This resulting mixture was then rolled up in a cloth and boiled for an hour after which pickle, white wine vinegar, strong beer, salt, whole black pepper, cloves and mace, were added to the liquid. The making of calves' foot jelly was more complicated.

> Take four Calves feet Cleaned washed & boned put a Gallon of Water, With four Ounces of hartshorn, boile it to a Jelly then run it through a bag & Clarify it with Six eggs whites, add to it a quart of White Wine & the Juice of five Lemons & Six pipins Sliced Sweeten it with the best Sugar to your taste, So boile it up & run it through your bag into Glasses

Other useful hints are included in 'My Book of Receipts' one of which is how to burn butter: 'put two ounces of butter over slow fire in a stew pan or sauce pan with out water when the butter is melted dust on a Little flour and keep it stiring till it grows thick and brown'. Sorrel was used to 'To take ironmolds[50] out of Linnen'.

---

49 A small earthen glazed pot.
50 Iron mould: rust stain

The leaves were bruised in a mortar then squeezed through a cloth and bottled for future use. When treating a stain, the juice was boiled in a silver or tin saucepan and the affected linen dipped in and then finished in cold water.

THE ART OF BAKING

Quantities of bread had to be made each day, for both the family and the servants and farm labourers, whose staple lunch diet was usually bread and cheese. Therefore yeast, and in this case, the frothy ale-yeast (barm), was an important commodity. Hannah Glasse left instructions as to how yeast was to be preserved.

> When you have Yeast in Plenty, take a Quantity of it, stir and work it well with a Whisk until it becomes liquid and thin, then get a large wooden Platter, Cooler or Tub, clean and dry, and with a soft Brush lay a thin Layer of the Yeast on the Tub, and turn the Mouth downwards that no Dust may fall upon it, but so that the air may get under to dry it.

Several coats are put on in this way until it is two or three inches thick. When the yeast is needed, 'cut a piece off, and lay it in warm Water, stir it together, and it will be fit for Use'. Yeast is also used in brewing and Glasse gives instructions as to how to proceed,

> If it is for Brewing, take a large handful of Birch tied together, and dip it into the Yeast and hang it up to dry, take great Care no Dust comes to it, and so you may do as many as you please, and when your Beer is fit to set to work, throw in one of these, and it will make it work as well as if you had fresh Yeast; you must whip it about in the Wort and then let it lie, when the Fat works well take out the Broome and dry it again it will do for the next Brewing.[51]

The method in 'My Book of Reciepts' is simpler and as it is written in a different hand must have been given by a friend or a member of the family. The yeast was put into a pot with cold water and skimmed off every day for a fortnight, and subsequently once a week. It would then keep ready for baking for nine months. A recipe given to Mary Bacon includes instructions as to how to make barm. The ingredients are two spoonfuls of ale yeast, two ounces of treacle and a pound of potatoes boiled and beaten to pieces with a spoon; this would make a sufficient quantity to bake a bushel of flour. Another more curious recipe uses alum: 'a pound of Barm to a bushell of flower a bit of allom as big as a small nut when barm is Searecy[52] put a spoonfull of Coarse sugar and an egg to take off bitterness bake a piece of bread and put it in the barm all night with a handfull of bran'.

One of the omissions from Mary Bacon's recipe book is bread; she may have

51 Glasse, *First Catch your Hare*, 151.

52 scarce

thought it unnecessary to include something so basic. As a farmer's wife, who sent her own wheat to the mill for grinding, she had no shortage of ingredients. In this she was fortunate in a way in which her poorer neighbours were not, especially during the war with France. During the 1790s there were six bad harvests which, compounded with the war and the necessity of feeding the growing militia, had a devastating effect on the price of bread and by 1800 the price was impossibly high. Drastic measures were needed and various ingredients were added to make the flour go further. A letter to the *Hampshire Chronicle*, 24 March 1800, gave a method of making bread flour go further with the addition of rice, itemising not only the method used, but also the cost.

To the Editor of the HAMPSHIRE CHRONICLE

SIR,

By inserting the following experiment made by a gentleman in this neighbourhood, in your useful and entertaining paper, you will much oblige A CONSTANT READER

Clearly to ascertain the cheapest method for the poor to make their own bread, I took a bushel of wheat, which weighed 59 lb from which 8 lb of bran was taken. It was mixed with rice, after the following method and proportion, viz To 28 lb of the flour were put yeast one pint, warm water one quart, and covered, and set before a fire two hours to rise. I put 4 lb of rice into six quarts of cold water, it boiled about an hour, until it became the consistency fit for pudding, it was poured into a kiever, and stirred about for half an hour. When it was about as warm as new milk, I put it to the dough, and kneaded them together. I made the oven thoroughly warm, and put the loaves in, which weighed 7 lb each, and baked them two hours. The dough weighed 50 lb when put into the oven; about 16 or 17 hours after baking, it was again weighed, and the produce of good bread was full 45 lb With the addition of only yeast and water, this was produced from 32 lb of materials. – I have made the following estimate of the expense, supposing the whole produce of the bushel of wheat to have been made into bread:

	s.	d.
Price of one bushel of wheat (at 29 *l.* per load)[53]		
which produced 5 *l.* of flour	14	6
Bran 8 lb. supposed to pay for the grinding etc.	0	0
Yeast, salt, and fuel about	1	0
Rice, 7 lb at 5*d.* per pound	2	11
	17	11

1 lb to be allowed for waste, &c.
28 lb baked,
22 lb remaining.

53 The letter '*l*' was used frequently in the eighteenth century to denote £.

51 lb. of flour with 7 lb. of rice thus mixed, will produce 80 lb of bread for 1*s*. 11*d*. not 2 ¼. per pound.

Some of the mathematical calculations are difficult to follow, but it is an example of philanthropy and of care for the poor among the gentry and aristocracy which is evidenced in the *Hampshire Chronicle* during this difficult period.

COSTS

Mary could afford a wide variety of ingredients in her recipes. Whereas she would have had flour, eggs, milk, butter and cream from the farm and could have grown or gathered herbs, she had to buy spices, sugar, dried fruits, oranges and spirits. She used ginger in food recipes and in cures both for humans and animals, costing approximately 1*s*. a pound. Spices, and especially ginger, were commonly used in eighteenth-century cooking. Mariana Starke, a London playwright, listed all the things she would need during her tour to the Mediterranean and included 'tea, loaf-sugar, fish-sauce, essence of anchovies, curry-powder, ketchup, soy, mustard, cayenne-pepper, ginger, nutmegs, oatmeal, portable-soup, sago';[54] many of these ingredients are included in Mary Bacon's recipes.

Although the Bacons had a pewter still, if they wished to purchase spirits, brandy would cost between 12*s*. 9*d*. and 11*s*. 3*d*. and rum about 8*s*. 6*d*. a bottle. These prices are approximate and fluctuated according to the market. There is evidence from the inventory that the Bacons drank tea and coffee, but had no chocolate pot, either because it was too fashionable a drink for them, or because Mary gave hers to her daughter Mary on her marriage. The prices of tea varied greatly, starting with the Common Bohea tea at the cheaper end of the market and rising to the best of the green teas, one of which was labelled Superfine Gunpowder and Cowslip. Coffee cost anything between 3*s*. to 7*s*. Mary Bacon worked hard in her kitchen, brewing beer and wines, endlessly beating cake batters, baking puddings, and preserving. Although she undoubtedly had help, she would have done much of the work herself. She must have spend a great deal of time in her kitchen, cooking and making her remedies, and it is surprising that she had the leisure to read and copy other material out into her ledger.

54 B. Dolan, *Ladies of the Grand Tour* (2001) 129.

Chapter Seven

Almanacs, chapbooks
and other printed material

ALTHOUGH MARY BACON'S spelling, punctuation, and grammar sometimes left much to be desired, she must have had a reasonable amount of
education in order to copy out the amount of material she did; she also seems
to have had the will and initiative to do so. The printed matter referred to in her
ledger, from both her list of books and other material, indicates a woman with wide
interests. Agriculture, farriery, history, geography, astronomy, astrology, human and
veterinary medicine, cookery, education manuals and, above all, religion, were all
the subjects of books she perused at her reading desk. The principal omission is
imaginative literature – there are no volumes of novels or poetry in her collection of
books. Either she read none, or she borrowed from a circulating library.

Mary was not alone in her desire to read and learn. Eighteenth-century middle-
class women had increasing recourse to a wide range of reading material, and used
it. The number of printed works rose throughout the period; scientific subjects were
very popular, although interest in mathematics and astrology waned as the century
progressed. During the 1750s circulating libraries began to open in England although
it was not until a decade later that they were to become available in Hampshire.
There were none in Basingstoke or Alton and if Mary had wanted to borrow books,
she would have had to go to Winchester. Reading material was increasingly available in bookshops in the provinces, as evidenced by the large number of advertisements for books and magazines in the *Hampshire Chronicle* from the time of its
inception in 1772. The county was served well by booksellers and there was at least
one open in Alton during the period in which Mary lived at Aylesfield farm. Apart
from books, other printed works could be purchased in these shops – almanacs,
broadsheets, weeklies, magazines, and newspapers.

Almanacs and chapbooks, from which Mary copied material, notably in the form

of long religious stories, had been common throughout the sixteenth and seventeenth centuries. They were very popular, were often sold uncut and unstitched,
and were readily available from peddlers at the door, or at the fairs which the
Bacons frequented. They became more instructive during the eighteenth century
and included accounts of classical mythology, natural theology, politics, history and
astronomy. These little publications were often illustrated with woodcuts, either
showing simple patterns, or with naive depictions. Mary would probably have
possessed or seen one of the yearly almanacs which were easily obtainable. Together
with diaries, memorandums and pocket books, they were advertised in local newspapers usually towards the end of the year, often in the form of cheap pamphlets
or broadsheets and containing a variety of information useful to farmers such as
times and seasons, and dates of festivals and fairs. Pocket books advertised in the
Hampshire Chronicle included the *Ladies Own Memorandum Book*, and *Walker's
Ladies Annual Journal or Complete Pocket book for the Year 1790*. Much more suitable
for a farmer's wife, and probably sold by her local bookseller, Mary would undoubtedly have preferred '*The Hampshire Pocket Book or Complete Ledger for Cash and Time
for 1790* [containing] besides great additions to the useful contents, new tables of
grain shewing the difference at one view, between the load and quarters at eight and
nine gallons to the bushel'.[1] She was unlikely to have purchased *The Ladies' Diary*,
founded in 1704, as it was aimed at the newly leisured middle-class woman and it is
difficult to imagine her having that amount of time on her hands. Not for her were
the beautifully leather-bound diaries of Eliza Chute of the Vyne in Hampshire,
which include in their end pages such useful bits of information as 'Twenty four
short rules for learning at Whist' or 'an artificial memory for those who play at
whist' (1792).[2] But it is possible that she might have found a 'short sketch of the laws,
as they now stand, relating to Hares, Partridges, Pheasants and other Game' useful.

Another source of reading material was newspapers. Augustin Kinchin's accounts
show that he paid the newsman regularly, indicating that he had a newspaper delivered at home. There is no evidence that the Bacons did the same, but Mary was probably used to seeing newspapers from an early age. During the eighteenth century
there was a substantial increase in the number of provincial newspapers. With the
improvement of main roads, transport was easier and the London news could be
relayed to the provinces with speed. The *Hampshire Chronicle*, one of the many new
newspapers, started production in 1772 and had a circulation of approximately 1,500,
with a very wide distribution area. It is thought that for every one copy of a such a
paper approximately fifteen people would have read it, whether at the coffee house,

1   *H C*, 21 December 1789.
2   Chute diaries, HRO 23M93/70/1/1-9

in the circulating library, delivered at home, or borrowed from a friend. It was an informative paper for farmers and the Bacons would have benefited from reading the monthly agricultural reports and the price lists of grains and pulses, both for the London market as well as for Basingstoke and Winchester. Mary copied out a similar agricultural report into her ledger, but not from the *Hampshire Chronicle* (see Chapter Three). No doubt the family enjoyed reading the local gossip in the Winchester column too and, like so many people in the eighteenth century, would have avidly read the accounts of trials at the assizes and the last words of prisoners about to be hanged. There were reports of local race meetings including a short report of a Mr Bacon losing a race on his pony at Winchester. Was this one of their sons?[3] The wedding of their daughter Sarah was also reported, which indicates that this was the newspaper they read.

It is interesting to see how some of the content of the paper is reflected, through advertisements and articles, in the more miscellaneous and less religious of Mary's writings or copyings. Her tastes related quite closely to those of the paper's readers; for example, she showed an interest in the West Indies, a subject which featured periodically in the newspaper, mainly in relation to military campaigns. On 17 September 1796 it was reported that the French fleet had arrived in the neighbourhood of Jamaica, and that there were fears that the colony might be threatened. The author goes on to add: 'In taking the view, however, … these apprehensions will naturally vanish, and in their stead the most pleasing prospect of permanent tranquillity presents itself, as results no less from our present approved military commanders, than the acknowledged abilities of our nautical chiefs'. There follows news of Martinique, Grenada, and St. Vincent, and a list of regiments remaining in the West Indies. This interest continued until at least the end of the century and in 1801 the Hampshire Chronicle reported of the island of Trinidad, 'our new possession is now an object of such general interest that curiosity greedily lays hold of everything that relates to it.'

There then follows an article on Trinidad and in the following year San Domingo is featured.[4] Mary was also interested in the West Indies and, using the kind of tabulated format found in almanacs, copied out the following tables into her ledger. There are so many likely sources for this table that it has not been possible to trace the one that she actually copied.

3   *H C*, 26 March 1796.
4   *ibid.* 24 May 1802.

West Indian Islands

Islands	len[5]	Brd[6]	chief towns	Belonging to
Jamaica	140	60	Kingston	Great Britain
Barbadoes	[021]	14	Bridgetown	'
St. Christopher	20	7	Basse-terre	'
Antigua	20	20	St. John's	'
Nevis and	each of them is		Charles-town	'
Montserrat	18 circumfer		Plymouth	
Barbuda	20	12		'
Anguilla	30	18		'
Dominica	28	13		'
S. Vincent	24	18		'
Granada	30	15	St. George's	'
Tobago	32	9		'
Cuba	700	70	Havannah	Spain
Hispaniola	450	150	St.Domingo	' and France
Portorico	100	40	Porto Rico	Spain
Trinidad	90	60		'
Margarita	40	24		'
Martinico	60	30	St. Peter's	France
Gadaloupe	45	38	Basse-terre	'
St. Lucia	23	12		'
St.Bartholom	all of			'
Desenda	them			'
Maragalante	inconsiderable			'
St Eustatia	29	circ	The Bay	Dutch
Curassao	30	10		
St. Thomas	15	circ		Denmark
St Croix	30	10	Bass-end	

5 length – it must be assumed that the figures relate to miles.
6 breadth – it must be assumed that the figures relate to miles.

American Islands

Newfoundland	350	200	Placentia	Great Britian
Cape Briton	100	80	Louisburgh	'
St. Johns	60	30	Charllotte	'
The Bermudas	20,000 acr		St. George	'
The Bahamas	very numer.		Nassau	'
Falklands				
Juan Fernandes	14	6	uninhabited	
Fuera				'
Chiloe	12	17	Castro	

According to Irene Collins, stargazing and an interest in astronomy were the result of Enlightenment teaching. Contemplation of the heavens through the newly invented telescopes convinced many that God was less remote than He had once seemed to be and archdeacons recommended the study of astronomy to the clergy as a suitable occupation for their leisure hours.[7] Compilers of almanacs argued that God was the first cause of all things, able if He wished, to overrule the stars. They explained that the contemplation of the universe led mankind to the worship of its Maker and that the motions and influence of the heavenly bodies pointed to the unimaginable skill of God the Creator.[8] Measurements were all important; figures were given for distances of the celestial bodies from each other and diameter of the moon and planets recorded in detail.

Diaries were one source of astronomical facts and figures. Among the information at the beginning and end of Eliza Chute's diaries are tabulated facts about the moon, the sun and the planets, including 'A Table of the Moon's Age' (1793) and 'A Table of the Planets, from Payne's system of Universal Geography, *just published*. This latter table contains such information as the 'Distance from the Earth in their Perigeon, or when <u>nearest</u> in English miles' and the 'Rate of motion through their Orbits by English Miles, in an Hour'.[9] Thomas Turner clearly had a strong interest in astronomy, with all the facts and figures that went with it, and noted in 1757:

> *Thurs. 30 June.* ... Today in reading *The London Magazine* for May, I find the following description of the comet that is shortly expected to appear, *viz.*, that it has appeared 6 times already, *viz.*, in the years 1305, 1380, 1456, 1531, 1607, and 1682, and

---

7 Collins, *Jane Austen*, 65.

8 B. Capp, *Astrology and the Popular Press, English Almanacs 1500–1800* (1979) 247, 255–6.

9 Chute diaries (1793).

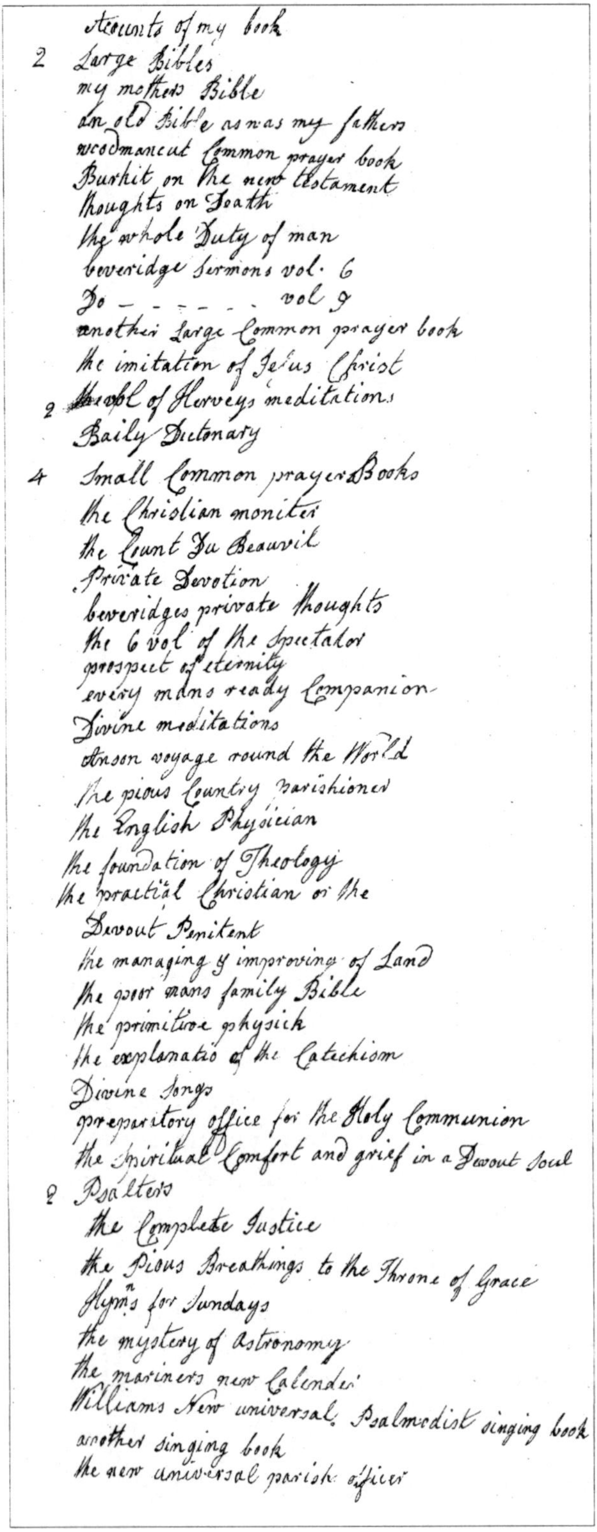

Accounts of my book
2 Large Bibles
my mothers Bible
an old Bible as was my fathers
woodmancut Common prayer book
Burkit on the new testament
thoughts on Death
the whole Duty of man
beveridge sermons vol. 6
Do ------ vol 9
another Large Common prayer book
the imitation of Jesus Christ
2 ~~the~~ ... of Herveys meditations
Baily Dictonary
4 Small Common prayer Books
the Christian monitor
the Count Du Beauvil
Private Devotion
beveridges private thoughts
the 6 vol of the Spectator
prospect of eternity
every mans ready Companion
Divine meditations
Anson voyage round the World
the pious Country parishioner
the English Physician
the foundation of Theology
the practical Christian or the
Devout Penitent
the managing & improving of Land
the poor mans family Bible
the primitive physick
the explanatio of the Catechism
Divine Songs
preparatory office for the Holy Communion
the spiritual Comfort and grief in a Devout Soul
2 Psalters
the Complete Justice
the Pious Breathings to the Throne of Grace
Hymns for Sundays
the mystery of Astronomy
the mariners new Calender
Williams New universal Psalmodist singing book
another singing book
the new universal parish officer

that it revolves about the sun at the intervals of 75 and 76 years alternately, and since the last period, viz., in 1682, was 75 years, it is presumed the present period will contain 76 years, and therefore its next appearance will probably be in 1758 ...

At one point the comet was likely to come very close to earth, 'and should that happen the 12th May, we should then be in a dangerous situation as the denser part of its blazing tail would envelop the earth.'[10] Another publication, *The Gentleman's Diary or the Mathematical Repository*, gave data of modern astronomy, the size of the universe, distance of the fixed stars and Halley's work on the periodicity of comets. Figures were noted, with so-called exact measurements. The sun, moon and stars were occasionally written about in the *Hampshire Chronicle*, the editor including information as to the exact time a planet could be seen and for how many days.

10 Diary of Thomas Turner, 103.

Figure 11
The first page of Mary Bacon's book list

(HRO 28M82/F1)

Against this background, it is not surprising that Mary Bacon copied detailed astronomical measurements into her ledger. She clearly had a strong interest in astronomy as she also had a mid seventeenth-century book on the subject. The title page is a good example of a belief that an appreciation of the greatness of God's works could come through a study of the universe, His creation:

The Mystery of
ASTRONOMY
Made plain
To the meanest Capacity
BY
An arithmetical Description of the
Terrestrial and Celestial Globes.
Briefly shewing (by way of Question and Answer)
the wondrous works of
God, from the earth
his Footstool, to his Throne of heaven
with Divine
Observations upon every part thereof
Also, Two TABLES: the one for
contents; the
other, for Explanation of Hard words.
By W.B. an honourer of ARTS & SCIENCES.

Jer. 10.12 *He hath made the earth by his power, he hath established the world by his wisdom, and hath stretched out the heavens by his discretion.*

Psal. 111.2 *The works of the Lord are great, sought out of all them that have pleasure therein.*

Psal.9.1 *I will shew forth all thy marvellous works.*[11]

The subject of the discourse is set out on the first page:

It is the most wonderful Frame of the whole World, both the heavens and the earth, created by God; and which comprehends all his other creatures, there being nothing visible without the limits thereof: so that whatsoever is betwixt the Seat of the ALMIGHTY, and the Centre of the Earth, is the proper subject of this Discourse.

The size of the earth is considered and the question asked, 'In what time may a man (having no lett) go round about the same (the Earth), after 16 miles a day?' The answer has been carefully calculated. 'In 3 years, nine months, and 3 days, he may compass the same.'

It has not been possible to trace the source of Mary's entry of astronomical

11 William Bagwell, *The Mystery of Astronomy made plain to the meanest capacity* (1655).

measurements into her ledger, as there are so many of these tables in many books and publications. As so often with the passages she copied out, there are frequent spelling mistakes and very little punctuation.

Mars is situated next above the Earth his Course being between the orbit of Jupiter and that of the Earth but very distant from both it is the least of all the planets, Mercury excepted has less lustre than any other star and appears of a dusky red hue Mars is considerably less than the Earth, its diameter, being only 4400, miles his distance from the sun is 129,000,000 of miles and he revolves about that central luminary in 687 days proceeding at the rate of 45,000 miles an hour

Jupiter is the largest of all the planets, but being very remote from the sun, would scarse enjoy any light. Had not the great Author of Nature provoided it in the four moons or Satelites, which revolves round it in different orbits the diameter of Jupiter is upwards of 80,000, of miles and mass of matter it contains is 220 times greater than our Earth, the distance from the sun is 424,000,000 miles, he revolves round his own axis in 9 hours and 56 minuets, round the sun in 11 years and 10 months and proceeds at the rate of 24,000 miles an hour

Saturn is the most distant planet in the whole System being 779,000,000 of miles from the sun he is 30 years in performing his revolution and yet moves at the rate of 18,000 miles an hour he is 61,000 miles in diameter Contains 94 times as much matter as the Earth, but his density is not more than a seventh part of the matter which composes our planet, as the light and heat in Saturn are not above a ninetieth part of what we enjoy from the sun, the wise Creator of the universe hath accommodated Saturn with five moons, which revolve round him in different orbs, but the most singular circumstance relative to this planet is his ring, this is a vast body of earth, of the thickness of near 800 miles, which surrounds Saturn in form of a circle, at the distance of 21-000, miles from its surface.

The Sun is a Globe of fire whose Diameter is equal to 100 diameters of the earth the thickness being 793=000 miles its surface is 10–1000 times Larger than the earth and its solidity is 1,000=000 Greater

Mercury is two thirds of the earth's Magnitude being 2700 miles in diameter distance from the earth is 98,000=000, of miles and from the sun 32,000,000 of miles his revolution round the sun is made in a little more than 88 days with the velocity of 100,00, miles in an hour, which is almost as Swift again as the earth travel We only go 56,000 miles in the same Space. The heat of the Sun in this planet is something more then Seven times Greater than the heat of the hottest part of the earth in the most Sultry summer, which is sufficient to make water boil

the planet Venus appears to the eye to be the brightest of all the planets and from its Superior lustre it cannot be mistaken for any of them, the distance of venus from the Sun is 60,000,000 of miles, her revolution round the Sun is performed in a little more than 224 Days and her motion in an hour is 70,000 miles

The Earth forms its revolution round the sun in 365 Days 5 hours and 49 minuets, which makes what we term a year, the Earth is near 80,000 miles in diameter, and distant from the sun about 81,000,000 of miles, the line which this planet describes in its annual motion is called the Ecliptic through which it proceeds from West to East according to the Signs of the Zodiac, and it is this motion which causes the different seasons of Spring, Summer Autumn and Winter, and of the various Lengths of Days and nights in those Seasons, the earth in passing through the ecliptic, always keeps its axis in a situation parallel to itself and equally inclined to the plane of the ecliptic, which is 23 degrees and a half. The rotation of the earth round its own axis makes it day in those parts, which are turned towards the sun and night in those parts which are turned from the Sun

The Moon which lights our Earth contains about the fortieth part of the quantity or mass of matter which compose the planet we reside upon it is near 2200 miles in diameter 240,000 miles distant from us, and its surface is about 14,000,000 of Square miles the Moon is the quickest in its Motion of all the planets, making its revolution in 27 days seven hours and three quarters, the light which this planet affords us at night is not the only benefit we receive from it, for it governs the waters and occasions the tides, which are of infinite benifit to mankind.

These figures are probably very arbitrary, and even if Mary Bacon's source were known, it would be impossible to assess their accuracy as they varied quite extensively from writer to writer. There is, for example, a significant variation between figures given in Eliza Chute's diaries and the ones copied out by Mary. The diary gives the diameter of Mars as 5,150 English miles whereas her source measured it as 4,400. In Mary's book, *The Mystery of Astronomy*, written more than a century earlier, the diameter of Mars is recorded as 9,450 miles. These figures also differ from Payne's *Universal Geography*, a further source.[12] According to Payne, the distance of Mars from the sun in English miles was 145,000,000, whereas Mary recorded it as 129,000,000. These differences are not important except to show the kind of variations which occur when the popular press takes over. What is important is that Mary was interested in facts of this kind and that she took the trouble to copy them out in detail.

One of the main functions of almanacs, especially in the sixteenth and seventeenth centuries, was that of astrological prediction, and although this was not so prevalent during the eighteenth century, some vestiges remained. It has not been possible to trace the 'curious prophecy' which Mary copied into her ledger but she clearly took it from a publication, most likely an almanac. Both Moore and

12 John Payne, *Universal Geography formed into a new and entire system…with a set of maps…and a great variety of copper plates* (1791).

Partridge, in their almanacs, included predictions of events such as the downfall of the French and the Pope. Mary's prediction also concerned the downfall of the French and reflects the common fear, especially prevalent during the 1790s, that France would conquer Britain. She treats the prophecy with some humour and it is difficult to think that anyone with her deep religious convictions could have taken Gog and Magog seriously. She has not dated the extract, but must have entered it in her ledger after the years mentioned, possibly in about 1800, as she wrote very little after that date.

> A curious prophecy was in circulation some years ago – we give it for the amusement of our readers:
> in the year 1790 – there will be a rebellion against the French King
> 1791 – there will be a war among many European Powers
> 1792 – More of the Christian powers engaged in the war against France
> 1793 – The war increases in Europe
> 1794 – There will be little or no form of Religion observed in France
> 1795 – there will be destructive divisions Among the powers of Europe
> 1796 – there will be great slaughter by sea and land
> 1797 – There will appear Gog and Magog that will make war against all the nations in the world
> 1798 – There will be a great destruction, which will thin the inhabitants of the earth
> 1799 – There will come a descendent of David who will perform such acts of grace from the power of heaven as to destroy Gog and Magog
> 1800 – He will cause the remnants of all nations to be of one religion and will banish war from the world: hence men will live in bonds of friendship, equality and love.

The subject matter has all the imprint of Moore's *Vox Stellarum*. An immensely popular publication, Moore was said to sell 82,000 copies a year, although this may have been an exaggeration. The 1789 edition of his publication reprinted *Hymns* by Isaac Watts, which might have attracted Mary to purchase it. The prophecies are for the following year and Henry Andrews, the editor, conceded that this material was what some of his readers liked to have included in his almanac. He remarked, 'in my line of writing many different tastes are to be pleased.' It was said after his death that his predictions were 'as much laughed at by himself, as by the worshipful company of Stationers for whom he annually manufactured them in order to render their almanacs saleable among the ignorant.'[13] Mary was not ignorant, but probably went along with the popular taste of her time and bought an almanac.

More evidence of Mary Bacon's enquiring mind is shown by the inclusion in her

---

13 Information about Moore's *Vox Stellarum* has been taken from Capp, *Astrology and the Popular Press* (1979).

book list of *The Mariner's New Calendar*,[14] although it is possible that the publication belonged to one of the men in her family. It is the most scientific work on the list, but has a similarity to some of her almanac material. The *Calendar* gives tide tables, tables of the Moon's age for the years 1762–70, and tables of latitude and longitude of the principal harbours, headlands and islands of the world. Material such as a 'Description and Use of the Sea-Quadrant, Necessary Problems of Plane-Sailing and Astronomy, The Course and Distances on the Coast of Great Britain, Ireland, France' and 'the soundings at coming into the Channel: With Directions for sailing into some Principal Harbours' seems a far cry from the every day world of a busy farmer's wife. Yet middle-class eighteenth-century women were reading widely and it is possible that Mary read at least some of this highly technical textbook for sailors.

Readers of the *Hampshire Chronicle* were clearly intrigued by criminals and misdemeanours of various kinds. The newspaper included scandalous stories of elopements and duels, as well as reports of trials at the assizes in Winchester, well-attended executions, and the prisoners' last words at the gallows. It was not uncommon for famous trials to be published and not surprising that Mary Bacon should have had a copy of *The Trial of Colonel Despard* in her possession. Published in 1803, it must have been one of the last additions to her library. She did not record whether it was the Dublin edition 'taken in short hand, by an eminent barrister',[15] or the London edition published by H. Reynall: *An Authentic Detail of the trial of Colonel E. M. Despard, and others, on a charge of high treason: tried at the Sessions-House, Newington, February 1803, before Lord Chief Justice Ellenborough: to which is prefixed His Lordship's charge to the Grand Jury.*[16] In the publication it is all there, the evidence, the legal argument, and the description of the terrible end of the accused, to be read by candlelight at the end of the winter, after a busy farming day. Colonel Edward Marcus Despard was born in 1751. He belonged to an Irish landowning family and had a distinguished military record. He served with Nelson on the Spanish Main, who is reported to have said at the trial at which he was a character witness,

> We went in the Spanish Main together; we slept many nights together in our clothes upon the ground; we have measured the height of the enemies' wall together. In all that period of time no man could have shown more zealous attachment to his Sovereign and his Country than Colonel Despard did.'[17]

Despard was accused of being a founder member of the United Englishmen, a secret

14 Colson, Nathaniel, *The Mariner's New Calendar*. There are several editions after 1770.
15 Dublin, 1803.
16 London 1803.
17 Despard, (1803), 174.

revolutionary society founded in 1797. Arrested for the first time in 1798, he was released and then arrested again in November 1802. He was charged with conspiring to form a revolutionary army and to kill the king. In 1803 he was finally brought to trial, found guilty of high treason, and executed together with six guardsmen. Fortunately for the colonel, the king commuted his sentence to beheading only, and he was spared being drawn while still alive and his entrails burnt in front of him. Innocent or guilty? – it was a controversial issue at the time.

The report of the trial is lengthy and very detailed, and was taken down word for word. The proceedings fell into two parts. The first trial was before a grand jury and started with an address from Lord Ellenborough, the Lord Chief Justice. He began by giving a legal explanation of high treason:

> The Statute of the 36th of the present reign, which particularly applies to the case that is to be submitted to your consideration, provides with peculiar care for the safely of his Majesty's sacred person ... By that statute it is, among other things enacted, that whosoever proposes, invents, or devises any bodily harm to his Majesty, shall be deemed a traitor and suffer all the penalties and forfeitures of high Treason.

The first jury had to decide whether 'there is a reasonable and probable ground for guilt on the part of the persons charged before you, and if so, to submit them to a final verdict.' It would then be the task of a smaller jury of twelve men to come to a final verdict in a second trial. Witnesses were called and a bill of indictment made against 13 of the prisoners.

The matter then came before the Attorney General who told the jury that 'no political party, no faction considers its interests at stake. There is no prejudice on either side; there has been no clamour; the public mind is completely at ease. You enter that box without prepossession, and without a wish further than that justice may be done'. Despard pleaded not guilty to the charges of 'compassing and imagining the death of the king', 'devising and intending the imprisonment of his Majesty's person' and 'conspiring to depose and dethrone the king'. He tried hard to interrupt during the proceedings and have his say about 'any unfavourable impressions which might have been made upon them by those villainous publications that had, at various times since his arrest, appeared against his character', but was not allowed to do so.[18] Witnesses were called again, including Nelson, but although the foreman of the jury recommended mercy because of his previous good character, Despard was condemned to the gallows. Did Mary buy the tract because she believed in his innocence, or was it because she, like so many other readers of the *Hampshire Chronicle* or of similar publications, enjoyed the scandal and drama of a trial?

18 *ibid.*

Disasters, catastrophes, shipwrecks, abductions, duels are all to be found on the pages of the *Hampshire Chronicle*, reflecting popular delight in all sorts of dramatic events. In the same way that trials were reported and circulated in tracts, so too were major disasters. One of these was the wreck of the *Halsewell*, a vessel caught in a storm in the English Channel in January 1786, the day after she set off for India. There is no evidence that Mary Bacon knew or was related to any of the sailors who are listed at the end of the tract but nevertheless she bought *A Circumstantial Narrative of the Loss of the Halsewell*.[19] Published by William Lane, known for his long production of 'trash' novels at the Minerva Press, this is probably the nearest that Mary got to having a novel in her book collection. The story is of the *Halsewell*, 'which was unfortunately wrecked at Seacombe in the Isle of Purbeck on the morning of Friday 6th January, 1786', and its captain, Richard Pierce, who perished. The record was 'compiled from the Communications and under the authorities of Mr. Henry Meriton and Mr. John Rogers, the two chief officers, who happily escaped the dreadful Catastrophe'. It is a dramatic and tragic tale, which was very popular, as it went into at least eleven editions. The tract begins on a sombre note,

> The melancholy Catastrophe which is intended to be the subject of the following pages, is of a nature so direful, that humanity recoils at the recollection of it; and among the various events of the same deplorable kind, which have blackened the annals of the last forty years, scarce one has been attended with so many circumstances of aggravated woe.

The story itself begins quite cheerfully,

> The Halsewell East Indiaman of 758 tons burthen, commanded by Richard Pierce, Esq., having been taken up by the Directors of the East-India Company to make her third voyage to Coast and Bay on the 16th day of November 1785, fell down to Gravesend, where she completed her lading; and taking the ladies and other passengers on board at the Hope, she sailed through the Downs on Sunday the 1st January 1786, and the next morning being a-breast of Dunnose, it fell calm…All appearances united to promise a happy and prosperous voyage, and not a cloud intervened to obscure the pleasing hopes, which are ever annexed to a life of Adventure, and which are the main springs of Industry.

Wealth, honour, public advantage and aggrandisement were all to be hoped for. The voyage was a commercial one, the objects being 'highly laudable, to extend the commerce, and to promote the revenue of the State'. The commander was distinguished, the crew excellent, the seamen the best. The passengers, seven ladies, two of whom were the captain's daughters, and one man, also had their merits. 'The young ladies were equally distinguished by their beauty and accomplishments … it is

19 Henry Meriton, (second mate), *A Circumstantial Narrative of the loss of the Halsewell* (1786).

hardly possible to conceive a more friendly and happy society nor one more calculated to join in diverting the tediousness of a long passage by little plans of rational
amusement …'. Unfortunately, these pleasurable amusements were not to last and
on Monday, 2 January thick weather started to close in and the crew had difficulty
with the sails, 'the snow falling thick, and freezing as it fell.' The following day they
bore down the Channel but by 10 at night there was a further deterioration in the
ship's situation. 'It blew a violent gale of wind at South,' there were large quantities
of water on the gun deck, five feet of water in the hold and the hawse bags were
washed away.[20] Wednesday was no better and at 2 the unfortunate seamen had to
cut away the mizzen mast and the main mast. Some hours later the fore top-mast
fell off, tearing the foresail to pieces. The rest of the day was spent working on the
sails and erecting a jury[21] main mast and mizzen mast. By Thursday the weather
deteriorated further and all attempts to get the ship into harbour failed. That night
the captain asked the second mate his opinion as to the probability of saving their
lives, 'to which he replied with equal calmness and candour, that he apprehended
there was very little hope, as they were then driving fast in the shore, and might
expect every moment to strike.' The boats were thought to be of no use, but it was
decided that the long boat would be reserved for the ladies and officers.

On Friday 6 January at 2, the ship was fast approaching the shore and disaster
was about to strike. Captain Pierce was 'expressing extreme anxiety for the pres-
ervation of his beloved daughters…' and the officers offered comfort to 'the fair
sufferers'. Then the ship hit the rocks on the Island of Purbeck between Peverel
Point and St Alban's Head:

> But at the particular spot the cliff is excavated at the foot, and presents a cavern of
> ten or twelve yards in depth, and of breadth upright as to be extremely difficult of
> access, and the roof formed of the stupendous cliff, and the bottom of it strewed
> with sharp and uneven rocks … It was at the mouth of this cavern that the unfor-
> tunate wreck lay stretched almost from side to side of it, and offering her broadside
> to the horrid chasm.

On board the ship the captain and passengers were gathered in the round house.
Mr Meriton, the second mate, found candles, and produced oranges so that the
ladies could suck the juice while they all awaited the dawn. All were composed
'except Miss Mansel, who was in hysteric fits on the floor deck of the round house'.
As the ship broke up, Meriton managed to swim to the rocks and drag himself up
to a little rock shelf in the cavern. On board, all was lost. 'Captain Pierce, with his

20 Hawse bags: prevent water from coming up the 'hawse holes' (through which run the anchor
   cables).
21 Jury mast: replacement or improvised mast in the event of damage.

great coat on, sat down between his two daughters, and struggled to suppress the parental tear which then burst into his eye.' Then the round house gave way and the ladies could be heard shrieking at intervals, 'as if the water had reached them, the noise of the sea at other times drowning their voices.' In the meantime, two of the mates grabbed a hencoop and were carried on a wave to the rocks, very bruised. In all, about 28 men reached the cavern. Then finally came the inevitable climax:

> But alas! their (the men in the cavern) apprehensions were too soon realised. In a very few minutes after Mr Rogers had gained the rock, a universal shriek, which still vibrates in their ears, and, in which, the voice of female distress was lamentably distinguishable, announced the dreadful Catastrophe; in a few moments all was hushed, except the warring winds, and beating waves; the wreck was buried in the remorseless deep, and not an atom of her was ever after discoverable.

The men in the cavern were left clinging precariously to small ledges in the rock, 'worn out with fatigue, weakened by bruises, battered by the tempest, and benumbed with cold'. Many dropped off and fell on the rocks or in to the sea below. Daylight came and a few men managed to creep along the side of the cave and to turn the corner and climb the very steep cliff, but some perished with the attempt. The quartermaster and the cook were first up the 200 ft high cliff and went for help to the Purbeck quarries from where quarrymen came to the rescue, saving some but not all of the survivors. Finally, Mr Meriton and Mr Rogers, third mate, arrived at India House on Sunday 8 January to tell the sad tale. Only 74 people had survived out of more than 240 passengers and crew. 50 went down with the ship including all the women and the Captain.

The tract ends with consolations to the afflicted and extols the merits of those who died.

> And above all, let the afflicted on the present occasion, remember that the friends they lament neither precipitated themselves to destruction by neglect, obstinacy, temerity, or even imprudence; but that the event, however melancholy in its operation, was the dispensation of that Being who '*rides in the whirlwind, and directs the storm*;' and that all his purposes, however unaccountable in this weak perception of human wisdom, are unquestionably wise, gracious, and ultimately merciful.

Novels were not included in Mary Bacon's list of books, but the sad story of the wreck of the *Halsewell* has all the trimmings of a Gothic tale, written to be read aloud by the fireside on a stormy winter's night. It is given here in some detail as it is illustrative of popular reading of the period.

Another dramatic tale, also to be found on Mary Bacon's bookshelf, which was very popular during the mid eighteenth century, reaching its fourteenth edition in 1779, was

A Voyage Round the World in the Years MDCCXLI, II, III, IV by George Anson
Esq., afterwards Lord Anson, commander in chief of A Squadron of his Majesty's
Ship the Centurion, in that Expedition with charts of the Southern Part of South
America, and Part of the Pacific Ocean. 14th ed. London in MDCCLXIX and of
the Track of the Centurion round the World.[22]

The squadron of ships sent off to harass the Spanish encountered many adventures,
but perhaps the most hair-raising was the rounding of Cape Horn, when heavy
storms were encountered. There was a succession of tempestuous storms,

> as surprised the oldest and most experienced Mariners on board, and obliged them
> to confess, that what they had hitherto called storms were inconsiderable gales,
> compared with the violence of these winds, which raised such short, and at the
> same time, such mountainous waves, as greatly surpassed in danger all seas known
> in any other part of the globe. And it was not without great reason, that this unusual
> appearance filled us with continual terror, for had any one of these waves broken
> fairly over us, it must, in all probability, have sent us to the bottom.[23]

Men were injured or killed and one man was swept overboard. Snow, sleet, frost
bite, frozen sails, all added to their misery.

Many of the books and tracts which Mary had in her possession were serious,
ponderous works of a religious nature but it seems that, like so many of those
around her, she could indulge in drama and excitement. Wild storms bring geography
to life, and there is drama in history too. Somewhere, at an agricultural fair, on
the doorstep, or at the booksellers in Alton or Basingstoke, Mary must have bought
a tract, which she copied into her ledger. This is in the form of a letter written by
Queen Charlotte (1744–1818), who came from Mecklenburg, to the king of Prussia,
whom she accused of overrunning and destroying her native country. Some doubt
has been cast over the authenticity of the document but it was in circulation at the
time. The original letter was published in the *Scots Magazine* in 1761 but Bacon's
copy, with the addition of an emotional and florid poem on the subject, was dated
1797, indicating that it had been around for a number of years and had got into
popular literature.[24]

> The following elegant epistle was written by the Queen of England to the King of
> Prussia during the late war
>> May it please your Majesty
> I am at a loss whether I should congratulate, or condole with you on your late victory, since the same success, which hath covered you with laurels, has overspread the

22 George Anson, '*A Voyage Round the World in the Years MDCCXLI, II, III, IV* (1745).
23 *ibid*, 106.
24 I am grateful to Janice Hadlow for this information.

country of mecklenburgh with desolation. I know, Sire, that it seems unbecoming my sex, in this age of vicious refinement to feel for one's country to lament the horrors of war or wish for the return of peace. I know you may think it more properly my province to study the arts of pleasing or to inspect subjects of a more domestic nature, but however unbecoming it may be in me, I cannot resist the desire of interceding for this unhappy people. It was but a few years ago, that this territory wore the most pleasing appearance; the county was cultivated, the peasant looked cheerful, and the towns abounded, with riches and festivity. What an alteration, at present, from so charming a scene! I am not expert at description, nor can my fancy add any horrors to the picture; but surely even conquerors themselves would weep at the hideous prospects now before me! The whole country (my dear country!) lies in frightful waste, presenting only objects to excite terror, pity, and despare. The Business of the husbandman and the shepherd are quite discontinued. The husbandman and the shepherd are become soldiers themselves, and help to ravage the soil they formerly cultivated the towns are inhabited only by old men, women, and children – perhaps here and there a warrior, by wounds or loss of limbs rendered unfit for service left at his door; his little Children hang around, ask an history of every wound and grow themselves soldiers before they find strength for the field. but this were nothing, did we not feel the alternate insolence of either army, as it happens to advance or retreat in pursing the operations of the Campaigns. It is impossible to express the confusion which even those who call themselves our friend create. even those from whome we might expect redress, oppress us with new calamities. from your justice, therefore it is that we expect relief. to you, even women and Children may complain, whose humanity stoops to the meanest petition, and whose power is capable of repressing the greatest injustice.

As the above epistle hath been elegantly paraphrased we shall subjoin some of the principal lines of the poetical version.

> While conquest seats you on the throne of fame,
> And marital deeds immortalize your name,
> On burnish'd arms, while glory brightly beams,
> And fields victorious fill the soldiers dreams;
> Trembling I view, from whence the glory springs,
> Of king-like heroes, or of hero-kings;
> Shock'd I behold the Source, whence dart those rays,
> Which shine on victors, and round conquerors blaze,
> Hence I'm in doubt, while prompted to express
> My weak ideas on your late success,
> Whether congratulations to bestow,
> Or melt to tears and swell the stream of woe;
> For all those laurels which your brows intwine
> Crown your success and bid your conquest shine,

Meant as immortal trophies to adorn
Were from my country's bleeding bowels torn:
While, in whats truly brave and greatly bold,
You outstrip heroes dignified of old:
My native Mecklenburg, a prey to arms,
Is desolated of her fertile charms:
No more her plains their plenteous verdure yield
No longer Cares decks the happy field;
Nothing is seen or heard where'er ye go
But Scenes of horror, and the signs of woe.
I know great Sire a patriotic theme,
In my weak Sex may unbecoming Seem;
For in an age so viciously refin'd
By folly led, and to caprice refin'd
Perhaps you deem the very name of arms,
The thought of rapine, and of wars alarms,
Of slaughter by contending armies made,
Or burnish'd swords for mortal ends displayed;
Of mourning widows, and of bleeding swains,
Of burning towns, and desolated plains:
Perhaps you deem such thought unfit for those,
Who should their minds to softer themes compose;
And court the prospect of domestic ease;
To inspect with care the finer art to charm.
And point the lighting when their eyes they arm;
To practise Smiles, by art to look serene;
Catch the free air, and dignity of mien;
To lose themselves in all that's idly vain,
The approbation of the world to gain:
If these, my Liege, are arts for females fit,
Who shou'd no other sentiments admit,
I must for once transgress, and, unconfin'd
Obey the dictates of a feeling mind;
I must by Soft humanity inspir'd
Express the thoughts from Shocking Scenes acquir'd
With truth, great Sire, permit me to unfold,
What I've beheld – ah: – what I yet behold
And while the natives of my country bleed,
For the unhappy people let me intercede.
A few years since, in Mecklenburg's domain,
Fair plenty smil'd on every fertile plain:
The placid years serenely fled away,

The fields were fruitful and the groves were gay
Now my dear county here the tear will flow
Now my dear country, is a waste of woe;
Depopulation makes a frightful void,
The peasant flies or staying is destroyed;
Turn to what part I will my aching eyes,
And all the horrors of the war arise;
The devastations of the martial train,
With streaming gore empurples every plain:
With native blood the silent rivers flow,
And in their bosoms streaming purple show;
While into camps the fertile fields are made,
And gloomy woods can scarce from danger shade;
And die each moment while from death they hide,
Who watch thro' fear, or thro' reflection weep,
And from exhausted Spirits borrow sleep;
Whose sweetest rest is but a troubled doze,
Who thank fatigue for ev'ry small repose;
A famish'd babe perhaps lifts up its eyes,
And for assistance to the mother cries;
The fainting mother ready to expire
Replies with tears and Supplicates the sire:
The Sire, unable to relieve their woe,
Can only answer with a briny flow;
And while his Silent sorrows grief express
Increase his own by sharing their distress;
Thus wing'd by fear no husbandman remains,
By cultivation to restore the plains;
No gentle shepherd tends his fleecy care
Both join the war and in the horrors share;
And soldiers grown, a strange reverse of fate,
Destroy those fields they us'd to cultivate;
With anguish'd age, the women sit and wail
As fears for husbands or for sons prevail:
Perhaps a warrior here and there is found
Debarr'd the field by many a rankling wound;
Or by the loss of limbs, not want of will
Deny'd the use of Sanguinary skill;
Round him the curious prattling children swarm
Hang on his tongue, and as he speaks grow warm;
Demand the history of each aching wound,
Devour each word and catch the martial sound

And while the soldier eagerly recites,
The rage of battle and the blood of lights;
The steeds loud neighing, and the clank of arms,
The rumbling drum, that beats to wars alarms;
The clangring trumpet and the cannons roar,
The dying groans and fields of streaming gore;
The little auditors erect their crests,
While a new ardor fires their youthful breasts,
To you, therefore, great Sire we make appeal
Whose justice only can our sufferings heal;
From you alone, great Sire, we hope relief,
Tis your compassion must assuage our grief;
To you ev'n helpless females may complain,
Nor shed their tears, nor plead their cause in vain;
And trembling babes with tender looks implore
The royal hand to open mercy's door,
To you, whose kind humanity stoops down,
To shield the peasant underneath the crown;
To guard the meanest who for justice press,
And give the humblest Supplicant redress
To you affliction speeds with tearful eye.
Whose power relieves, and bids injustice fly.
                    Finis June 28 = 1797   Mary Bacon

More accounts of history are to be found in another of the books entered in Mary's list. Rapine's *History of England*, 'A New History of England by Question and Answer extracted from the Most Celebrated English Historians, particularly M. Rapin de Thoyras for the Instruction and Entertainment of our Youth of both Sexes.'[25] The Dedication was by John Lockman:

I here give a succinct account of the reigns of our several monarchs, from the earliest times, extracted from authors of reputation: and have endeavoured to set the whole in such a light, as may inspire the readers with an ardent love of our pure religion, and its darling attendant, liberty; and, on the other hand, with a just abhorrence of popery, and its companion, slavery.

'A just abhorrence of popery' was a common theme of the period, as will be evident in the next chapter.

Mary Bacon both read printed material, copied from it, and enjoyed a library of books and tracts. Although she must have had some education, she lacked refinement in her literary skills. Her punctuation was almost non-existent and she frequently made some very basic mistakes of both spelling and grammar. However,

25 Paul Rapin de Thoyras, *History of England*, 16th edition (1770).

she did have the means to improve these skills, if she wished to do so. An appropriate book to help her was 'every mans ready companion' which she entered in her list of books. Although I have been unable to find an exact match, it is likely that she was referring to *Every Young Man's Companion*.[26] This is a book from which she may have derived great benefit as it encompasses so many of the skills which she needed to aid her in her lengthy copying. The book includes directions for spelling, reading and writing English, together with a section on instructions in the art of penmanship. The reader is taught appropriate body posture when writing:

> Let your Seat be so high, as that you may sit easy, without either your Legs hanging, or throwing them from you. Let your Desk or Table be about the Height of your Middle. Thus seated, lay your Book or Paper awry; that is, let it incline towards our Left Arm or Side, instead of being strait before you. The more it inclines, the more your slope will be. If you write upright, then lay your Book or Paper even before you. Fix your body directly before your Desk or Table, with both Right and Left Elbows on it; notwithstanding the general Method is, that your Left Arm only should rest thereon.
>
> Thus seated, and having your Book and Paper before you, you may write with all the Freedom and Ease imaginable: No *Nervous Flutterings*, no numbness, or Stiffness that a too frequent Sitting with the left Side towards the Desk or Table, and leaning the Stress of your Body on your Left Arm, on occasions, will attend you. This Method will suit all Sizes; the Fat or the Lean; the Tall, or the short; Men of Bulk, and Ladies laced in their stays …'

There are plenty of examples of pious prose and poetry for the student to copy out in order to improve on skills, including, 'All human Things are subject to decay And when Death summons, Monarchs must obey' and 'Nature is nothing but the Voice of God: A bright Display of that Divine Wisdom, which demands an eternal tribute of Wonder and Worship.' Arithmetic, algebra, geometry and logarithms are all included in this book. A chapter on 'the Circles of the Sphere or Globe, and of the fixed Stars, Planets and Comets' gives very similar measurements to Mary in her almanac tables. In addition the book has a gardener's calendar with instructions as to which plants to grow each month, a section on farriery, and another on recipes, all of great interest to Mary. Finally there is a very useful table of measurements, reproduced in Appendix One.

Further aids to literary improvement entered on Mary's list were two old spelling books, which would also have helped with writing skills, but her greatest asset was Bailey's *Dictionary*. It was described as 'A universal etymological dictionary of the English language … to which is prefixed a grammar of the English language by N.

26 William Gordon, *Every Young Man's Companion* (1759).

Bayley, Edinburgh 1764.' There was an earlier edition of 1730. Nathan Bailey also wrote a '*Dictionarium Domesticum*, being a new and compleat household dictionary. For the use of both city and country' (1736). There were many further editions, the 25th being printed in 1790. I prefer to think that Mary Bacon possessed the domestic version, as it would have undoubtedly suited her better. We do not know if Mary was fat or lean, tall or short, or if she was laced in her stays as she sat reading at her book stand. No records confirm whether she wrote in her ledger at a table, or at her bureau. However, it is clear that she had an inquiring mind, and like many middle-class women of her generation covered a range of subjects in her reading experience. But there was one subject which seems to have been central in her intellectual world – religion.

Chapter Eight

The importance of religion

LIKE MOST OF her contemporaries, religion was central to the life of Mary Bacon. The majority of her books had a religious content and the subject matter of more than half the material she copied into her ledger was concerned with religious stories, hymns, and meditations. She lived in an age when sermons were published prolifically, books of biblical criticism abounded, and the publishing of religious books flourished. The *Hampshire Chronicle* is full of advertisements for Bibles, prayer books, catechisms and a diverse variety of other meditation books. From 1700 to 1790 an average of 230 books on religion were published annually and 8,800 sermons were printed between 1660 and 1751.[1] One of the more prolific writers was John Wesley who, reaching a wide audience, produced cheap abridgements intended for family reading. Magazines such as *The Idler, Spectator* and *The Rambler* regularly printed religious articles. Tracts abounded and would have been available to Mary through fairs and peddlers. Some of these preached good conduct, and advocated that faults had to be righted, as in, *An Help for Recovery from the detestable HABIT of Profane Swearing and Cursing*, published by E. Robertson at Edinburgh. Others contained exhortations to read God's holy word, to avoid the Baits of Sin and adhere to the path of duty, 'and shun the Cruel as you'd shun a Bear.' A number warned about the excesses of Roman Catholicism. 'Rules for a Christian Life' was one of these:

> Let ev'ry Day at least begin and end
> With humble Pray'er to God thro' Christ thy Friend,
> [Bow to no Images; invoke no Saints;
> Make Christ thine Advocate in all thy Wants]

Yet another attacked the use of Latin in the Roman Catholic service. 'Nor worship God in Language quite unknown, This is but mocking the Almighty ONE'.[2]

1   From an article by T. Preston in I. Rivers ed., *Books and their Readers in Eighteenth-century England* (1982) 98.
2   Tracts (1757–79) British Library 4375.df.9.

Social conduct and the proper upbringing of the family were important, especially as extolled by Wesley, but other writers gave the same message. *The Christian Monitor*,[3] one of Mary's many religious books, was a popular work, going into numerous editions. The author exhorted good Christian conduct:

> When you come from Church, spend not the Remainder of the Day in sports and Idleness, much less in Drinking and Gaming, as too many do: but if you have a Family let some Time be spent with them, in praying, in reading God's Word, and some good Book; and let Children and Servants be instructed in their Catechism ...

Mary Bacon's own background was one of churchgoing: two of her uncles were clergymen and a third, Augustin Kinchin, was a churchwarden. In her early years she would have been taken to the little church at Woodmancott, next to her uncle's house, and near the end of her life still had the *Woodmancot Common Prayer Book* in her possession. After her father died when she was only four years old, her mother married Joseph Husbands, the parish clerk in Dummer, who no doubt brought additional religious influence into her young life. After she was married, Mary would have had some distance to travel to church. It has not been possible to establish the exact location of the Bacons' farm at Cliddesden, although it is likely that it was not situated near the church in the village itself, but at a point where three parishes met, as discussed in Chapter Two. In 1791 the family moved to Aylesfield farm, approximately three miles from Alton parish church (St Laurence) where they almost certainly worshipped. Their daughter Sarah married there, and William Bacon was an Overseer of the Poor in 1798.

Churches were not very comfortable places to arrive at after a long journey. The building would have been unheated giving little opportunity for the Bacons to warm up or dry out after what would often have been a long and muddy walk, although some of the family may have ridden or travelled in a horse-drawn vehicle. Conditions were worsened by very severe winters, with high snowdrifts sometimes lasting for weeks. It is therefore possible that there were times when the Bacon family met with neighbours nearer to home to worship, as it was not unusual in the eighteenth century for small groups to get together in this way.

Services of Morning and Evening Prayer were held every Sunday and parishioners were expected to take Holy Communion at least three times a year, one of which had to be Easter. The morning service could be up to three hours long, especially if there was a sermon; it was a long time to sit on hard pews. Although the Bacons were well respected and reasonably well off, they were not gentry, and

3 John Rawlett, *The Christian Monitor, containing an earnest exhortation to an holy life*, earliest recorded edition was published in 1672.

would not have had a private pew near the front of the nave, nor are they on the list in the church records of those paying for seats in the gallery. They would have been able to sit where they liked, but would have had to pay the church rate, levied for the upkeep of the nave. The service, consisting of the liturgy, the Litany and Ante-Communion, started with the General Confession followed by a psalm of praise and thanksgiving, lessons from the Old and New Testaments, and the Apostles' Creed.[4] The psalm was sometimes sung, the parish clerk singing a line, as many of the parishioners could not read. It would then be repeated by the congregation and inevitably took a long time. It was not the normal practice to hold services on Ash Wednesday or Good Friday and there was no Harvest Festival. There is evidence in the ledger that business was done as usual on Christmas Day. Bell ringing was an important activity and the Alton churchwardens' minute book lists the payments made to the ringers usually paid at the rate of 8*s.* a session. Bells were rung to celebrate the Queen's birthday, the Prince of Wales's birthday, the anniversaries of the King's coronation, his Accession, the King's Restoration, and the Gunpowder Plot. When the news of peace with France was announced in 1801 a guinea was paid in order to provide beer for the ringers.

The list of books owned by Mary Bacon shows how important her faith was to her.[5] She had at least five Bibles, including 'my mother's Bible,' 'an old Bible as was my father's' and *The Poor Man's Family Bible*. Her six prayer books and three Psalters would have equipped the family well for church; included in her list are *Williams New Universal Psalmodist*[6] singing book, and two others of a similar nature. Although Mary owned hymn books, they would have been of less use than Psalters, as singing hymns in the Church of England was discouraged. It is possible that family and servants sang hymns at home at the farm as Mary possessed a volume of *Hymns for Sundays*,[7] which includes the well known hymns sung today, 'Joy to the world, the Lord is come' and 'When I survey the wondrous Cross'. 'Praise to God for our Redemption' must have been a favourite hymn of Mary's which she personalised by substituting the word 'I' instead of 'we' in the last verse, when she copied it into her ledger. It was in her book, *Hymns for Sundays,* as well as in a tract she owned, which also contained the story of Judas Iscariot. (see below)

4 Collins, *Jane Austen,* 45–49.
5 see Appendix Two
6 Popular in the late 1760s, early 1770s, this book went into a number of editions.
7 This book has been difficult to trace as there are not many hymnals listed for the eighteenth century. The most likely title is *Hymns for several Sundays and festivals of the year, for thr (sic) sacrament and other public solemnities.* (*c.* 1770).

Praise God for our Redemption

1   Bless the wisdom and the power,
    The justice and the grace
    That join'd in counsel to restore
    And save our ruin'd race

2   our father eat forbidden fruit
    and from his glory fell
    and we his children thus were brought,
    to death, and near to hell,

3   Blest be the God who sent his Son,
    to take our flesh and blood
    He for our lives gave up his own,
    To make our peace with God

4   He Honourd all his father's laws
    which we have disobey'd
    he bore our Sins upon the cross,
    And our full ransom paid

5   Behold him rising from the grave
    Behold him rais'd on high:
    He pleads his merit there to save
    Transgressors doom'd to die.

6   There in a glorious throne he sits
    And by his power divine,
    Redeems us from the slavish chains,
    Of Satan and of Sin

7   Thence shall the Lord to judgement come
    and with a sovreign voice,
    shall call and break up every tomb,
    while waking Saints rejoice

8   O may I then with joy appear,
    Before the judges face
    And with the blest assembly there
    Sing his redeeming grace

Throughout her life, Mary would have used books of preparation for Confirmation, for the Holy Communion service and for church services in general. There were many tracts and books published during the eighteenth century with questions on and explanations of the Catechism; Mary's title in her list, 'the explanation of the Catechism' is one of many. Catechisms were written to instruct young people and were also read by adults for spiritual guidance. Thomas Turner, recorded in 1758 that: 'In the even finished reading Wake's Catechism, which I think a very good book and proper for all families, there being good instructions in it and also something which is prodigious moving … And so far as I can judge there is everything contained in it necessary to a man's salvation.'[8] Another of Mary's books, *The Church Catechism Explained by way of Question and Answer* by John Lewis (1712) was a very popular book, reaching its 24th edition in 1753. This edition had an added section on Confirmation and was probably still in circulation when she was confirmed. Church services had to be prepared for and there was much in the way of spiritual assistance for Mary on her bookshelf. 'Private Devotions', from the book list, has been difficult to identify, but it is probably either *Private Devotions for several Occasions ordinary and extraordinary*[9] or *Private Devotions in the Church, fitted to employ some short time before divine service begins; and also on occasion of receiving the Holy Sacrament. By a divine of the Church of England*.[10] Both were printed before Mary was born and if one of them was the book she referred to, could have been inherited from one of her Kinchin relatives. She also entered in her book list 'preparatory office for the communion'. Studying the scriptures with a commentary was a common practice in the eighteenth century and these books were very widely read. To help her study the Bible, Mary had William Burkit to turn to and could read, *Expository notes with practical observations, on the new Testament of our Lord and Saviour Jesus Christ*,[11] a very popular book in the eighteenth century. Advertised in the *Salisbury Journal* on 25 September 1752, price 6*d*., it is possible that this was another of Kinchin's books. Perhaps the meditation on religion which Mary copied out helped her in her spiritual preparations.

Thoughts on Relligon

There is but one God, the author, the creator, the governor of the world; almighty, eternal, and incomprehensible.

The Sun is not God, though his noblest image, He enlightenth the world with his brightness; his warmth giveth life to the products of the earth: admire him as the creator, the instrument of God; but worship him not.

To the one who is supreme, most wise, and beneficent and to him alone belong worship adoration, thanksgiving, and praise Who hath stretched out the heavens with his hand; who hath described with his fingers the course of the stars.

Who setteth bounds to the ocean, which it cannot pass and saith unto the stormy

8 *Diary of Thomas Turner*, 149.
9 Anon, *Private Devotions* (Dublin 1723, London 1724). There is also a *Private Devotions for several Occasions* printed with R. Allstree, *The Whole Duty of Man*. Editions dated from 1675.
10 Anon, *Private Devotions in the Church* (1712).
11 It is not possible to know which of the many editions Mary Bacon owned.

winds, be still. Who shaketh the earth and the nations tremble; who darteth the lightnings, and the wicked are dismayed Who calleth forth worlds by the words of his mouth; who smiteth with his arm, and they sink into nothing O reverence the majesty of the omnipotent, and tempt not his anger, least thou be destroyed. The providence of God is over all his works; he ruleth and directeth with infinite wisdom.

He hath instituted laws for the government of the world, and each by his nature conformeth to his will, in the depth of his mind he revolveth all knowledge; the secrets of futurity lie open before him. The thoughts of thy heart are naked to his view; he knoweth thy determinations before they are made. With respect to his prescience, there is nothing contingent: with respect to his providence, there is nothing accidental.

Wonderful is he in all his ways: his counsels are inscrutable, the manner of his knowledge transcendeth thy conception.

Pay, therefore, to his wisdom all honour and veneration and bow down thy self in humble and submissive obediance to his supream direction.

The Lord is gracious and benificent; he hath created the world in mercy and love. His goodness is conspicuous in all his works: he is the fountain of excellence the center of perfection. The creatures of his hand declare his goodness, and all their enjoyments speak his praise; he clotheth them with beauty, he supporteth them with food, he preserveth them with pleasure from generation to generation.

If we lift up our eyes to the heavens, his glory shineth forth; if we cast them down upon earth, it is full of his goodness; the hills and vallies rejoice and sing; fields, rivers, and woods, resound his praise.

But thee, O man! He hath distinguished with peculiar favour, and exalted thy station above all creatures, he hath endowed thee with reason to maintain thy dominion; he hath fitted thee with language to improve thy society, and exalted thy mind with the powers of meditation, to contemplate and adore his inimitable perfections.

And in the laws he hath ordained as the rule of thy life, so kindly hath he suited thy duty to thy nature that obedience to his precepts is happiness to thyself O praise his goodness with songs of thanksgiving, and meditate in silence on the wonders of his love: let thy heart overflow with gratitude and acknowledgement; let the language of thy lips speak praise and adoration, let the actions of thy life shew thy love to his law. The Lord is just and righteous, and will judge the earth with equity and truth.

He hath established his laws in goodness and mercy and shall he not punish the transgressors thereof. O think not, bold man! Because thy punishment is delayed, that the arm of the lord is weakened neither flatter thyself with hopes, that he winketh at thy misdoings.

His eye pierceth the secrets of every heart, and he remembereth them for ever; he respecteth not the persons nor the station of men.

The high and the low, the rich and the poor, the wise and the ignorant, when the soul hath shaken off the cumberous shackles of this mortal life, shall equally receive from the sentence of God, a just and everlasting retribution, according to their workes.

Then shall the wicked tremble and be afraid, but the hearts of the righteous shall rejoice in his judgements.

O fear the Lord, therefore, all the days of thy life, and walk in the paths which he hath opened before thee Let prudence admonish thee, let Temprance restrain thee, let justice guide thy hand, benevolence warm thy heart, and gratitude to heaven inspire thee with devotion These shall give thee happiness in thy present state, and bring thee to the mansions of eternal felicity in the paradise of God.[12]

Not only had a devout Christian to prepare for church services, but also for daily life itself. To help her Mary had *The Pious Country Parishioner*, 'being directions how a Christian may manage every day through the whole course of his life … with safety and success'.[13] Further spiritual assistance was provided in *The Practical Christian or Devout Penitent* by Richard Sherlock D.D.[14] and *The whole duty of man laid down in a plain and familiar way for the use of all, … with private devotions*, which went into more than 30 editions, first published in 1659 and continuing throughout most of the eighteenth century.[15] It was widely used by Anglicans, quoted in sermons, and frequently distributed by the Society for the Propagation of the Gospel. A reduction of the price was offered to 'those Gentlemen and Ladies, who, out of a tender regard to promote the Eternal Welfare of their Poor and Uninstructed Neighbours and Servants, are disposed to give them away'.

Sermons were listened to at length in the eighteenth century and were also widely read. Another of Mary's books was Beveridge's *Sermons* in which homilies were written on a diversity of Christian subjects such as fasting, prayer, receiving of the blessed body and blood, idleness, gluttony, drunkenness, envy, ire and so on.[16] Allegedly, it was a hard read and there is a warning in the introduction that, 'perhaps there is not one clergyman in ten thousand that is capable of reading the

12 Robert Dodsley, *The Oeconomy of Human Life* Part 1 (1783) 64. The first edition of this very popular work was published in 1751.
13 Anon, *The Pious Country Parishioner*. The 5th edition is the earliest listed (1731).
14 Richard Sherlock, *The Practical Christian* (1682).
15 Richard Allestree, *The Whole Duty of Man* (1658).
16 Bishop Beveridge, *The Thirty Nine Articles of Religion Established in the church of England with Expository Observations on some of the most Important, relating to Divine Faith and Eternal Salvation* (1710).

whole of this Bishop's Book, it is to be hoped they will have so much modesty as not to gainsay or contradict the plain matter contained therein.'

There are no commentaries on the Bible included in the book list, which is surprising as such works were often advertised in newspapers. The nearest was *The History of the Jews*, by the Count de Beauville, a large tome of weighty reading.[17] The book starts with an account of 'The state and Government of *Judea* under the Race of the *Herrods*', and includes the '*Patriarchs* that govern'd in *Judea*'. It goes on to describe, 'The works and Character of the *Talmudists, Gemarists, Pyrrhonists*, or Doubters, *Excellents*, or *Gaons, Masorets, Cabbalists*, with the particulars of the *Cabbala*, and of the famous *Rabbins*'. Various creeds, theologies, and philosophies continue to be listed throughout the table of contents, such as '*The true Origin of Spinosism, the Precepts of the Noachides*'. The book goes on to give '*A general Account of the Dispersion of the Tribes in Assyria, among the* Medes *and* Persians, *in the* Indies, America, Aethiopia, Egypt *and* Arabia, *in the* Greek *and* Ottoman Empire, *among the* Tarturs, *in* Italy, Spain, Germany France, *and* England'. The work is finally brought up to date with a description of the state of the Jews in various parts of the world in the two to three centuries prior to the eighteenth. The book was advertised in the *Hampshire Chronicle*, 7 December 1789, as containing 'the antiquity of the Jews, in twenty books, with their wars, memorable transaction, authentic and remarkable occurrences, their various turns of glory and misery, or prosperity and adversity &c., from the creation of the world'.

Many of Mary's books were for children, as well as adults, and reflect the menacing threats made as to what the afterlife might be like for those who did not mend their ways. This is the way you behave, or else the retribution is terrifying, roared the writers. There is no penitence after death and you are to be judged entirely by the way in which you have acquitted yourself on this earth. Two very popular books on the Catechism for children, which were on Mary's booklist, were in use through much of the eighteenth century and well into the nineteenth century, and could have been used by her or her children. *The Young Communicants Catechism … With a proposal for publick renewing of the Baptismal Covenant* [18], by John Willison, had gone into the 27th edition by 1776 and the book remained in print until at least 1845. It even crossed the Atlantic and there was a printing in New York in 1824. Advice is given both to parents and young persons. Parents are exhorted to teach their children to read and pray and to set them a good example; they were to be told of the frequency of the evil of sin and the excellency of godliness. Above all children's

17 Count de Beaville (Mr Basnage), trans. Thomas Taylor, *The History of the Jews* (1708).

18 John Willison, *The Young Communicants Catechism, or a help both short and plain for instructing and preparing the young* (1731).

souls must be saved, the statistics were against their reaching four score years and ten, and the judgement of the Almighty might come as early as next week. Life was fragile and life was short and children must be prepared to meet their Maker. They must have nothing to do with sin and Satan and must be serious about offering themselves to the Lord. Catechisms were hard work for children and young people. In *The Young Communicants' Catechism* alone there are 160 questions and answers, followed by a further 40 questions, all of which had to be learnt by heart. The religious teaching of children started young and 'The first sett of Catechisms and prayers: or, the religion of little children under seven or eight years of age. Collected out of the larger books of Prayers and Catechisms for childhood and youth'[19] almost certainly equates with Mary's entry, *a set of catechisms & prayers for Little Child.* The children's hymn book, *Divine Songs, in easy language for the use of children*, was also on the book list.[20]

As well as her own books, Mary Bacon's reading also included bought or borrowed tracts, some of which she copied into her ledger; the majority of them had a religious content. The eighteenth century was a time when folklore still abounded. Literature of the people, age old in content and in tradition, was contained in tracts and chapbooks which were sold at fairs or by wandering peddlers. There were little books of riddles, old rhymes and folk tales; potted histories were circulated which were not necessarily about historical characters, but heroes of the imagination like Robin Hood. Emanating from oral tradition, some of these stories and songs were much older than popular print and over time had emerged in a number of different versions. A good example of one of these religious tales is that of Judas Iscariot, copied out by Mary into her ledger. It is the Oedipus version of the story in which Judas kills his father and marries his mother, a continuation of mediaeval tradition going back to at least the eleventh century and possibly as early as the second century. Translated into every Western European language, the only surviving early translation in English was by William Caxton in 1483. The story lingered on into the eighteenth century, but disappeared early in the nineteenth. *A Dictionary of Biblical Tradition in English Literature* makes reference to the *Golden Legend* in the context of this tale:

> The legendary life of Judas – from his birth and *enfance* to his eventual suicide, including the pseudo-Oedipal story of how he came to be an honoured member of Pilate's court, unwittingly murdered his father and married his mother, sought

---

19 Isaac Watts, *The first set of catechisms and prayers, or, the religion of little children under seven or eight years of age* (1734). By 1788 the book had reached its 20th edition.

20 Isaac Watts, *Divine songs, attempted in easy language for the use of children* (1715). See also Chapter Two.

out Jesus to seek pardon for his sins, and became an apostle – is recounted in the
popular late-13th cent. *Legenda Aurea* by Jacobus de Voragine (trans. in the 15th cent.
by Caxton)… The medieval Judas legend continued to circulate in England well
into the 18th cent., when it was widely distributed in five distinct versions in several
editions of chapbooks and in ballads. [21]

Mary Bacon, then, was one of the last in a long tradition of Christian worship-
pers to value and to want to keep this dramatic, and at times, lurid tale of supersti-
tion, murder, and greed. No doubt her motives were moral and sound and she took
more heed of what was taught than of the dramatic content. It certainly attracted
her interest, for it is a long tale to copy out by candlelight.

> To the Reader
> What here is writ pathetically shews
> young Judas strange and most Stupendious birth,
> Tells his parents Sorrows grief and woes,
> For that they knew his sad untimely death:
> With projects vain they Strove to anticipate
> The thing that was decreed, his certain fate.
> Inclos'd in wood amidst impetuous waves.
> Where roaring billows rapidly do run,
> Where many thousands find untimely graves,
> There was the infant left to be undone:
> A royal king by chance the child did find
> Who prov'd a father, generous and kind.
> But when at age, the king's dear son he kill'd,
> And then escaped into a land unknown
> Where by his hand his fathers blood was spill'd
> And wed his mother when the crime he'd done:
> Then turn'd disciple, but he after this,
> Betray'd his blest Redeemer with a kiss.
> He is the argument of what I write,
> Concluding with the manner of his end,
> The various griefs and passions I indite,
> Of Christ who proves his best and dearest friends:
> May no such as Judas ever interpose,
> To sell as he has Sold, the Church his Spouse.

---

21 J. D. Lyle, ed., *A Dictionary of Biblical Tradition in English Literature* (1992) 419–420.

The History of Judas Iscariot

––––––––

Chapter the first Of his Parents

The father of Judas was one Maccabeus, a worthy Merchant, being of the tribe of Issachar, who was betrothed to one Bernice, a beautiful and rich maiden living at Herapolis; after the nuptials were Solemnized after the Jewish custom, he brought his Spouse home to Joppa, his own habitation, where they lived very happily together, and she soon after conceived: but one night she dreamed, that the child she then went with, should be that perfidious wretch, who according to the several prophecies of the prophets, should betray the blessed Lord and Saviour of the world. This frightful dream so disturbed her, that she was very restless, and awaked her husband in great agony: and he being much troubled thereat asked her the reason of that perturbation of mind which he found her in. she weeping bitterly, replied, that in a dream it was revealed to her, that the child now in her womb, should bring upon their happy state a great deal of trouble, in that he should be the person who was to fulfil the predictions of the prophets by betraying the Lord of Life and Glory, for which treacherous deed, a most heavy judgement would fall on him. at this narration the father was much troubled, and after long consultation, in so great an exegency, they concluded to destroy the child as soon as it was born, to prevent so great a calamity falling upon them.

Chapter the 2 The Birth of Judas

Now when Bernice's full time was come that she should be delivered, she brought forth a Son; which was two years before the birth of our Saviour, and according to Bircklet's computation, in the year of the world 1769, the child was very beautiful, and of a lively aspect, and by its comely features, so won the parents hearts, that they in great measure, repented of their tragical purpose, however, to avert the heavy judgement that hung over their heads, in case it should live to grow up, and [betray] the Saviour of the world, as it was ominously presaged to his mother they resolved to adhere to their first tho' inhuman resolution: whereupon a box was provided for that purpose, and as they were putting it in, its innocent smiles drew tears from them both, who, after kissing it, nailed up the box, and by a faithful Servant, whom they could trust, had it conveyed to a river and thrown in. now to conceal the intended murder, the parents after circumcision, pretended they had sent it to nurse afar off, and about a month or two after, gave out that it was dead, and seemingly shewed great grief for the loss of the infant, which so blinded the eyes of their friends and relations, that no further enquiry was made about it; for they being married and in a flourishing situation in life, able to maintain children without other circumstances they could not suppose otherwise than as they had reported.

However the eternal decree of the most High cannot be frustrated, their intent to destroy the infant could not avert the purpose, tho' the parents of Judas thought he had been drowned, yet it happened otherwise, for one Valerius, a Roman counsellor, and King of the Island of Iscariot, having built a large and Spacious house, on a mountain near to the banks of the river into which Judas had been put, spied the chest floating upon the water, and supposing some ship had been cast away, he sent out a boat to take it up, no sooner was it brought to him and opened, but to his great surprise, he found an infant wrapped in soft linnen the chest being lined with oil-cloth, and on his breast was written, Judas is my name, to which the King added Iscariot, the name of the Island whereon he was saved; but whence he came, or to whom he belonged, not the least mention was made of it: however a nurse was provided, and strict charge given to be very tender of him. In due time the child grew strong and healthy and being of a beautiful countenance, rejoiced the King's heart so much, that at five years of age he took him home, provided the best instructors for him and treated him in every respect as if he had been his own son, and indeed his winning behaviour and pleasing countenance, gained him the respect and esteem of all who knew him.

Chapter the 3

The Education and preferment of Judas, and how unfortunately he killed the King's son.

Judas being put to School, his inclination to learning induced the prince to spare no cost in his education, he was well skilled in different languages, as well as philosophy and mathematics: and having finished his juvenile studies, the King made him a companion for his son, and as soon as he arrived at years of discretion, made him one of his counsel, and at length he became his chief favourite; he advanced him to the greatest places of honour and profit, in which he became vastly rich, and by his obliging conversation and genteel deportment, gained him the hearts of all: and having great influence over valerius he gained much honor with the people, by soliciting him in the affairs in which he was always successful.

Though Judas was now about twenty years of age, he knew nothing of his own origin, or where he was born, nor how valerius came to be his foster father, yet he was very dutiful to him, and behaved with the greatest respect, which won the King's affections, it happened that the King's son and he was going to some pastime out of the town, they had a dispute, and words arising they drew their swords, and pushing furiously at each other, the King's son was slain, and their left weltring in his gore and Judas making his escape on board a ship arrived at Joppa where his own parents lived.

Chapter the 4

How Judas was intreated to serve a Gentleman and how unfortunately he killed his own Father

Judas lived lived not long without any Service for being tall and handsome, he was persuaded by a great man there to be his servant, where he stayed not long before he committed another most henious crime which was in this manner:

The gentleman's lady had been walking for the benefit of the air, near to her own habitation and seeing a lofty building very pleasantly situated near a cool spring, with gardens, curious orchards, and abundance of fruit trees, loaded with the finest fruit she had ever seen; and being desirous of some, she called Judas, and gave him money to buy her some; he accordingly went to the place, but resolved to steal some of them, and keep the money for himself, so getting over the wall, he was espied by the gentleman who was his own father, who went to secure him, on which they fell to blows, and Judas getting the old man under him, stabbed him, to the heart, and left him bleeding on the Ground. he had no sooner committed this inhuman murder but he fled from his habitation, and wandered about like a vagabond upon the face of the earth, for he knew not wither to go.

Chapter the 5
Judas returning in a years time to Joppa went and courted his own Mother and married her, and how she knew him to be her son, by the mark she had perceived at his birth

About a years time after, Judas returned to Joppa and finding he was not known in that town, settled himself to business and gained the love and esteem of most people, and was of very great esteem, having given himself another name. His father whom he had slain, had been dead above a year, when he went and courted his widow, who was his mother, who gave him encouragement, and a little time after gave her consent to be his lawful bride: the marriage rites being over they lived together in love and great plenty, untill one morning he arising out of bed and putting on a clean shirt, she, to her great surprise, beheld the fatal cross and gibbet, for by those marks she knew he must needs be her own child, that was sent adrift in the little chest: where upon she examined from whence he came who were his parents, and what was his name; for said she when I behold that cross and gibbet, it puts me in mind that you are my child, truly my dear I cannot tell who are my parents, or from whence I came; be who they will, they were most unkind, for I was tossed into the sea, and was taken up by a King on the coast of Iscariot, Judas was I named by my unkind parents, to which the King added that of Iscariot; I was greatly beloved by him, and was made chief minister of state, but I unfortunately killed the King's son, from whence I came to this town, where I was not long before I killed your husband, and some time after I married you, this is all the account I can give. She upon these very words was confirmed of her suspicion, and immediately burst out into tears, and from that time she made a resolution never to cohabit with him again, and exhorted him to lead a new life, which to all appearence he did. His mother knowing within herself what fatal ills would befall him, did not acquaint him with his fatal doom in betraying the Son of God, they lived together till our blessed Saviour appeaed upon the earth.

Chapter the 6
Judas being made an Apostle, betrayed his Lord and Master Jesus Christ, and

afterwards hanged himself

After this, Judas hearing the fame of our blessed Saviour Jesus Christ, and having a remourse of conscience for what he had done in his life time, but particularly for the murder of his father, he by his mother's persuasion, of desiring him to take up and amend, followed our Saviour, and in process of time became one of his apostles; so it happened that Jesus came that way, and Judas seeing many of his miracles, and hearing what he had preached, mightily admired his doctrine, and was so zealous a professor, that our Saviour admired him, although our blessed Lord knew before, that he was to betray and sell his life, yet he admitted him a disciple, and when he had chosen twelve, to be as it were the foundation of the church in future ages, he honoured them with the title of the Apostles, as being sent to preach in his name, and spread his gospel through the world. Among the twelve was Judas Iscariot elected, who above all the rest coveted to carry the bag, or purse for the lucre of pinching the money. Soon after our Saviour made his choice, he led them up to a mountain, being followed by a great multitude of people, and there made the famous discourse called the Sermon on the mount, Matthew the fifth chapter and the 6 and 7 verses. Our Saviour having finished his many miraculous, and great wonders, for confirming his Apostles, disciples and followers in the faith, and the time for the redemption of lost sinners drawing near, he commanded his disciples to prepare for the passover, to which feast it was but two days, and furthermore declared the great desire he had to celebrate it with them before he instituted the divine Supper

They having prepared accordingly, the Redeemer of the world sat down with them, and knowing what Judas would do, said, verily one of you shall betray me, at which words they were very sorrowful, and began every one to say unto him, Lord is it I. he said, he that dippeth his hand with me in the dish, the same shall betray me, the son of man goeth as it is written of him, but woe unto the man by whom the son of man is betrayed, it had been better for that man had he never been born. Then Judas said master, is it I. Jesus said unto him thou hast said, and when Judas had received the sop, the Devil entered into him, and he left the company and went to the chief priest, with whom he bargained for thirty pieces of Silver to betray his Lord and Master, saying he whom I shall kiss, is he whom ye shall lay hands on.

Our saviour shortly after going into the garden of Gethsemane, according to his usual custom, to pray: after he had done, being exceedingly afflicted with grief, he cometh to his disciples and found them asleep, and said unto Peter, what could you not watch with me one hour. watch and pray lest ye enter into temptation; the spirit indeed is willing but the flesh is weak. then he went and prayed a Second, and a third time and prayed, saying O my father, if this cup may not pass away from me except I drink, thy will be done. Then cometh he to his disciples and said, sleep on and take your rest, behold the hour is at hand, and the Son of man is betrayed into the hands of Sinners; rise, let us be going, behold he is at hand that betrays me

He had no sooner done Speaking to them than Judas appeared at the head of a great number of people, armed with clubs and staves and approaching our Saviour, treacherously kissed him, saying, Hail master, our Lord replied, Judas betrayest thou the Son of man with a kiss and then went to meet those that came to take him; asking whom they sought with a powerful voice, that made them fall to the ground, but nevertheless, he surrendered himself into their power. And though Peter drew his sword and cut off the ear of Malchus the high-priest's servant, yet so far was our Saviour from making any resistance, that he instantly healed the wound and rebuked the Apostle. Our Saviour then being secured in the hands of the Jews, his disciples fled and left him alone, so being carried before Annas, father in law to Caiphas, who was high priest that year, there the chief priests were assembled to form his accusation, and to suborn false witnesses upon the occasion at last two false witnesses came, who swore that our Saviour said, I am able to destroy the temple of God and build it again in three days, to which our Saviour made no defence, but being asked, art thou the Son of the blessed, he answered and said, I am: and ye shall see the Son of man Sitting on the right hand of power, and coming in the clouds of heaven. Then the high priest having heard these words rent his cloaths, and said, what need we any further witness, ye have heard the blasphemy, what think ye, and they all condemned him guilty of death; so our Saviour being led to Pilate, arrayed in a gorgeous robe who would have released him, but the people cried out, Crucify him, and accordingly being sent to mount Calvary, he was crucified.

This Judas was surnamed Iscariot from a little town on the Island of Judea, where he was found, and also from being cast upon the coast, when he was thrown into the sea to be drowned, or else so called by the Evangelist to be distinguish him from Judas Lebbeus who is the same as Thaddeus one of the twelve apostles. But after the dismal tiding of Christ's death and passion came to Judas Iscariot's ears, he went and Slung down the thirty pieces of silver he had of the Jews and went and hanged himself, likewise before he was cut down from the tree, his bowels burst out of his belly.

Thus wickedly lived and died the impious Judas, who having sinned above aggravation and commited one villany in betraying the Lord of Life, which cannot be expiated, and charged as you may see by authentic historians, with the murder of his reputed brother, parricide with his father, and incest with his own mother; and Judas, who was born in the reign of Augustus, hanged himself; that he perished in the fifth year of Caligula, we shall not raise a doubt, although Asenius discoursing the point produces the testimony of thophylaci and Buthyonicao that he died not by the gallows, but under a cart wheel; Barjonium also declares, that this was the opinion of the Greeks, and derived as high as Papis one of the disciples of Saint. John: altho' how hard is the expression of Saint. Mathew, reconcilable to that of Saint. Peter, that he plainly hanged himself, with that, falling head long, he burst asunder in the middle; with many others as the learned Grotius plainly doth acknowledge; however there are criticisms, we cannot be bound to adhere to human testimonies, but

belive the fate of Judas to be according as Scripture delivers to us. There are those
that are so very particular that they acquaint us with the manner, and that it was
done with a cord, Antiochus Laurensis, that it was done in a fig-tree, at Bada. some
acquaint us with the time it was done, viz the day after he had given the kiss so Saint
Chrysostom says in his first homily but there are others that tell us that hanging did
not kill him, but that either the rope broke, or he was cut down, and afterwards cast
himself headlong as it is related in the Acts.[22]

Other versions vary slightly but the basic story is the same. In one edition, printed
in London by John Hambleton in 1784,[23] Judas's mother consults a magician, who
brings in a character named Rot to help him. Through the magician's connivance,
she tells her husband that the child is dead.

> She accordingly put this scheme into practice at night, when her husband did all
> he could to comfort her, telling her that as they were young, they might be parents
> of many children; and going upstairs to see the child (the maid then pinched its
> neck until it was black in the face) and thinking it was a convulsions, gave it over
> for death.

The *Legenda Aurea* (*The Golden Legend*) version makes Judas so bad that he must
be consigned to the air. 'Moreover, Judas perished in the air, so that the one who
had offended the angels in heaven and men on earth was kept out of the regions
belonging to angels and to men, and was left in the air in the company of demons.'
A tract printed by H. Galbraith and sold at his printing house in the West Bow,
1776, shows a few variations, which is what is to be expected from such an ancient
tale.[24] Judas is put to sea in a boat 'with a cabin in it and all manner of conveniency
as conveniently could be made in it…' Rather than partake of a gory fight with the
prince's son, Judas kills him by pushing him down a well. In this version, Judas does
not stab his father in the heart, but throws a stone at him and knocks his brains out.
Judas' end is graphically described,

> It is known when a malefactor commits high treason against the king, that the
> executioner rips open his belly, and takes out his heart, and holds it in his hand in
> view of all the spectators, crying out, Behold the heart of a traitor. And for Judas,
> who was a traitor to the King of kings, it was no wonder that the ream of his belly
> did burst asunder, that all that passed by might behold his treacherous heart.

To someone living in the eighteenth century there was little shocking in this kind
of description. People were used to watching executions and to reading about the
last words and actions of criminals in the newspapers.

22 British Library catalogue 1078.i.27 printed Durham 1750?
23 BL 1078.k.21
24 BL RB.23.a.834

Following the story of Judas Iscariot, in the version which Mary copied out, there is in the same tract a tale of Pontius Pilate, which she also carefully wrote into her ledger.

The Life and Death of Pontius Pilate
Who Condemned the Lord of Life to Death

Pontius Pilate came of worthy parents in the city of Rome, where he was born and educated, and being preferred in the army, for his signal services, abroad, in defence and honour of the Roman Empire, he succeeded Valerious Grotious in the precidentship of Judea, where he resided governor for eight years, and then in the eighth year of his government, Christ was delivered up to him by the Jewish rabble but he knowing that for envy they did accuse him he seemed the more willing to release Christ, by asking them, would ye that I release you unto Barrabas or Jesus, who is called Christ, for it was the custom of the governor to release at the feast a prisoner, whome they would; moreover, when he sat down to the judgement seat, his wife sent unto him saying, Have thou nothing to do with just man, for I have suffered many things this night in a dream because of him. Which message made Pilate some what fearfull and cautious, and willing to release Christ yet were the multitude more vehement for his crucifixion: saying to Pilate if thou let this man go thou art not Caesars friend whoso maketh himself a king speaketh against Caesar. at this threatening he delivered him up to be crucified, and as he could prevail nothing, but rather a tumult was made, he took water and washed his hands before the multitude, saying. I am innocent of the blood of this just person, see ye to it likewise Pilate wrote the title, which was put upon his cross, in Hebrew, Greek and Lattin, which writing was Jesus of Nazareth king of the Jews

Two years after the death of our Saviour, for killing the innocent Samaritans he was removed from his own office, by Vitellis, president of Syria, and another being instituted in his place, was carried prisoner to Rome, to purge himself before the judgement seat of Caesar, of the accusations laid against him by the Samaritans, but before he arrived at Rome, Tiberius was dead, and Caiuis was constituted in his place. it is likewise to be noted that when Tiberius was alive, he governed under the Romans of the miracles of Christ, of his fame and of his life and doings, Pilates letter was shewn to the senators in the time of Caligula Herod the Tetarch coming from jury to Rome, he was banished by that Emperor from Rome to Lugdinum, a town in france, and falling into disgrace, he was reduced to such miseries and calamities, that he was very wretched in this world and never satisfied in his conscience, which so terrified him, that he often attempted to lay violent hands on himself, but was prevented, Neverthless the wrath of God pursued his troubled soul; Pontious Pilate wandered to seina, in Italy, and being no longer able to Survive the tortures of his insupportable aflictions, he there drowned himself in a lake which still bears his name, and where he every year appears on the banks, in the judical habit, wherein he judged our Saviour, but whosoever man or woman happens to see this apparition, he or she within that year surely dies; besides of such a wonderful nature is the water of that lake, that if any person throws any thing into it, it swells so boisterously that the water overflows its bounds, and drowns a great part of the country, to the destruction of man and beast. Wherefore there is a law that forbids either man, woman or child to throw any thing in upon pain of death, furthermore it is to be noted that in less than three years after the death of Pontius Pilate, his whole generation and family, by one untimely end or other, was entirely extinct, so implacable was the wrath of God, that he extripated the whole lineage of him and Judas, who had a hand in betraying and condemning our Saviour of the earth.

A third biblical tale copied out by Mary relates to the Old Testament and tells the story of Joseph and Jacob. It has not been possible to trace the source, but it is written in the popular style and was probably another tract bought at a fair or from a travelling peddler. At the end, Mary has written, 'Mary Bacon wrote this' and it cannot be ruled out that it was indeed her own composition. There are enough spelling mistakes and the punctuation so lacking that this may have been the case. Capital letters were commonly used at the beginning of nouns, but not usually with words such as When, Could, Go, Quickly, and some of the names in the story begin with the first letter in lower case. It is difficult to believe that even in a tract 'were' was spelt 'where' and 'here' spelt 'hear'; two, instead of to, is a mistake sometimes made by Mary. There is a similarity to some of the careless writing which is found in the recipes, but not enough definitive proof to be sure that she was the author. It is quoted here in full as there are few opportunities for most readers to view tracts or chapbooks of this nature.

Joseph and Jacob

Joseph the son of Jacob he
Did dream in his Minority
He told unto his Brethren all
His Sheaf would Stand but theirs would fall
Then Joseph Dreamed another Dream
And that was of a higher Strain
the Sun the moon and Stars to boot
Should bow their heads at Josephs foot
Then Jacob he could not forsee how
Joseph should advanced be
But Jacob kept these Dreams in mind
And Still to Joseph he was kind
He had a many Coulered Coat
by which his Brethren did Denote
That Jacob loved Joseph more

than all the Sons he had before
For which his Brethren did him hate
Not knowing what might be the fate
They Could not speak to him in Peace
Nor did their malice to him Cease
Now Joseph was to Sechem sent
At Jacobs word away he Went
He heard to Dothan they where gone
Away his Journey he goes on
To see his Breathren there he goes
Tho they to him are mortal foes
As I will make it plain appear
in the Sequal as you shall hear
When Joseph was a great way of
His breathren at him made a Scoff
Yonder the Dreamer Comes they say
Come let us take his Life away
And then his Dreams will have an End
And we to him shall never bend
But Ruben said it is not good
For us to shed our Brothers blood
What will our aged Father say
If we should take his Life away
Then Joseph in a pit was Cast
And out again was drew at Last
His cruel Brethren sold him then
Unto the Ishmaliteish men
for twenty Pieces of Silver they
Did send their Brother far away
They stript him of his Curious Coat
and Dipt it in the blood of a Goat
Which they Did to there Father shew
If he Could own the Coat or no
This is my Sons then Jacob said
Who at the Sight was much Dismayed
Saying my Son is in Pieces tore
And I shall never see him more
Jacob would not be Comforted
Supposing Joseph had been Dead
But now I must to Egypt Go
To hear if he be dead or no
No sooner I arrived their

But I this Piece of News did hear
That Joseph to Potipher was sold
I Cannot tell for how much Gold
But Let the Price be Less or more
God a Blessing had for him in store
His Master found that he was Just
With all his heart he did him trust
He had a Blessing for his sake
And then he did him Steward make
And when he was his Steward made
His Misstress as it is said
Upon Joseph Cast her eye
And said to him Come with me lye
But Joseph being full of grace
Would not be Charmed with her face
At Length his misstress grew so bold
Upon his Garment to take hold
That Joseph would no longer stay
But from his mistress run away
She kept the Garment in her sight
till potipher Came home at night
And then she forged a pack of Lyes
Which put him in a great Surprise
But When he saw the piece of Cloth
It made him with his Steward wroth
Then Joseph was to prison sent
And God Almighty with him went
Altho he was in Prison bound
He favour with the keeper found
Who made him under Jaylor then
And Gave him Charge of all the men
For in the Prison or the Hall
The keeper took no Care at all
And now I must to Pharohs Court
To hear what there be done of note
No sooner I arrived there
But I this Piece of news did hear
The Chief Butler & Chief Baker they
Where both Commited in one Day
And each of them to prison sent
Where they Lay under Discontent
These men had Each of them a dream

And Joseph Quickly drew the same
He could unto the Butler tell
Never fear with thee all will Go well
Thy Master he will thee restore
Unto the Place thou hadst before
Thou shalt before King Pharoh stand
And Give the Cup into his hand
And when thou art from Prison free
I pray thee then remember me
the Baker hearing that was Glad
Tho he had reason to be sad
For Joseph said I tell to thee
Thou Shalt be hanged on a tree
As Joseph said it Proved true
the Baker was hanged up in View
The Butler Joseph soon forgot
For that he was a silly sot
But Gods time is the best we know
When Joseph must from Prison go
King Pharoh first must have a dream
Magisions where to Draw the same
They nothing knew of Pharoh kind
For Magick art is not Divine
The butler then Could call to Mind
To Joseph he had been unkind
He Could unto King Pharoh tell
I know a person very well
That in the Prison now doth Lye
That soon the King Can satisfy
Joseph was sent for to the Court
He Shaved his face and Changed his Coat
And when before the King he came
He soon Did prove a man of fame
The King no sooner told his Dream
But Joseph Quickly drew the same
The seven kine so fat and Lean
He told king what they did mean
The seven Kine so fat and fair
That seven years of plenty Where
The seven kine so Lean and poor
It did foretell a Famine sore
Then Joseph did to pharoh show

What it was best for him to do
Let pharoh Chuse a person Just
That will be faithfull to his trust
To lay up Corn one part in five
And that will thousands keep alive
The King replied no one so fit
As thee a man of grace and wit
I Chuse no other man but thee
Therefore thou shalt be next to me
Only I will Except the Crown
But thou shall be of great renown
In my Second Chariot thou shall ride
my Servants waiting by thy side
Now Joseph is advanced high
And you have heard the reason why
leave him now to hoard up store
Till he Could number it no more
then Jacob called his sons ten
But would not part with Little Ben
He said in Egypt there is Corn
But little thought to him was born
A son that did Lay up in store
till he Could number it no more
He gave them money there to pay
for what they bought and brought away
Now when they into Egypt Came
They saw a man of mighty fame
but who it was they did not know
Not thinking then of their brother Jo
Joseph knew them they knew not him
Altho their eyes they where not Dim
He Spake unto them very Rough
They wondred he should be so Grough
To Charge them all with being Spies
Which put them in a great Surprise
They said my Lord we are not Spies
We Came not hear to tell thee Lies
We came not of our own accord
Our Father sent us hear my Lord
Have you a father then said Jo
When I the truth of that will know
Or any Brethren more than ten

One more my Lord his name is Ben
We once another Brother had
Who went away when but a Lad
That they need not to Joseph tell
For they where the men that did him sell
then Joseph put them all in ward
They thought that measure very hard
their Consciences did them accuse
How they their Brother did abuse
Three Days they all in Prison Lay
then Joseph unto them did say
I take my tythe one out of ten
And nine shall go to bring me Ben
And if you do not bring him Down
Do not pretend to Come to town
By the life of Pharoh I have swore
that you shall see my face no more
Except you bring your Brother ben
it is in vain to Come again
Simeon was bound before their Eyes
To make them prove they were not spies
Then Joseph did to his Steward say
Go fill their Sacks send them away
Return them all their money back
Convey it into each man sack
They knew not who put it their
Which put them in a panick fear
When they did to Canan Come
They told old Jacob what was Done
that they had brought their mony back
They found it put in Each mans sack
Now they had Corn two save their Lives
For them their Children and their Wives
But at Last their Stock grew Low
They must again to Egypt go
Then Jacob unto them Did Cry
We must have food or else we Die
Take Double money in your hand
And then you may with Courage stand
Perhaps it was some over sight
Which that you soon may put two right
And take a present down with you

Some balm and nuts and Honny to
And God Almighty with you be
That I again may Simeon see
Then Juda to his Father said
to Go again we are afraid
Except we take our Brother Ben
it is in vain to go again
Then Jacob said you did not well
The Lord of Egypt for to tell
That you another Brother had
What made you deal with me so bad
They said the man did ask us then
If we were any more than ten
Thou wouldest not have us tell him Lies
Who took us all before for Spies
Then Juda was to Jacob bound
To bring ben back both safe and sound
At Last old Jacob gave Consent
And then they all together went
And when they into Egypt Came
They did Consult what must be Done
The presents then they did prepare
And that with Diligence and Care
Whence Josephs House they did Come near
Before their Lord for to appear
Like men of Breeding you must know
They Bowed before him very Low
Joseph received the presents then
The finest was his Brother Ben
He saith how doth your Father Do
Is he alive as well as you
They said thy Servant he is well
And that we Can with Comfort tell
And is your younger Brother Come
God Gracious be to thee my son
Then Joseph did to his Steward say
Prepare a feast for me to Day
And see you get it ready soon
These men shall Dine with me at noon
The Steward did as Joseph said
When on the table it was Laid
He set them down in order then

From Ruben unto Little Ben
they wondred how he did to know
the Elder from the younger so
He messes sent to all the ten
But Gave the bigest unto Ben
They eat and drank and had their fill
And Joseph kept the secret still
then Joseph did to his steward say
Go fill their sacks send them away
Return them all their money right
And send them of by morning Light
The Silver Cup which I drink in
Put in the sack of Benjamin
The Steward did as Joseph said
And the men was not at all afraid
But mark after did befall
When Joseph did his steward Call
And said to him persue these men
And make them all come back again
Tell them that they ungratefull be
to Steal from such a man as me
To take my Silver Cup so fine
In which I Drank and do Divine
The Steward did them overtake
Which made them to both fear and Quake
And told them what his master said
Then the men was sore afraid
saying God forbid that we should Act
Or Guilty be of such a fact
They all with one Consent did Cry
The Man that stole the Cup shall Dye
The Steward said so let it be
To what you say now Let me see
He made them all their sacks unload
And set them Down upon the Road
At Rubens Sack he did begin
And Searched down to Benjamin
And when Bens sack he did untie
His Masters Cup he there did Spy
They rent their Cloaths and were in amaze
And did upon each other Gaze
Saying God has found us out this Day

What shall we Do what must we say
Their Asses they Did Load Again
the innofencive theif was Ben
When Joseph's house they did Come near
Before their Lord for to appear
With faces then as pale as Death
They bowed themselves down to the earth
Then Joseph said what have you Done
What steal and then away you run
To take my silver Cup so fine
In which I Drank and do Divine
[The next three lines are erased]
Then Ruben said my Lord I see
That we thy Bondsmen now must be
Our Asses and we all must be
My Lord in bondage unto thee
But Joseph said unto them nay
I shall not do as you do say
For on the man the Cup was found
He only with me shall be bound
But you may Load and go with Speed
Your Father and your friends to feed
Then Juda said my Lord I pray
Hear what thy servant has to say
If Benjamin in Egypt stay
Our Father's Head which now is Grey
With Sorrow will be Laid in Grave
I am sure his Life we Cannot save
Then Joseph hearing him say so
He said unto his Servants Go
Avoid the room a Little while
And I will make you all to smile
I have a Secret for to tell
I am sure twill please these Hebrews well
Then Joseph to his Brethren said
Come near to me be not afraid
I am Joseph whome you sold
I want not your Silver nor your Gold
It was not you that sent me here
It was my God whome I do fear
He sent me hear you to preserve
That you might not by famine starve

For five more years there are to Come
No work in Harvist Can be Done
They trembled at his presence More
than all the times they had Done before
He Changes of Raiment gave to ten
But gave the finest unto Ben
Three hundred silver pieces bright
He gave his Brother ben at sight
When Pharohs servants heard the thing
They Presently did tell the King
Which he was pleased for to hear
That Josephs Brethren were so near
There was Plenty of Provisions Sent
And Wagons unto Canan went
And when they Did to Canan come
they told old Jacob what was Done
That Joseph he was then a Live
And that he did in Egypt thrive
the men did Jacob so surprise
He fainted down before their eyes
But when the Wagons Came in view
Then Jacob thought the news was true
Then Jacob's Spirits did Revive
and said if Joseph is yet alive
I will go and see him Ere I Die
But first unto my God I will Cry
So Jacob went and Little Ben
With all the rest threescore ten
I dare not make a Longer detail
For fear my memory should me fail
If more of Jacob you would know
You may unto your Bible go
Where you may have the History at Large
And you may Read it at a Little Charge
Mary Bacon wrote this

October 4: 1788 If I should have any Grand Children Let them Learn this

Mary Bacon was not without humour and copied a further tale into her ledger. Although *A Story Concerning a Pack of Cards* has a religious base, it is nevertheless a light and amusing story. It was circulating in tracts and had probably been around in popular religious literature for some time. Mary's version of the story is dated 20 April 1762 but its popularity clearly continued after that date as it is included in

a tract of other amusing tales or anecdotes, dated *c.*1780. Bill Peterson, an aquaint-
ance of mine, remembers meeting a naval chaplain at HMS *Blenheim* in Alexandria
during the second world war. He is certain that it was he who referred to the soldier
and the pack of cards in one of the 'evangelical' visits he made to the 'lower deck' of
various ships. It seems as though this story carried on at least until the 1940s.

As well as 'A very ingenious Article, called, The CARDS SPIRITUALIZED
and shewn to answer the various Purposes of BIBLE, PRAYER-BOOK, AND
ALMANACK,' the tract includes 'The Witty Exploits of George Buchanan,
commonly called the Kings Fool And also, A very curious SERMON ON THE
WORD MALT'.[25] There are two versions of the soldier's story, usually indicating a
popular circulation. The earlier version, as written down by Mary Bacon, is livelier
and sounds like an oral relation, while the later version is literate; it has become a
text. On the whole, Mary's spelling and grammar are more or less accurate in her
other narrative pieces, which she copied out. Here, however, there is a distinct ring
of the vernacular and it reads more like a story remembered from an oral or written
source, than one which has been copied. Mary also used the shortened version of
'and' – '&' – in her weather reports and sometimes in the recipes, but never in the
long pieces which she copied, a further indication that this was material from out
of her head.[26]

A Story Concerning a Pack of Cards April the 20, 1762

There was one Richard Middleton a soldier which was at Glasgow Church in
Scotland with the rest of the Rigment and when the Parson took his text all the
Soldiers that had Bibles pulled them out to find the text, but the above middleton
had neither Bible almanack nor Common Prayer Book, but he pulled out a pack
of Cards spread them before him in the Desk as he sat and while the Parson was
Preaching he looked one Card & then at another the sergant of the Company saw
him and said Richard put up your Cards which he refused then the sergant of the
City saw him and said soldier put up your cards which he Likewise refused so after
Churching was over the City sargant had Richard before the mayor, saying I have
brought a soldier before your Honour for playing at cards in the Church, well soldier if you can clear your self well and good if not you shall be Punished the worst
that ever a Man was, I hope your Honour will give me Leave to speak for my self,

25 BL 1078.k.21. There is no date, but its position in the document, which contains a number of tracts
    would indicate *c.* 1780.
26 The entry in Wikipidia for the *The Deck of Cards* has not taken earlier versions of this story into
    account, dating it to the late 1940s in America and stating that it was popularized in both country
    and popular music (www.wikipedia.org, consulted August 2010). It does, however, refer to the fact
    that 'the story is based in part on an excerpt from a piece of 19th century British literature called
    The Soldier's Almanack, Bible And Prayer Book.' It is clear from the dating of Mary's version that the
    tale was in circulation as early as the middle of the eighteenth century.

speak man and welcome and Please your honour I have been 8 days upon the march I have but 6 pence a day allowed me, which will scarsely maintain me in Eating and drinking washing and Lodging & necessaries that a man may want and with Bible Almanack Common prayer book or any thing thats good but a pack of Cards, any thing that's good out of a pack of Cards I never knew the like in all my life said the mayor there the Soldier pulled out a pack of Cards & spread them before the mayor, and began with the ace, when I see the ace it puts me in mind there is one God, & when I see the duce it puts me in mind of father & son & when I see ye 3 it puts me in mind of father son & holy ghost and when I see the 4 it puts me in mind of the 4 evangelists, that read the Gospel, Mathew mark Luke & John, and when I see this 5 it puts me in mind of the 5 wise virgins that trimed their Lamps, there was but 10 but their was 5 foolish that was shut out, and this 6 puts me in mind, that in 6 days the Lord made heaven & earth, & this 7 puts me in mind that on the 7 day, God rested from all his works which he had Created & made, Wherefore the Lord, blessed the 7 day & hallowed it & this puts me in mind of the 8 Righteous persons that God saved when he drowned the world noah his wife his 3 sons and there wives and when I see this 9 it puts me in mind of the 9 Lepors that was Cleansed by our Saviour, there was 10 cleansed but there was 9 went away that never returned God thanks & when I see this tenth Card it puts me in mind of the 10 Commandments that was gave to Moses, on the mount of olives on the two tables of ston and he took the knave and Laid him aside & past to the Queen, and when I see the Queen it puts me in mind of the wise queen of Sheba that came from the farthermost parts of the world to hear the wisdom of wise king Solomon, for she was as wise a woman as he was a man, for she brought 50 Boys and 50 Girls all cloathed in Boys apparel to show them before the king for him to tell which was boys and which was Girls & he could not untill she Called for water to wash them and the Girls washed up to there elbow & the boys round the wrist of there hands, and king Solomon told by that when I see this King it puts me in mind of the great King of heaven and earth & of his Majesty King George the third, well said the mayor you have given a good description of all the Cards but one, I can give your honour as good description of that Card as any in the pack if your honour want be angry with me Well said the mayor, if you firm(?) me the knave, well says the soldier, the greatest knave is the sergeant of the city that brought me before your honour I don't know says the mayor whether he is the greatest knave or no but I am sure he is the greatest fool than said the Soldier when I count how many dots there is in a Pack of Cards there is 365 so many days in a year, and when I count how many Cards there is in a pack there is 52 so many weeks in a year and when I count how many tricks there is in a pack of Cards there is thirteen so many months in a year, and this pack of Cards is both Bible and Almanack Common Prayer book and a pack of Cards for me the mayor called for his Servants and ordered them to entertain the Soldier well and give him a piece of money and said he was the finest fellow as ever he heard in his Life. Finis

And so to the end of life and the good Christian must think of what lies beyond. One of the most important messages in Mary's books is the need to prepare for the afterlife. Mortality was a subject much written about in this period, both in prose and poetry, in notably the 'graveyard' genre, best known from the works of Edward Young whose most celebrated poem, *The Complaint, or Night Thoughts on Life, Death and Immortality* was published in 1742–5. It was a didactic and meditative poem in blank verse and went into nine books. Mary's *thoughts on death* was therefore in keeping with the reading of her time, but it is difficult to make a clear identification. It is possible that she was referring to *Thoughts on Mortality occasioned by the death of* … , (1789) published anonymously, but actually by the Revd William Davidson.

One of the best known works of the eighteenth century, concerned with the idea of meditating on death while in a churchyard, is Hervey's *Meditations*; it was also included in Mary's list. An edition of 1793 written in the style and manner of Hervey's *Meditations*, has an introduction by George Wright:

> Though the language of Hervey's meditations may be accounted by some too florid for common conversation, and abounding with redundant epithets, still it must be generally acknowledged to be pleasing in the reading, and has evidently been acceptable to thousands, from their extensive sale; the subject matter of them is truly interesting and important, and well deserves the serious attention and regard of all.[27]

One of the sections in this particular volume is entitled, 'A Soliloquy written among the Tombs'. It starts with:

> The beauties of nature may please the eye, and justly attract our admiration; flowers may regale our smell, fruits may court our taste, music may please our ears, and all our senses may be alive to the various scenes presented to our view; but the *soul*, the rational and immortal soul of man, cannot be satisfied with any thing short of spiritual enjoyments and celestial pleasures, suitable to its nature, and eternal, as its existence.'

The passage goes on to reflect that the writer will shortly die and appear before God in judgement, exhorting the reader to be ready. 'Oh! then let it be my solicitous concern, as well as my earnest prayer, to believe in Jesus Christ, who is the *resurrection* and the *life*; in whosoever liveth and believeth in him shall not die *eternally*.' Constant warnings abound such as 'Death justly may be stiled the king of terrors to that man, who has spent his life pursing the hours of the solemn and momentous concerns of his dying soul.'

Hervey's *Meditations* are calm, thoughtful and gentle compared with some of

---

27 George Wright, *Pleasing Melancholy, or a walk among the tombs in a country churchyard in the style and manner of Harvey's Meditations* (1793) 204–5.

the works included in Mary's list. Sometimes the warnings are severe and the consequences of sin are dire, terrifying and everlasting. One such book is *Divine Meditations*, which contains 'Description of the Four Last things viz Death, Hell, & Judgement, Heaven' and is written in blank verse. The author affirmed categorically that every man, as soon as he is born, is entered upon a State of Everlastingness. 'The native Nobleness of the Soul, whose Capacities are too large for any Thing in this World to satisfy, can only be Happy in the Supreme Good.' He warned that 'Nothing but an effectual Change by Divine Grace, and an Interest in the redeemer, can fortify the Soul against the Terrors of Death and prepare it for Eternity.' Then comes the dreadful warning, 'Every man receives his final Doom, immediately after Death, and is fix's in an unchangeable State for ever.[28] The picture of Hell, declaimed in blank verse is grim indeed:

> ...Those furious Fiends
> That with Heav'ns State, all heav'nly Graces left,
> Revengeful seize her strait, and down she's hurl'd
> To their infernal, fiery, dark Abode
> Plung'd in eternal Flames! Too late awake,
> Struck with the sudden dreadful Change, her vast
> And everlasting Thoughts around she throws
> And drinks immortal Woe, and pines, and Shrieks,
> Wrapt in strong Chains of fire, Despair and Death.[29]

Yet another book on the Bacon shelf warns of terrible torments. The opening chapter of *The Whole Duty of Man (with Private Devotions for several Occasions)* is a treatise on 'The Necessity of caring for the Soul' in which the author, Richard Allestree, warned against the terrors of eternal damnation and the importance of looking after the soul.[30]

Hymns, meditations, Bible tales and a quirky story all formed a part of Mary Bacon's religious life. I like to think that when this remarkable farmer's wife lay dying, she was sufficiently at peace with herself to believe not in the terrors of eternal damnation, but in the words of the beautiful meditation on the soul which she copied out into her ledger. It is very carefully copied and does not have some of the spelling and punctuation errors evident in some of her entries. It comes from *The Oeconomy of Human Life. Translated from an Indian manuscript written by an Ancient BRAMIN*, a very popular work in two parts which went into a number of editions.

28 Anonymous, William Bond, *Divine Meditations. Description of the Four Last Things viz Death, Hell & Judgement, Heaven in blank Verse* (1719) 5–6.

29 Bond, *Divine Meditations*, 103.

30 Allestree, Richard, *The Whole Duty of Man* (1698).

The first part is by Robert Dodsley, but according to the British Library catalogue, the second part is attributed to John Hill. The extract which Mary copied into her book is by John Hill. For me, it is her epitaph.

The Soul of Man, its origin and Affections.

The blessings, O man of thy external parts, are health,
vigour, and proportion, The greatest of these is health.
What health is to the body, even that is honesty to the soul.
That thou hast a soul is of all knowledge the most certain
of all truths, the most plain unto thee. Be meek, be grateful
for it. Seek not to know it perfectly, it is inscrutable.

Thinking, understanding, reasoning, willing; call not these the
Soul. They are its actions but they are not its essence.
Raise it not to high, that thou be not dispised. Be thou not
like unto those who fall by climbing; neither debase it to
the sense of brutes; nor be thou like unto the horse and the mule,
in whom there is no understanding.

Search it by its faculties, know it by its virtues, They
are more in number than the hairs of thy head, the stars
of heaven are not to be counted with them.

Think not with Arabia, that one Soul is parted among
all men; neither belive thou with the sons of Egypt,
that every man hath many: know that as thy heart,
so also thy soul is one.

Doth not the sun harden the clay, doth it not also soften
the wax, as it is one sun that worketh both, even so is it
one Soul that willeth contrarities.

As the moon retaineth her nature, though darkness spread
itself before her face as a curtain, so the soul remaineth
perfect, even in the bosom of the fool.
She is immortal; she is unchangeable; she is alike in all, Health
calleth her forth to shew her loveliness, and application
anointeth her with the oil of wisdom.

Although she shall live after thee, think not she was born
before thee. She was created with the flesh and formed with
thy brain.

Justice could not give her to thee exalted by virtues. nor
mercy deliver her to the deformed by vices. These must be
thine and thou must answer them.

Suppose not death can shield from examination
think not corruption can hide thee from enquiry He who
formed thee of thou knowest not what, can he not raise
thee from thou knowest not what again
Perceiveth not the cock the hour of midnight, exhalteth he
not his voice to tell thee it is morning; knoweth not the
dog the footsteps of his master, and flieth not the wounded
goat unto the herb that healeth him: yet when these die
their spirit returneth to the dust; thine alone Surviveth.
Envy not these of their Sences because quicker than thine own
Learn that the advantage lieth not in professing good things,
but in knowing to use them.
Hadst thou the ear of the stag, or were thine eyes as strong
and piercing as the eagles: dist thou eaqual the hound in
smell, or could the ape resign thee his taste, or the tortise
her feeling; yet without reason, what would they
avail thee; Perish not all these like thy kindred.

Hath any one of them the gift of speech; can any say unto
thee, Therefore did I so.

The lips of the wise are as the doors of a cabinet; no sooner
are they opened, but treasures are poured out before thee.
Like unto trees of gold, arranged in beds of silver, are
wise sentences uttered in due season.
Canst thou think to greatly of thy soul, or can too
much be said in its praise; it is the image of him who gave it.

Remember thou its dignity for ever; forget not how great
a tallent is commited to thy charge.
Whatsoever may do good may also do harm.
Beware that thou direct its course to virtue.

Think not that thou canst lose her in the crowd; suppose
not that thou canst bury her in thy closet; Action is her
delight, and will not be withheld from it.

Her motion is perpetual; her attempts are universal; her
agility is not to be suppressed, is it at the uttermost
part of the earth, she will have it: is it beyond the
region of the stars, yet her eyes discover it.

Inquiry is her delight as one who traverseth the burning
sands in search of water, so is the soul that thirsteth
after knowledge.

Guard her for she is rash, restrain her for she is irregular;
correct her, for she is outrageous: more simple is she than
water, more flexible than wax, more yielding than air.
Is there ought that can bind her,
As a sword in the hand of a madman, even so is the
Soul to him who wanteth discretion.

The end of her search is truth; her means to discover it
are reason and experience. But are not these weak,
uncertain, and fallacious, how then shall she attain unto it.
General opinion is no proof of truth; for the generality
of men are ignorant.

Perception of thyself the knowledge of him who created
thee, the sense of thy worship thou owest unto him,
are not these plain before your face; and behold what is
there more that man needeth to know.[31]

---

31 John Hill, attributed to, *The Oeconomy of Human Life*, Part 2 (1783) 75. The first edition was in 1751.

Appendix One
Table of measurements

A load of timber unhewed,	40 Feet
A hogshead of Wine	63 gallons
A Hogshead of Beer	54 gallons
A Barrel of Beer	36 gallons
A Barrel of Ale	32 gallons
A Tod of wool	28 pounds
A packet of wool	240 pounds
Pole or Perch	5 yards and a half
A Furlong is	40 perches
A Mile is	8 furlongs

An Acre of Land is 40 Poles or Perches in Length, and four in Breadth

A Truss of Hay	56 pounds
a Load of ditto	39 Trusses

(note: New Hay in June and August ought to be 60 pounds to the Truss, as per Statute of 2d William and Mary 1693)[1]

from Eliza Chute's Diary, 1799 [2]
Dry Measure

2 gallons = 1 peck
4 pecks = 1 bushel
2 bushels = 1 strike
8 bushels = 1 quarter
4 quarters = 1 wey or load
Sack = 28 stone or 364 lb

1 William Gordon, *Every Young Man's Companion* (1759) 443.
2 HRO 23M93/70/9.

Appendix Two
Mary Bacon's list of books

MARY BACON ENTERED all the books she owned in a long list covering a page and a half of her ledger. As she only wrote down titles, which were often inaccurate, but rarely the name of an author, some of her books have been impossible to trace. Her titles are given below, in italics, but with some added information taken from the main reference catalogues, to include further details of the extended title, date of publication, publisher/bookseller, etc. These catalogues do not always list the first edition, or indeed all the subsequent editions. I have included enough of the further editions in order to convey a general idea of the popularity of the book and the time-scale of its publication. The list is not alphabetical, but in the order Mary entered them herself, and with her spelling. Where a book has been difficult to trace, I have tried to find a similar work, in order to give an overall picture of her reading and the sorts of topics she was interested in. Most of the titles are included in the text of this book, which includes some details of their contents.

Accounts of my book

2 Large Bibles

my mothers Bible

an old Bible as was my fathers

Woodmancut Common prayer book
A prayer book taken from Woodmancott Parish Church.

Burkit on the new testament William Burkit.
Full title: 'Expository notes with practical observations, on the new Testament of our Lord and Saviour Jesus Christ' ... Endeavoured by William Burkitt. Editions: 1st 1700; 7th edition 1719; Birmingham, 1789.

thoughts on Death
This title is may be either 'Thoughts on Mortality occasioned by the death of ...' (1789). Anonymous by William Davidson (Rev), or one of the religious tracts circulating at the time.

the whole Duty of man Anonymous, by Richard Allestree.

Full title: 'The whole duty of man, laid down in a plain and familiar way for the use of all, … with private devotions' (1703). 31 further editions from 1705 to 1797.

another large Common prayer book

beveridge Sermons Vol 6 and Vol 9 William Beveridge, Bishop of St. Asaph.
Full title: 'A choice and select collection of sermons, taken out of the various works of William Beveridge, Wolverhampton' printed by Mary Wilson 1757.
A popular writer, his works went into a number of editions.

the imitation of Jesus Christ Thomas a Kempis.
There are a number of editions. Editions in 1790 and 1800 were subscription issues and can probably be ruled out.

2 the vol of Hervey's Meditations James Hervey.
Volume 1 'Meditations among the tombs' and 'Reflections in a flower garden'.
Volume 2 'Contemplations on the night' and 'Contemplations on the starry heavens'.
The idea of meditating on death in a churchyard was a common theme now remembered in the 'graveyard' genre of poetry. A noted example of this genre was *The Complaint, or Night Thoughts on Life, Death* and *Immortality* by Edward Young (1683–1756), a poem extremely popular both in England and Europe. Lines by Young are included in the *Meditations*. First printed in 1746.

Baily Dictionary Nathan Bailey.
'A universal etymological dictionary of the English language … to which is prefixed a grammar of the English language' by N Bayley, Edinburgh 1764. I prefer to think that Mary Bacon possessed the domestic version, 'Dictionarium Domesticum being a new and compleat household dictionary. For the use of both city and country' By N. Bailey London 1736.

4 Small Common prayer Books

the Christian monitor
'The Christian Monitor, containing an earnest exhortation to an holy life with some directions in order thereto' … London: 1701. This short book, or tract, was 'written in a plain and easie style, for all sorts of people.' It was first published in 1686 with continuing editions in 1776 and 1777. In 1800, it was included in Religious Tracts dispersed by the Society for the Promotion of Christian Knowledge, Vol. III.

The Count du Beauvil. Basnage, Jacques, Sieur de Beauval.
'(Histoire des Juifes) the History of the Jews, from Jesus Christ to the present time: containing their antiquities, their religion, their rites, the dispersion of the ten tribes in the East, and the persecution this nation has suffered in the West. Being a supplement and containing the History of Josephus.' Written in French by Mr. Basnage. Translated into English by A. M. Taylor (1708).

Private Devotion

There are two possibilities for this title, where the dates would be appropriate, and the subject matter in tune with the general tenor of the religious works in Mary's list.

1. 'Private devotions for several Occasions ordinary and extraordinary' Anon (1723). Later editions are by the author of *The Whole Duty of Man* i.e. Richard Allestree.

2. 'Private Devotions in the Church, fitted to employ some short time before divine service begins; and also on occasion of receiving the Holy Sacrament.' By a divine of the Church of England (1712).

beveridges private thoughts

'Private Thoughts' William Beveridge, Bishop of St. Asaph

Part I upon religion digested into twelve articles; with practical resolutions form'd thereupon. Part II upon a Christian life.

This was a very popular work and it ran into many editions, the 16th being printed in 1753.

the 6 vol of the Spectator

prospect of eternity

'A Prospect of Eternity; or, Man's Everlasting Condition opened and applyed.' John Wells, Minister of St. Olave Jewry, London 1655.

This identification is tentative. Unless Mary inherited it through her Kinchin family, it is unlikely that it was available for sale during the mid to late eighteenth century. It was not a popular work as there is only one edition listed. It may have been one of the many religious tracts in circulation.

every mans ready companion

There were two 'Every young man's Companion', one for mathematics and one for writing etc. They were published in several editions during the 1750s and the one on mathematics was still in print as late as 1777.

1. 'Every young man's Companion ... with a great variety of cuts and tables, accurately drawn and made for the more ready performance of the different operations taught in this treatise.' William Gordon, teacher of Mathematics. (1755).

2. 'Every young man's Companion: containing directions for spelling, reading, and writing English ... The third edition, corrected, with large additions.' William Gordon, teacher of Mathematics. (1759). Although Mary's spelling and grammar left much to be desired, and Mr. Gordon failed her in some respects, I prefer to think that the book she possessed was the second.

Divine meditation

The subject of meditation was a very common one during the eighteenth century and, with only part of the title, it is impossible to be certain as to which book or tract Mary owned. The following two examples are both possibilities and are works which someone like her could have read. As the title is listed separately, it is unlikely that it refers to Hervey's *Meditations*.

1. 'Divine meditations on the following subjects, viz. The Tombs in Westminster Abbey, The Christian's Felicity. The joys of eternity. Printed in the Spectator, in the year 1715. To which is added a meditation on the works of the creation…By the author of the Description of the four last things.' William Bond (?) London, printed for John Clark 1719.

2. 'Divine Meditation: or a key to the Scriptures. A sermon…from Psalm lxxvii.12.' Henry Lee LLB.

Anson voyage round the World. George Anson, Baron Anson of Soberton.
'A voyage round the world in the years MDCCXL I II III IV' by George Anson Includes the South Seas and other parts of the world. (1748) This was a very popular work as it went into 17 editions between 1748 and 1796. It is impossible to know when Mary acquired it.

the pious Country parishioner
'The Pious Country Parishioner, being directions how a Christian may manage every day through the whole course of his life…with safety and success.' An extremely popular book, it went into many editions; the earliest recorded is the 5th edition, 1732.

The English Physician. Nicholas Culpeper.
The work was extremely popular and is still in print today. (1653).

the foundation of Theology
I have been unable to trace this entry. It was probably a tract.

the practical Christian or the Devout Penitent
'The Practical Christian or the Devout Penitent' by Richard Sherlock D.D. (1693).

the managing of improving of Land
'The whole art of Husbandry; or, the way of managing and improving of land' … by Tho. Mortimer (Farmer) (1707). The book went into many editions.

the poor mans family Bible
Not traced.

the primitive physic. Anon, by John Wesley.
'The Primitive Physick or an easy and natural method of curing most diseases.' (1747).

the explanatio of the Catechism
There were many tracts and books published during the eighteenth century with questions on and explanations of the Catechism and it has not been possible to identify the one in Mary Bacon's possession. There were also other sorts of catechisms concerned with asking questions about biblical matters.

Divine Songs
> There are a number of eighteenth-century hymnals listed in the catalogues. The most likely is 'Divine Songs: in easy language for the use of children' by Isaac Watts (1715).

preparatory office for the Holy Communion
> It is difficult to identify this book with any certainty, but the following title was very popular during the latter half of the seventeenth century and carried on until 1753, 30th edition.
> 'Officium Eucharisticum, A preparatory service to a devout and worthy reception of the Lord's Supper' by Edward Lake D.D. The earliest edition recorded is 1678.

the Spiritual Comfort and grief in a Devout Soul
> 'The Returnes of Spiritual Comfort and grief in a devout Soul. Represented, by intercourse of letters, to the Right Honourable' the Lady Letice, Vi-Countess Falkland, in her life-time And exemplified with the holy life and death of the said ... Lady, etc. By John Cuncon (1648).

2 Psalters

the Complete Justice
> '[The Complete Justice] A Manuall: or Analecta. being a compendious collection out of such as have treated of the office of Justices of the Peace. Formerly styled The Complete Justice: but now corrected and purged from a multitude of errors ... with diverse and sundry new additions ENGLAND Departments of States and Official Bodies. Justices of the Peace' (London: Miles Flesher & Robert Young, 1642).
> I have given the above edition as an example, but it is not possible to know which one Mary had. It was probably inherited from a Kinchin or Terry ancestor. The first edition was in 1638 and editions continued until 1660.

the Pious Breathings to the Throne of Grace
> 'Pious Breathings. Being the meditations of St. Augustine, containing iv books. Collected for the benefit of mankind in general.' Made English by George Stanhope (1751). There were earlier editions, starting in 1701.

Hymns for Sundays
> There are not many Protestant hymnals listed for the eighteenth century and it was unusual to sing hymns during the Sunday services. I have only found one possible title:
> 'Hymns for several Sundays and festivals of the year, for the sacrament, and other public solemnities.' (1770).

the mystery of Astronomy
> 'The Mystery of Astronomy made plain to the meanest capacity, by an arithmetical description of the terrestrial and celestial globes' ... by W.B. (Will Bagwell) an honourer of Arts and Sciences (1655).

the mariners new Calender

'The Mariners New Calender, containing the principles of arithmetic and practical geometry ... the whole revised and adjusted' ... by William Mountaine F.R.S. This was originally by Nathaniel Colson (1763). The first edition was in 1726 and publication continued up to 1784.

Williams New Universal Psalmodist singing book

Not traced.

another singing book

the new universal parish officer

'The New Universal Parish Officer. Containing all the laws now in force, relating to parish business' ... the second edition ... By a gentleman of the Middle Temple (1764?). The fourth edition in 1774 had the addition of 'four Acts of Parliament made in the last session; concerning the highways and turn-pike roads.' It is not possible to know which edition Mary Bacon owned.

the English Horseman and complete farrier

No title equates with the one listed. The most likely is 'The Compleat Horseman: or Perfect Farrier' Written in French by the Sieur de Solleysell. Abridged from the folio done into English by Sir W. Hope. With the addition of several excellent receipts ... Illustrated etc. (1702).

The Gentlemans Jocky & approved farrier

'The Gentleman's Compleat Jockey: with the Perfect Horseman, and Experienced Farrier' ... by A. S. Gent (1697).

the Great importance of a Religious Life

'The great importance of a religious life; with the complete family prayer book: or manual of family and private devotion ...' by William Melmoth (1711). Further editions were published well into the nineteenth century.

2 old spelling books

another Common prayer book

the Church Catechism Explained by way of Question & answer

This book was first published in 1688, reaching its twenty fourth edition in 1753. The following edition is given as an example as it has the addition of a section on Confirmation and was nearer to the date when Mary herself might have been confirmed.

'The Church Catechism explained, by way of question and answer' ... Collected by John Lewis ... The twenty fourth edition; to which is added a section on Confirmation (1753).

Rapines History of England

written in French by Mr. Rapin de Thoyras. translated into English, with additional notes, by N. Tindal (1727).

There were further editions and the work was brought up to date to the year 1786.
The title varied: 'New History …' 'impartial History …' abridgements, and some
included extracts from other writers, including T. Smollett.

a Circumstantial Narrative of the Loss of the Halsewell
'A Circumstantial Narrative of the Loss of the Halsewell … Compiled from the com-
munications, and under the authorities of Mr. Henry Meriton and Mr. John Rogers'
… By Henry Meriton, Second Mate of the Halsewell, East Indiaman. (William
Lane, 1786)

The Trial of Col Despard
'An Authentic Detail of the Trial of Colonel E. M. Despard, and other, on a charge
of high treason: tried at the Sessions-House, Newington, February 7th, 1803, before
Lord Chief Justice Ellenborough: to which is prefixed His Lordship's charge to the
Grand Jury.' (1803)

The young Communicants Catechism John Willison.
'The Young Communicant's Catechism…With a proposal for publick remewing of
the Baptismal Covenant.' The earliest edition listed is the 5th edition, Edinburgh:
1731). This was a popular book and editions carried on up to 1845 with a printing in
New York in 1824.

a set of Catechisms & prayers for Little Child Isaac Watts.
'The first sett of Catechisms and prayers: or, the religion of little children under seven
or eight years of age. Collected out of the larger books of Prayers and Catechisms
for childhood and youth' … Earliest edition listed: 5th edition, 1734.
This little book of twenty or so pages was also very popular, a 20th edition appeared
in 1788. It carried on well into the twentieth century.

Although *First catch your Hare – the art of cookery made plain and easy by a lady,* Hannah
Glasse, 1747, is not in Mary Bacon's list, she must have either owned the book, or at
least read it very substantially. Approximately one third of her cooking recipes are
taken from this work, indicating a detailed knowledge of the book.

Appendix Three
Herbal remedies

SOME OF THE ingredients listed in Mary Bacon's cures, both for humans and for animals, had to be purchased but a great many of the plants she used grew in Hampshire and could be collected by her, or for her, with very little trouble. An indication that some of the plants were collected is given in the instruction in the recipe for Green Oil, 'takeing none but the fine green Leaves and tender tops.' In another recipe there is an instruction that herbs were to be gathered when at their best, 'in perfection'. It will be seen from the following list that Mary used a large number of plants for her remedies which could be gathered from woods, down land, marshy areas, old marl pits and from the hedgerows. A few of the plants are difficult to identify as not all local names are recorded in the dialect dictionaries, but the majority of the names remain the same. Much of my information and Latin classification has been taken from *The Flora of Hampshire*,[1] Brewis, Bowman, and Rose and *The Concise British Flora in Colour*, W. Keble Martin.[2] Culpeper's *Complete Herbal* has been an invaluable asset, especially where the identification of plants was difficult. Mary Bacon's nomenclature and spelling is given first.

CAUTION: *Great care should be taken in making any of Mary Bacon's recipes using these ingredients. Some identifications are speculative and proper quantities are not given in the recipes.*

ADDERSTONGUE, ADDERSTUNG Adder's-tongue (*ophioglossum vulgatum*). A fern, which was used by Mary when 'in perfection'.

AFSSMART, ARSENART *polygonum* family. Culpeper refers to this plant as Ars-smart, giving two species in his herbal either of which Mary may have used. According to Culpeper, 'the hot arssmart is called also water-pepper, or culrage' (*polygonum hydropiper*). 'The mild arssmart is called dead arssmart, perciaria, or peach-wort, because the leaves are so like the leaves of a peach-tree'. From his description, this plant may be identified as Common Persicaria (*polygonum persicaria*).

1 Brewis, Anne, Bowman, Paul, Rose, Francis, in collaboration with the Hampshire Flora Committee, *The Flora of Hampshire* (Colchester : Harley in association with the Hampshire and Isle of Wight Wildlife Trust, 1996).
2 Keble Martin, W. *The Concise British Flora in Colour* (1965).

AISHEN WOOD Ash (*fraxinus excelsior*), a very common tree in Hampshire, especially on the chalk.

ALCOST. See **COSTMARY.**

ALLHEAL, ALHEAL (*stachys* family) Given in Culpeper, but not in modern herbals. He also referred to it as Hercules's wound-wort or opopane wort. He described it as having yellow flowers, which is not a characteristic of the common woundworts which grow in Hampshire. It is therefore difficult to identify.

ANGELICA Wild Angelica (*angelica sylvestris*). Common in the wild, but, according to Culpeper, also grown in gardens.

BAY, BAYBERRIES, OIL OF BAYS (*myrica cerifera*) This plant is rare in the wild and would have been garden grown.

BEECH LEAVES.

BRAMBLE, RED There are many brambles in the rubus family and it is impossible to know which Mary used. Culpeper does not make any distinction.

BROOM, GREEN BROOM Broom (*cytisus scoparius*). Locally very common in Hampshire. If one believes Culpeper, this shrub cures anything from toothache to kidney ailments.

BUGEL, PLANATINE BUGLE Bugle (*ajuga reptans*). Highly recommended by Culpeper: 'This herb belongeth to dame Venus. If the virtues of it make you fall in love with it (as they will if you be wise), keep a syrup of it to take inwardly, and an ointment and plaister of it to use outwardly, always by you'.

BURDOCK Either Greater Burdock (*arctium lappa*) or Lesser Burdock (*arctium minus*). Greater Burdock is rare, but Lesser Burdock is commonly found. Culpeper used the seeds, leaves, and roots

CELENDINE, CELINDINE Greater Celandine (*chelidonium majus*) or Lesser Celandine (*ranunculus ficaria*).

CENTUARY Common Centaury (*centaurium erythraea*). Grows in pastures and chalk downs, so it should have been easy for Mary to find. There are other centauries, but they are rare in Hampshire.

CHICKWEED (*stellaria media*).

CLEAVERS (*galium aparine*) Known in my family as 'sticky grass'.

CLOWN WORT, CLOWNSWOUND-WORT This must be one of the Woundworts (*stachys* family). Culpeper referred to Clown's Woundwort and recommended it for the healing of ulcers etc.

CORIANDER, CORIANDER SEEDS (*coriandrum sativum*) Although this plant grows in Britain, it is not listed in *The Flora of Hampshire*. It is possible that Mary grew it in her garden, or bought the seeds.

COSTMARY Mary wrote, 'One Blade Alcost or Balsam herb is called Costmary'. According to Culpeper, it was a common plant which he did not feel it necessary to describe. It is not therefore possible to identify which of the balsam family it was. Orange Balsam (*impatiens capensis*) and Indian Balsam (*impatiens glandulifera*) are both locally common in Hampshire.

COTTON Probably common cotton grass (*eriophorum angustifolium*).

CUMPHERY Common Comfrey (*symphytum officinale*).

DOCK, REDDOCK, WHITE DOCK, PLAIN DOCK There are several possibilities within the *rumex* family. Mary Bacon's 'plain dock' is probably Common Dock. She used both the leaves and the roots.

ELDER, DWARF ELDER (*sambucus nigra*) Both bark, leaves and flower were used.

ELICOMPANE, ELECOMPANE Elecampane (*inula helenium*), a garden plant which flowered in June and July. It is possible that Mary gathered this in her own garden, but she also bought it by the pennyworth. It grows in the wild, but is rare in Hampshire, although not elsewhere.

ELM, INNER PEEL OF Probably English Elm (*ulmus procera*), although Wych Elm (*ulmus montana*) is common in hedgerows. Leaves, bark and roots were used.

FENNIGREEK Fenugreek (*trifolium ornithopodioides*), a leguminous plant with seeds used in farriery. It grows on sandy heaths, near the sea, and so it is unlikely that Mary gathered the seeds herself.

SWEET FENNEL Fennel (*foeniculum vulgare*). Culpeper differentiates between Common Fennel and Sweet Fennel but as he does not give a description of either, it is impossible to make a clear identification. As Fennel is only usually found near the coast in Hampshire, it is likely that Mary grew it in her garden, as Culpeper recommended that people should do.

FERMETORY Fumitory (*fumaria* family). There are a number of fumitories, most of which are rare in Hampshire. Common fumitory (*fumaria officinalis*) is the most likely. This plant also fits the description in Culpeper very well, 'A pretty wild plant, with bluish divided leaves, and spikes of little purple flowers: it grows ten inches high … the leaves are large, but they are divided into a vast number of little parts, which are blunt and rounded at the ends; their colour is a faint green.'

FETHERFOY, FEATHERFEW, FEVERFOY Feverfew (*chrysanthemum parthenium*), which appears in Culpeper. It was originally introduced as a herb which grew in eighteenth-century gardens, but is now a common wild flower. According to Culpeper there were four species of this plant: Sea, Sweet, Corn and Common Feverfew. All were efficacious, 'the virtues of any sort of feverfew are beyond all praise, and above all value.'[3] W. Keble Martin, lists only one feverfew, better known as Batchelor's Buttons (Plate 46).

FOXGLOVE (*digitalis purpurea*).

GARLICK Garlic (*Allium* family). This was probably the garden variety, although there

3 Culpeper , *Complete Herbal*, 57.

were several wild varieties growing in Hampshire. Culpeper comments, 'The offensiveness of the breath of him that hath eaten garlic will lead you by the nose to the knowledge hereof, and (instead of a description) direct you the place where it groweth in gardens.

GROUNDIVY, GROUND IVY Ground Ivy (*glechoma hederacea*). Very common.

HALEBAR, WHITE Hellebore. Culpeper only uses Black Helebore and refers to that as growing in gardens. There is the White Helleborine, but it is more likely that Mary gathered the Green Hellebore (*helleborus viridis*) which grows on the chalk in the south of England.

HENLOCK, HEMLOCK (*conium maculatum*)

HONNYSUCKLES, HONNYSUCKELS (*lonicera periclymenum*)

HOREHOUND This is probably White Horehound (*marrubium vulgare*) which was used in cough medicine and is now a very rare plant. It grows on downs and chalk cliffs and the Bacons' farm being on down land, would have been easy for Mary to collect.

HOUNDSWORT, HOUNDWORT This is probably Houndstongue (*cynoglossum officinale*), which grows on down land and at the edges of woods.

HEMLOCK, HENLOCK Hemlock (*conium maculatum*).

HYSOP, HYSSOP (*hyssopus officinalis*) Rare in Britain.

JACOBS LADER Jacob's Ladder (*polemonium caeruleum*).

JUNIPER (*juniperus communis*) Mary only mentioned the berries, which according to Culpeper, seem to cure most ailments.

LAWRELL This is probably the common Cherry Laurel (*prunus laurocerasus*).

LAVENDERSPIKE, LAVENDER COTTON Lavender. Oil of spike was very strong and according to Culpeper 'it is cautiously to be used, some few drops being sufficient.'

MADDER This is almost certainly Field Madder (*sherardia arvensis*) as Wild Madder (*rubius peregrina*) did not grow in the northern part of Hampshire.

MAIDEN HAIR, SYROP OF It is likely that Mary purchased this syrup, as Maidenhair Fern is not listed in the British floras cited.

MALLARDS, MALLARD FLOWERS Marshmallows, mashmallow, mashmallards, wild mallows, single mallows, oyle of mashmallows. There are several wild mallows; musk mallow (*malva moschata*) and common mallow (*malva sylvestris*) are common. Marshmallow (*althaea officinalis*) grows in marshes, often near river estuaries and the roots are used to make the sweetmeat. It is difficult to identify exactly which mallows Mary used.

MARYGOLD, MERRYGOULD Marigold. This is either Corn Marigold (*chrysanthemum segetum*) or the garden variety. Both were said to have healing properties.

MINT Spear Mint (*mentha spicata*) commonly naturalized from gardens. Culpeper recommended this plant for a variety of ailments, including the bite of a mad dog.

MISSLETO, OAK Mistletoe (*viscum album*).

MUGWORT (*ARTEMISIA vulgaris*). This herb is still used as an aid to depression and as a digestive stimulant.

NIGHT SHADE Black Nightshade (*solanum nigrum*). Deadly Nightshade is included in Culpeper, but only in order to give a strong warning as to the extremely poisonous properties of the plant.

OAK BARK This is usually listed with other ingredients which had obviously been purchased. It was certainly available locally.

ORPEN Orpine (*sedum telephium*).

PARSLEY, GARDEN PARSLEY Grown in the garden.

PENNYROYAL (*mentha pulegium*). It used to grow in old marl-pits or in heavily trodden or grazed sites and is now rare.

PILEWORT Pillwort (*pilularia globulifera*). Not surprisingly, this plant is recommended by Culpeper to use in the alleviation of haemorrhoids.

PLANTONY, PLANTINY, PLANATINE, PLANATERY PLANTINE One of the plantains from the *plantaginaceae* family. Nine plantains are listed in Culpeper and it is not possible to identify the one, or ones, used by Mary. Five grow in Hampshire, all of which are relatively common.

RED DOCK, REDDOCK It is mentioned in Culpeper who gave the alternative name of bloodwort. There are a number of docks, but it is not possible to identify which this one is.

REDWEEDS, RED WEED There is no common name today for this plant. Redshank (*persicaria maculosa*) and Red Rattle are possibilities, although speculative, both growing in Hampshire.

ROSE LEAVES, ROSEBUDS These could either be from wild or garden roses.

ROSEMARY This would have been grown in the farm's garden. Bog rosemary is a possibility, though not likely as it has not been recorded in Hampshire.

RUE, RHUE Rue. This is almost certainly Common Meadow Rue (*thalictrum flavum*), which grows in damp meadows, ditches and by streams. The other rues are located in more northerly areas of the country. Mary Bacon used this for sheep rot, or liver fluke. Culpeper gives two varieties: Wild Meadow Rue (*thalictrum flavum*) which grows in damp meadows, ditches and by streams, was advocated for lice, worms, and 'vermin', and Garden Rue, which seemed to be for almost everything. The former is the more likely.

SAGE, SAGE TEA This must be Wild Sage (*salvia nemorosa*) rather than Wood Sage (*teucrium scorodonia*), which is rare in Britain. Mary used 'red sage', which would fit in with the red flower of the Wild Sage but also used 'green sage'. It is also possible that she grew sage in the garden.

SAINT JOHNWORT St. John's-wort. Member of the *hypericum* family of which there are several varieties growing in Hampshire, Perforate St. John's-wort (*hypericum perforatum*) being the most common.

SEDWELL A local herb as it had to be collected when it was 'in perfection'. It was almost certainly Setwall, or red valerian (*centranthus ruber*), which was used medicinally.

SHEPHERDS POUCH This is probably Shepherd's-purse (*capsella bursa-pastoris*).

SMALLAGE Listed in Culpeper but not in modern herbals. He described it as having a carrot-like root and a yellow flower, but it is difficult to identify.

SOLOMAN SEAL Solomon's Seal (*polygonatum multiflorum*). According to Culpeper, distilled water from the whole plant is good for facial blemishes, 'leaving the place fresh, fair, and lovely' for which purpose it is much used by the Italian dames.'[4]

SORREL, GARDEN SORREL OR THE COMON SOREL Common Sorrel (*Rumex acetosella*). Culpeper also refers to a Mountain Sorrel grown in Gardens, with much the same properties.

SPEARMINT (*mentha spicata*) Mary referred to 'a top or two' implying that she was able to gather it. It probably grew in her garden.

STININGNETTLES Stinging Nettles.

SULENDINE Celandine. Both Lesser (*ranunculus ficaria*) and Greater Celandine (*chelidonium majus*) appear in Culpeper. This is probably the Greater Celandine (*chelidonium majus*) which Mary used to cure a 'squat or swelling'. It is still used to cure warts.

THYME Mary may have cut Thyme from her garden, or collected Wild Thyme (*thumus polytrichus*) from the surrounding chalk lands.

TORCHWORT Probably Toothwort (*lathraea squamaria*), which grows in Hampshire in old woods and copses on the chalk. According to Culpeper, it heals wounds and bruises although he does not mention burns for which it is used by Mary.

TUTSEN, TUTSON, TUTSAR Tutsan (*hypericum androsaemum*).

VALERIAN ROOT Valerian (*valeriana officinalis*).

WALNUT Mary used the leaves only. It is likely that she had a tree in her garden as she pickled the nuts and need them to be white and young.

WICHAZEL, INNER PEEL OF Probably Hazel (*corylus avellana*).

WINTER SAVORY (*satureja Montana*). Now very rare in Hampshire.

WORMWOOD, ROMAN WORMWOOD Wormwood (*artemisia absinthium*)

4   *ibid.* 166

Appendix Four Family tree

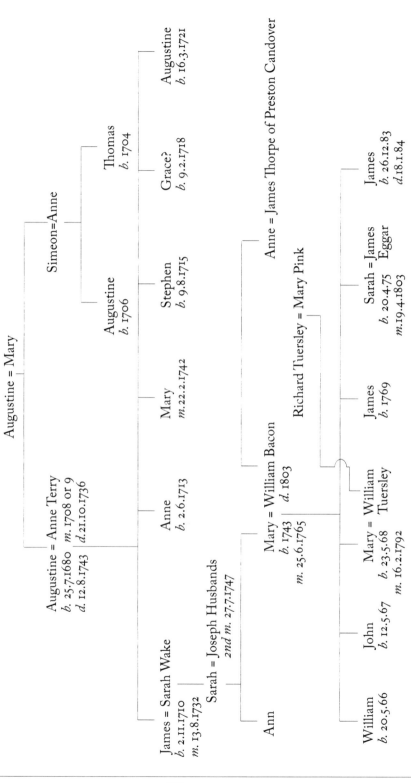

191

Appendix Five   Mary Bacon's inventory

December 21, 1807

This is an account of my Goods at Mrs Baldings

three feather Beds and three bolsters

one bedstead with red and white check furniture

one bedstead with patch furniture

one Clock a Larg looking Glass in a brown frame

a Weather Glass, a looking Glass with two drawers in a mahogany frame,

a book stand two small Looking Glasses. a dressing glass

a Japan tea board & two waiters. a tea chest and

a Mahogany tea board. one beaurow

six stained Chairs, six ashe Chairs two arm Chairs

two Chairs with roded bottoms, one Chair with a [?] bottom

a Childs Chair a old low Chair,

a Mahogany teatable, another teatable one Coffee mill

a Square Dineing table, one spice box

one pair of brass Candlesticks one brass flat Do

two pair of iron Candlesticks a pair of Snuffers

one Copper Coffee pot and a tin Do, a brass mortar

and pestle flower box and pepper cast one steel

a Copper saucepan one dozen of Scuers, a sugar hatchet

one pair of sugar nippers, a pair of tobacco tongs

one Long Skuer a pair of Clams a bread grater

another pair of Snuffers, one Safe a bodkin

four flat irons & stand a Corner Shelves

a warming pan, a fire pan & tongs & a pair of angers

a pair of tongs with a brass head and a poker

a kitchen firepan & tongs & fender a cupiron

two pair of bellows a gridiron another pair of angers

my Granary a Cleaver a Chopping knife 2 Iron rings

a Cottrell a Crane & four hooks,

a bread basket a broiling tin a driping pan

a nest of drawers a brown Quilt under my sisters bed

two Cloaths Horse a Drip box a wash Tub

a stand for the mash tub a Little Stand

a Dozen of knives and forks in a box

a beaufet a Japan Snuff tray

a toasting fork two Long hair brushes

an Iron bound half hogshed a Iron bound Six Gallon barell

Seven pillows in my room a Large Chest

a travelling trunk a box with one drawer

a Iron bound 16 Gallon barell another Iron bound 30 Gallon barell

one Iron bound 10 gallon barell one Iron bound

eight Gallon barrel a tun bowl hopstrainer

Huckmuck[1] with stick & plug a mash Stirrer

a Little powdering tub a Dutch oven a Chafindish

a Lanthorn a tender box a pewter still & Iron pot

a oval boiler a Little boiler

1   Huckmuck is a strainer used in the mash tun in brewing

Bibliography

PRIMARY SOURCES

Adair, J. M. *Essays on Fashionable Diseases* (1790)

Allestree, R. *The whole duty of man laid down in a plain and familiar way for the use of all ... with private devotions* (1703)

Ancient Brahmin, An (attributed to Robert Dodsley and John Hill) *The Oeconomy of Human Life* (1783) First edition 1751

Anon, *Divine Meditations* (1719)

Anon, *The Farmer's Wife, or Complete Country Housewife* (1780?)

Anon, *Hampshire Notes and Queries*, Vol. IV (1889)

Anon, *Hampshire Repository*, Vols. I and II (Winchester, 1799–1800)

Anon, *Hymns for several Sundays and festivals of the year, for the sacrament and other public solemnities* (ca. 1770)

Anon, *The Life of Judas Iscariot*, BL 1078.i.27 tract (Durham, 1750?)

Anon, *The Life of Judas Iscariot*, BL 1078.k.21 tract (London, 1784)

Anon, *The Life of Judas Iscariot* BL RB.23.a.834 tract (London: 1776)

Anon, *The Life and Death of Pontius Pilate*, tract (1720?)

Anon, *The Mystery of Astronomy, made plain ...* (1655)

Anon, *The New Universal Parish Officer* (1769)

Anon, *The Pious Country Parishioner* (1732)

Anon, *Private Devotions for several Occasions ordinary and extraordinary* (1724)

Anon, a divine in the Church of England. *Private Devotions in the Church, fitted to employ some short time before divine service begins; and also on occasion of receiving the Holy Sacrament* (1712)

Anon, *A Story Concerning a Pack of Cards* (1762)

Anon, *Twelve True Old Golden Rules* (1800)

Anson, G., Esq., *A Voyage Round the World*, 14th edition (1769)

Baldwin, R. et al. *The Complete Farmer; or a general dictionary of husbandry by a Society of Gentlemen* (1769)

Basnage, Mr. (the Count de Beauville) *The History of the Jews*, translated into English by Thomas Taylor (1708)

Beveridge, Bishop, *Sermons, or The Thirty Nine Articles of Religion* (1757)

Billingsley, J. *A General View of the Agriculture in the County of Somerset* (1794)

Buchan, W. *Domestic Medicine*, 3rd edition (1774)

Burkit, W. *Expository notes with practical observations, on the new Testament of our Lord and Saviour Jesus Christ*, 4th edition. (1709)

Cadogan, W. *An Essay upon Nursing* (1748)

Cadogan, W. *A Dissertation on the Gout* (1771)

Davidson, Rev. W. *Thoughts on Mortality occasioned by the death of ...* (1789)

Davies, J. *The Innkeeper and Butler's Guide, or, a Directory in the Making and Managing of British Wines* (1808)

Despard, E. M. *The Trial of Colonel Despard* (1803)

Driver, W. and A. *General View of the Agriculture of the County of Hants with Observations on the means of its improvement* (1794)

Ellis, W. *The Country Housewife's Family Companion* (1750)

Ellis, W. Farmer, *The Modern Husbandman, or , the Practice of Farming etc.* (1744)

Falkland, Viscountess, *The Returns of Spiritual Comfort* (1648)

A Farmer, *Rural Recreations or Modern Farmer's Calendar and Monthly Instructor* (1802)

Gent, A. S. *The Gentleman's Compleat Jockey with the Perfect Horseman and Experience'd Farrier* (1717)

Gibson, William, *A new Treatise on the disease of horses* (1754)

Gordon, W. *Every Young Man's Companion* (1759)

Henderson, William Augustus, *The Housekeeper's Instructor, or Universal Family Cook* (ca 1800, tenth edition)

Hervey, J. *Meditations and Contemplations* (London: Millar, 174–?)

Hill, J. *The Useful Family Herbal* (1754)

Hill, John and Dodsley, Robert attrib. *The Oeconomy of Human Life*, Part 2 (1783)

A Lady, *The whole duty of a woman: or a guide to the female sex* (1695)

Lewis, John, collected by, *The Church Catechism Explained by way of Question and Answer* (1753)

Lisle, E. *Observations in Husbandry* (1757)

Marriott, T. *Female conduct, being an essay on the art of pleasing to be practised by the Fair Sex, before and after marriage* (1759)

Meriton, Henry, *The Circumstantial narrative of the Loss of the Halsewell* (1786)

Mortimer, J. Esq. F.R.S. *The Whole Art of Husbandry, or the Way of Managing and Improving of Land*, 6th edition (1761)

Payne, J. *Universal Geography formed into a new and entire system…with a set of maps…and a great variety of copper plates* (1791)

Rawlett, J. *The Christian Monitor, containing an earnest exhortation to an holy life* (1696)

de Reamur, René Antoine Ferchault, *The art of hatching and bringing up domestic fowls* (1750)

Sherlock, R. D.D. *The Practical Christian or Devout Penitent.* 5th edition (1699)

Smith, E. *The Compleat Housewife: or Accomplished gentlewoman's companion: being a collection of upwards of five hundred of the most approved receipts in cookery…to which is added a collection of near two hundred family receipts of medicines …* 2nd edition (1728)

de Sollysell, Sieur, written in French, *Compleat Horseman: or Perfect Farrier*, abridged from the Folio done into English by Sir William Hope. 4th edition (1729)

Stanhope, G. *The Pious Breathings* (1701)

de Thoyras, Rapin, *History of England*, 16th ed. (1770)

Tracts 1757–79, British Library Catalogue 4375.df.9

Vancouver, C. *General View of the Agriculture of Hampshire including the Isle of Wight* (1813)

Watts, I. *Divine Songs: Attempted in Easy Language for the use of Children* (1715)

Watts, I. *The first sett of Catechisms and prayers: or, the religion of little children under seven or eight years of age.* (1734)

W. B. *The Mysteries of Astronomy* (1655)

Wesley, J. *Primitive Physick: or an Easy and Natural Method of Curing most Diseases* (1759). Taken from edition of 1843

Willis, A. J. *Wills, Administrations, and Inventories with the Winchester Diocesan Records* (1968)

Willison, J. *The Young Communicants Catechism … With a proposal for publick renewing of the Baptismal Covenant* (1734)

Wright, G. introduction, *Pleasing Melancholy, or a walk among the tombs in a country church-yard in the style and manner of Harvey's Meditations* (1793)

Young, A. *The Farmers' Kalendar* (1771)

Young, A. 'A Six Weeks' Tour Through the Southern Counties of England and Wales' *The Annals of Agriculture*, No. 157 (1768)

Hampshire Record Office

Anonymous Notebook 3M51/607

Anon, Veterinary notebook 5M50/2244

Anon, Veterinary recipes 5M50/2245

Churchwardens presentments (Micheldever) 21M65/B2/539–542

Cliddesden Parish Records 31M82/M52 PR1,2,3; M52 PR4 PR6; M52 PR9; 44M69M/2/61

Deeds of lands of the Earl of Portsmouth, 1763, 7M48/1

The Diaries of Elizabeth Chute 1790–1799, 23M93/70/1/1–9

Earl of Portsmouth papers 21M65/B4/3/35

Eggar family notebook 28M82/F2

Farmer of Cliddesden 1785, 18M76/PO1/20

Glebe Terriers 35M48 16/81–84, 150–1

Hampshire Allegations for Marriage Licences 1689–1837 (Harleian Society Publications)

Hampshire Marriage Licences 1669–1680 from records in the Diocesan Registry, Winchester

Heathcote papers 63M84/235

Hen and Chicken betting records 12 M98/1–3

Land Tax Assessments Q22/1/1/14/5

Lands in Cliddesden 1652–1803 11M49 E/T3; ET 7–13

Lease of Swallick farm to Charles Hoare 15M84/3/1/1/39

Mary Bacon's List of Books 28M82/F1

Mill at Binstead belonging to James Eggar 57M78/E/T371

Moens, W. C. J., *Hampshire Allegations for Marriage Licences, granted by the Bishop of Winchester, 1689–1837* (1893)

Parish Register Returns 1813, 21M65 F6/23

Schedule for Shalden, Defence of the Realm Act 1798, Q22/1/2/5

Visitation return 21M65B4/3/35

Visitation return 44MB4/3/35

Voters' List 1734, 44M69/G2/278

Will of James Kinchin, Wills Index: 1748B/063
Yalden, Richard, Diary and Memorandum of Richard Yaldon, Vicar of Newton Valence
     1761–1785 and rector of Greatham 1754–1785, 33M66/P17

Journals and newspapers

The Farmers' Magazine, 1807
The Gentlemen's Magazine
Hampshire Chronicle
Henry's Winchester Journal or Weekly Review
Salisbury Journal

Meteorological Office

Meteorological Register kept at Nodbury Devonshire by Mr. John Andrews (snr) from 1788
     to 1822. Ms

Museum of Rural Life (MERL)

Diary of a female member of the Sutton family MERL DEV 3/8/1
Farmer's Diary MERL LAN 1.1
Diary of George Brigham of Lindy Hill Farm, Cleveland, Yorkshire MERL YOR 13.1

Wiltshire Record Office

Kinchin leaseholds in Wiltshire 221B 2216, 212B 2202

Winchester College Archives

Winchester College Archives, Ref. 21448, 1761. Isaac Taylor map
Winchester College Monuments, Vol. III item 29466

Maps (Hampshire Record Office)

Isaac Taylor map of Hampshire, 1759, Scale 1" to 1 mile. HRO County Maps sheets 9 and 11
Thomas Milne map 1791 Scale: 1" to 1 mile. HRO County Maps sheet 15
6" Ordnance Survey sheet 27, 1870–71

SECONDARY SOURCES

Agricultural History Review, Vol. 35, part 1 (1987)
Altick, Robert D. *The English Common Reader* (1957)
Anderson, B. L. and Latham, A. J. H. *The Market in History* (1986)
Anon, *Some features of Interest in the Twelfth Century Church of All Saints Dummer.* Leaflet
Armstrong, A. *Farmworkers: A Social and Economic History 1770–1980* (1988)
Ashton, J. *Chapbooks of the Eighteenth century* (1966). First published in 1882
Austen, Jane, *Mansfield Park* (1949). First published in 1814
Barley, M. W. *The English Farmhouse and Cottage* (1961)
Barry, J. and Brooks, C. eds. *The Middling Sort of People, Culture, Society and Politics in
     England, 1550–1800* (1994)
Beckett, J. V. *The Agricultural Revolution* (1990)
Birdwood, V. ed. *So Dearly loved, So Much Admired, Letters to Hester Pitt, Lady Chatham, from
     her relations and friends 1744–1801* (1994)

Blamey, M., Fitter, A. and Fitter, R. *The Wild Flowers of Britain and Northern Europe* (1974)

Bland, D. S. *Chapbooks and Garlands in the Robert White collection in the Library of King's College* (1956)

Bourne, G. *A Farmer's Life* (1922)

Boyd, Lizzie, ed. *British Cookery* (1976)

Brewis, A., Bowman, P. and Rose, F. *The Flora of Hampshire* (1996)

Capp, B. *Astrology and the Popular Press* (1979)

Chambers, J. D. and Mingay, G. E. *The Agricultural Revolution 1750–1880* (1966)

Chapman, C. R. *Using Newspapers and Periodicals*, (Birmingham: Federation of Family History Societies, 1993)

Chapman, John and Seeliger, Sylvia, *A Guide to the Enclosures in Hampshire* (1997)

Child, M. *Farms Fairs and Felonies, Life on the Hampshire–Wiltshire Border, 1760–1830* (1967)

Coates, R. *The Place Names of Hampshire* (1989)

Collins, I. *Jane Austen, the Parson's Daughter* (1998)

Cope, Rev. Sir William H. *A Glossary of Hampshire Words and Phrases* (English Dialect Society, 1883)

Culpeper, Nicholas, *Complete Herbal and English Physician*, ed. Christopher Hedley (1997). First published 1653

Davison, M., Currie, I. and Ogley, B. *The Hampshire and the Isle of Wight Weather Book* (1993)

Defoe, Daniel, *A Tour through the whole island of Great Britain*, ed. Pat Rogers (1971). First published between 1724 and 1724

Dolan, B. *Ladies of the Grand Tour* (2001)

Drummond, J. C. and Wilbraham, A. *The Englishman's Food: A history of five centuries of English diet* (1957). Revised by Dorothy Hollingsworth 1991

Dudek, L. *The searching image* (1952)

Dyke, I. *William Cobbett and Rural Popular Culture* (1992)

Edwards, P. *Rural Life, Guide to Local Records* (1993)

Edwards, P. *Farming: Sources for Local Historians* (1991)

Emsley, C. *British Society and the French Wars* (1979)

Encyclopedia Brittannica Online Library version (http://library.eb.co.uk)

Evans, E. J. *The Contentious Tithe: the Tithe Problem and English Agriculture 1750–1850* (1976)

Fergus, J. 'Women, Class and the Growth of Magazine Readership in the Provinces 1746–1780' *Studies in 18th Century Culture* Vol. 16 (1986)

Fiennes, Celia, *The Journeys of Celia Fiennes* Morris, C. ed. (1947). Travels from 1684–1703

Fussell, G. E. F. *The English Dairy Farmer 1500–1900* (1966)

Garnett, J. and Matthew, C. eds. *Revival and Religion since 1700* (1993)

Gilboy E. W. 'The Cost of Living and Real Wages in 18th Century England', *Review of Economic Statistics* Vol. 18 (1936)

Glasse, Hannah, *First Catch your Hare, the art of cookery made plain and easy by a lady*, ed. Jennifer Stead and Priscilla Bain (1995) First published 1747

Grigg, D. B. *Population Growth and Agrarian change: an Historical Perspective* (1980)

Grundy, G. B. *Saxon Land Charters and Place Names of Hampshire* (1921–1930)

Hammond, J. L. and B. *The Village Labourer 1760–1832* (1911)

Hampshire County Council, *Hampshire Treasures* (1982)

Hardy, M. *Mary Hardy's Diary*, ed. B. Cozens, Norfolk Record Society Vol. 37 (1968)

Hecht, J. *The Domestic Servant Class in Eighteenth-century England* (1956)

Hill, B. *Servants: English Domestics in the Eighteenth century* (1989)

Horn, P. *A Georgian Parson and his village: the Life of David Davies* (1981)

Horn, P. *The Rural World: Social Change in the English countryside* (1980)

Hoskins W. G. *The Making of the English Landscape* (1953)

Hughes, Anne, *The Diary of a Farmer's Wife* (1964). First written in 1796, 1797

James, T. B. *Winchester* (1997)

Jeffrey, D. L. general editor, *A Dictionary of Biblical tradition in English Literature* (1992)

Keble Martin, W. *The Concise British Flora in Colour* (1965)

Kerridge, Eric, *The Agricultural Revolution* (1967)

Kussmaul, A. *A general view of the Rural Economy of England 1538–1840* (1990)

Kussmaul, A. *Servants in Husbandry in early modern England* (1981)

Lamb, H. *Historic Storms of the North Sea, British Isles and North West Europe* (1991)

Lavers, J. *A Dictionary of Isle of Wight Dialect* (1988)

Long, W. H. *A Dictionary of the Isle of Wight Dialect* (1886)

Maclean, V. *A Short-title catalogue of household and cookery books published in the English tongue 1701–1800* (1980)

Malcolmson, R. W. *Life and Labour in England 1700–1780* (1981)

Malcolmson, R. W. *Popular Recreations in English Society 1700–1850* (1973)

Malcolmson, R. and Mastoris S. *The English Pig: A History* (1998)

Marshall, William, *The Rural Economy of Glocestershire* (2005). First published 1789

Mattias, P, *The Transformation of England: Essays in the Economic and Social History of England in the Eighteenth century* (1979)

Milner, A. B. Vicar of Micheldever-cum-Stratton, *History of Micheldever* (1924)

Mingay, G. E. ed. *The Agrarian History of England and Wales* Vol. vi, 1750–1850 (1989)

Mingay, G. E. 'The Land Tax Assessments and the Small Landowner', *Econ. Hist. Rev.* 2nd series, Vol. xxviii (1975)

Mingay, G. E. 'The Size of Farms in the Eighteenth century' *Econ. Hist. Rev.* 2nd series, Vol. xiv (1961–2)

Monkton, H. A. *A History of Ale and Beer* (1966)

Morris, Claver, *The Diary of a West Country Physician* (ed. Edmund Hobhouse 1934)

O'Neill, G. V. *The Golden Legend* (1914)

Page, W. ed. *The Victoria History of the Counties of England: Hampshire* (1973)

Porter, R. *English Society in the Eighteenth century* (1982)

Porter, R. 'Sick People, Health and Doctors in Georgian England', *The Historian* Vol. 21 (1988–89)

Porter, R. 'Lay Medical Knowledge in the Eighteenth century: the Evidence of *The Gentlemen's Magazine*', *Medical History* Vol. 29 (1985)

Preston, C. and Michael J. eds. *The other print tradition. Essays on chapbooks, broadsides and related ephemera* (1995)

Pullar, Philippa, *Consuming Passions: A history of English food and appetite* (1971)

Raven, J., Small, H. and Tadmor, N. eds. *The Practice and Representation of Reading in England* (1996)

Raven, J. *Judging New Wealth. Popular Publishing and Responses to commerce in England 1750–1800* (1992)

Richardson, Samuel, *Clarissa*, Penguin Classics, (1985). First published 1747–8

Rivers, Isabel, *Books and their Readers in 18th Century England* (1982)

Roebuck, 'Leases and Tenancy Agreements', *The Local Historian* Vol. 10 No. 1 (1972)

Rushton, Jill, *A Hundred years of Progress* Hampshire Country Council (1989)

Ryder, M. L. *Sheep and Man* (1983)

Samuel, R. *Village Life and Labour* (1975)

Sheppard, L. *The History of Street Literature* (1973)

Snell, K. D. M. *Annals of the Labouring Poor* (1985)

Southam, B. 'The charm of Mrs. Norris' *Jane Austen Society Report* (2002)

Stead, Jennifer, *Food and Cooking in 18th Century Britain* (1985)

Stirling, A. M. W. ed. *The Diaries of Dummer* (1934)

Stone, L. *The Family, Sex and Marriage in England 1500–1800* (1977)

Summerfield, Geoffrey, *Fantasy and Reason: Children's Literature in the Eighteenth century* (1984)

Symons, Michael, *A History of Cooks and Cookery* (2001)

Tadmor, N. *Family and Friends: Household, Kinship and Patronage in Eighteenth-Century England* (2001)

Tannahill, Reay, *Food in History* (1988)

Taylor, J. A. ed. *Weather and Agriculture* (1967)

Terry, Stephen, *The Diaries of Dummer: Reminiscences of an Old Sportsman* (1934)

Thirsk, J. ed. *The Agrarian History of England and Wales* vol 6 (1984)

Thirsk, J. *The Rural Economy of England* (1984)

Turner, B. Carpenter, *A History of Winchester* (1992)

Turner, M. 'Agricultural Productivity in England in the Eighteenth century: evidence from crop Yields' *Econ. Hist Rev.* 2nd series Vol. 35 (4) (1982)

Turner, M. *English Parliamentary Enclosure* (1980)

Turner, M. E., Beckett, J. V. & Afton, B. *Farm Production in England 1700–1914* (2001)

Turner, T. *The Diary of Thomas Turner 1754–1765* ed. D. Vaisey (1994)

Verdon, Nicola 'Subject deserving of highest praise: farmers' wives and the farm economy in England, *c.* 1700–1850' *Agricultural History Review* Vol. 51, part 1 (2003)

Vickery, Amanda, *The Gentleman's Daughter, Women's Lives in Georgian England* (1988)

Victorian History of Hampshire, University of London reprint 1973, ref. Hants *N & Q* ix.20

Virgin, Peter, *The Church in an Age of Negligence, 1700–1840* (1989)

Voragine, Jacobus de, *The Golden Legend* selections by Christopher Stace, (1998). First published in Latin *c.* 1260

Watts, Isaac, *Divine Songs in easy language for the use of children* ed. J. H. P. Pafford (1971). First published 1715

Weiss, Henry, *A Book about Chapbooks; the People's Literature of bygone times* (reprinted USA: Folklore Associates, 1969)

White, Gilbert *The Journals of Gilbert White 1784–1793* ed. F. Greenoak (1989)

White, R. *Popular Literature in eighteenth and nineteenth century Britain* (1985)

Woodforde, James, *The Diary of a Country Parson: the Reverend James Woodforde, 1758–1802* ed. J. Beresford (1924–31)

Index

Mary Bacon's World

servants 4–8, 26, 29, 32–34, 49–50, 72, 76–78, 80, 97, 102, 111, 118, 145
  wages 49–51
sheep 7, 11, 13–14, 20, 22, 27–28, 40, 44–47, 54, 56–59, 63–64, 71–72, 114, 189
  cures for diseases of 63–65
  purchases 46
Steventon 99
Sutton family diary 5

T

taxes 20, 28–29, 32, 35, 42
  land tax 20, 28, 35
tea 17, 24–25, 83–84, 91–92, 99, 108, 120, 189, 192
Terry, Stephen 41, 98, 99
tobacco 25, 64, 71, 93, 192
Tuersly, William
  marriage to Mary Bacon (daughter) 30–31
Turner, Thomas 15, 27, 43, 46, 79, 91, 98, 125, 126, 146, 147

V

Vancouver, Charles 13, 46, 49–50, 59, 60–65, 72, 104
vegetables 5, 28, 33, 36, 98, 115
Verdon, Nicola 1, 2

W

wagons 35, 47
War with France 33–35, 46
  threats of invasion 33–34
Watts, Isaac 20, 130, 151, 182, 184
weather 2, 6, 7, 8, 24, 43, 47, 51–57, 58, 68, 134, 170
  Mary Bacon's reports of 54–58
Wesley, John vi, viii, 77, 79–82, 93, 99, 115, 143, 181
wheat 7, 14, 39, 43–46, 50, 57, 58, 119
White, Gilbert 54–56
Winchester i, viii, 11, 12, 13, 14, 34, 36–40, 57, 121–123, 131
Winchester College i, viii, 11
wine 8, 14, 15, 60, 64, 66, 72, 80, 83, 90, 91, 93, 100, 105–117
Woodforde, Parson James 23, 24, 26, 35, 56, 80, 84, 112, 117
Woodmancott 7–8, 11–14, 16, 114, 144, 178
wreck of the *Halsewell* 133–136

Y

Young, Arthur 3, 4, 36, 66, 72